How People Talk About Politics

How People Talk About Politics

Brexit and Beyond

Stephen Coleman

BLOOMSBURY ACADEMIC
LONDON • NEW YORK • OXFORD • NEW DELHI • SYDNEY

BLOOMSBURY ACADEMIC
Bloomsbury Publishing Plc
50 Bedford Square, London, WC1B 3DP, UK
1385 Broadway, New York, NY 10018, USA
29 Earlsfort Terrace, Dublin 2, Ireland

BLOOMSBURY, BLOOMSBURY ACADEMIC and the Diana logo
are trademarks of Bloomsbury Publishing Plc

First published in Great Britain 2021
This paperback edition published in 2022

Series design by Adriana Brioso

A catalogue record for this book is available from the British Library.

A catalog record for this book is available from the Library of Congress.

ISBN: HB: 978-0-7556-1879-8
PB: 978-0-7556-3560-3
ePDF: 978-0-7556-1881-1
eBook: 978-0-7556-1880-4

Typeset by Deanta Global Publishing Services, Chennai, India

To find out more about our authors and books visit www.bloomsbury.com and sign up for
our newsletters

Contents

Preface

When I think back to moments in which I have been engaged in political talk, my mind is flooded by emotions, reminding me that to speak is to declare oneself present in the world. I recall occasions in which I have struggled to find the right words for intensely felt thoughts, and others in which I have become conscious of my values only as I have begun to articulate them. And others still when I have been so engrossed that I was unable to distinguish between speaking and listening. In all of these moments I was acutely aware that to talk about how the world is and should be is an exhilarating challenge – a reminder of both agency and vulnerability.

'*Speak, you also/speak as the last/have your say*,' writes Paul Celan in one of the finest of his poems. This is a book about what it feels like to take up Celan's invitation. It is a book about why people speak as they do; why some hardly speak about politics at all; and why most of us speak more politically than we might realize or admit. It is a book about how we learn to talk politics as a social practice, replete with tacit customs and rules. It is not a book about technologies of political talk. Questions about whether newspapers, television or social media are 'good for democracy' have been asked by countless scholars, nearly all of whom have concluded that 'it depends on what sort of newspapers, television or social media we have'. Before political talk can be printed, broadcast or circulated, it must be enunciated. How well this happens depends upon that most sophisticated of technologies: the voice. This is a book, therefore, about voices in their most common context of interaction: face-to-face talk.

I could not have written this book unless people had consented to speak with me about their memories and experiences of political talk. In fact, they more than consented. I soon discovered that for many of my interviewees, telling stories about their experiences of political talk allowed them to access biographical streams that took them to the core of their identities. It follows from this that the present book is not only about what it means to talk about politics but also about how it feels to adopt one's own position in the world. Doing so entails mustering the courage and confidence to take a stand, and how that can be encouraged is the theme of the book's concluding chapter.

It will be clear from each of the following chapters that I could not have written this book without learning from many thinkers whose names are liberally referenced. I have read some of them with such appreciation and/or misgiving that I feel as if I have been in protracted conversations with people I have never met. I hope they will forgive me for my excitability during these imaginary exchanges. I have been very lucky to have had more direct conversations over the years with friends, colleagues and students who have encouraged me to work through some of the ideas presented in this book. They include Jay Blumler, John Corner, Roderick Hart and, more recently, Tom Wright and the excellent team of researchers working on the AHRC-funded 'Speaking Citizens' project.

I am grateful to the British Academy for funding the research which led to this book being written. The assistance I received at various times throughout the writing process from David Wright, Malaika Cunningham, Andy Irving, Katie Peate and Angeline Dresser is much appreciated. I wish to thank Tomasz Hoskins and Nayiri Kendir at Bloomsbury Press for their confidence in this project and Mohammed Raffi for his diligent attention to the text. My PhD students have always inspired me to think harder, so I thank them. And without the stimulating intellectual environment of the School of Media and Communication at the University of Leeds, I would have felt less motivated to write.

Over the past ten years I have taught undergraduate courses designed to develop students' confidence in speaking. I want to thank all the students who have taken those courses for demonstrating what is involved in speaking courageously.

As I write this Preface, society is going through an exceptional period – a grand 'lockdown' in which we have all had to become acutely aware of the limits of our personal agency. We are having to learn to act in new ways, distanced physically and yet thrown socially into a common conversation. There has been much speculation about what life will be like after this. Allow me to express one hope: that when this is all over we might learn to become a more confident democracy, saying what we mean to say, excluding no voices from our public discourse. That, anyway, is the normative thrust of what follows.

I dedicate this book to Bernadette, Safi, Kari, Simon and Olivia.

Political talk as social practice

In 2016, the British people engaged in a grand act of national catharsis: a referendum that was about their status; their borders; their fantasies of self; their grievances of decline; their interests; their emotions; their long-standing mutterings of 'and another thing that really annoys me'; their right to piss off the government; their historic destiny; and, tangentially, whether to remain members of the European Union.

People were told that there was to be a 'national conversation' in which they would 'have their say'. In preparation for this critical deliberation, newspaper editorials offered instructions on how to behave: 'In the coming months, we are going to have to endure a great deal of disagreement – and must try to do so politely and with good humour, recognising that it is a sign of democracy in motion' (*Daily Telegraph*, 6 March 2016). The 'endurance' of disagreement was presented as an imagined risk. Would it lead to fights in the street, bricks through neighbours' windows or angry divorces? The prime minister David Cameron appealed to the democratic maturity of the British people: 'We should all be big enough to have an honest and open, but polite disagreement, and then come back together again afterwards.' Here again, the emphasis was upon resilience to endure the stress of dissensus. Political articulation was conceived as a temporary interruption of social accord, but its disruptive candour could only be sustained long enough to prepare the ground for renewed consensus: coming back together again afterwards.

The days and months leading up to the referendum entailed the playing out of a stock metaphor of 'the people having their say'. Emerging languidly from the murky inattention that had prevailed in the days before plebiscitary responsibility was thrust upon them, non-politicians were invited to give voice to their interests and longings as if they could make a difference. This was democracy in its most potent symbolic register, bringing into being a *demos* capable of asserting, deliberating, demanding and resolving, while at the same time standing as a conspicuous addressee and vulnerable object of persuasion.

Assured in their belief that *this time* they could not be ignored, people found themselves talking with an energy that many had forgotten they possessed. It was as if words might change everything.

What transpired turned out to be less like a national conversation than a fractious cultural convulsion. People began to fall out. There were whispered suspicions and shaming accusations, each side disappointed by the insensibility of the other. Strangers worked hard to ignore one another and then felt stranger than ever. Even loving partners and close families found themselves drawn into the enveloping animus:

> So my partner said he felt like I was being racist. But I'm not being racist – because I'm not a racist person. But because I'd said 'I do think it's time we did say no to everyone coming in – and there are people that are working, but there are people that are scrounging, and to me it is time as a country that we said no' . . . he just thinks that I'm being racist. . . . So we had arguments about that. It was pretty heated. . . . And yeah, it does insult me – because I'm not racist. I don't see myself as a racist in that I don't value everyone the same, because I do. . . . So yeah, it does insult me. I don't think it's fair. (Abbey, 26-year-old shop worker)

> We spent about three hours on the phone between me, my mum, my dad and my brother, all on loudspeaker. My brother and me are very pro-staying in the EU, I don't really believe in country boundaries and stuff like that. I think it's all made up, to be honest. Great Britain is a boundary that we've made up. France is a boundary that we've made up. And we're just deciding to keep these boundaries drawn, basically, by stepping out of the EU. And my mum and dad feel like it was better, we had so much more business, but for me, all those industries, like coal mining, all that, it's kind of dead. There's nothing we can do about it, it's dead. But I don't think cutting ourselves off from the world, as I said to them, is really helping us. Basically, the argument ended in my mum and dad putting the phone down, and we didn't speak for a couple of days. (Will, thirty-year-old office worker)

In the sobering aftermath of the vote people found themselves looking at one another nervously, feeling like members of a split jury that had both made a decision and locked itself into irreconcilable disagreement. Sophie, aged twenty-two, spoke about how her initial enthusiasm for the long-awaited decision began to dissipate as she came to terms with its affective ambivalence:

> I was excited. But then when you hear how upset other people were about it, it kind of took a bit of a toll. You felt a bit flat, rather than excited, because it was

clear that it wasn't the whole country wanting one thing . . . I thought it would be a bit more of a celebration. But instead, you had all the people that had been trying to persuade you to vote leave resigning, or going back on what they were saying, and it was just really disappointing.

Some people began to wonder whether they had merely been playing at being citizen-jurors, adopting theatrical civic voices derived from trace memories of crowded meetings in mythical village halls and fictitious insurgencies staged to amuse viewers of the black-and-white film classic *Passport to Pimlico*. Drawing upon such popular imaginaries of vibrant democracy, they had convinced themselves that there was a direct correspondence between public expression and institutional efficacy. Critics who regarded the referendum as a 'depressing, divisive, duplicitous political event' (Robert Harris on Twitter, 16 June 2016) began to suggest that what had been celebrated as 'the people speaking' had amounted to little more than the people listening to politicians speaking and then stumblingly mimicking their most mendacious gestures. The normative character of the public as addressee was well defined, but it began to appear that the expressive and reciprocating role of citizens was radically under-rehearsed. Questions about the cultural mechanics of plebiscitary sovereignty began to be asked. If the vote was merely the end point of a national conversation, when was the starting point? What was a national conversation supposed to sound like? What constituted meaningful political talk about a decision that would affect everyone? How were citizens supposed to attain the confidence and competence to speak with an authority that would justify the force of their decision? What is political talk for? Where might it lead?

This book is about how people talk about politics – how turbulent topics and deadlocked disagreements come to be aired in a culture where there are no reliable scripts to turn to. It is not about the political machinations that led to Brexit but it seeks to explore how it feels for people when their voices (and silences) become integral to political dramas that enfold them. It might be imagined that in any society calling itself a democracy most people would find it easy to speak confidently about political issues and values, but what follows suggests otherwise. It was within the hum of millions of mundane conversations that Brexit was translated into the lexicon of personal experience, as people formed and firmed up their positions through stuttering starts to speech, pregnant pauses, semi-revealed thoughts and lingering memories of conversations past. Through such talk, political predilections leaked out as expressions of personal troubles. This is an observation to which we shall return often in this book, for the ways in which political talk moves fluidly between private identity and public sociality forces each into the orbit of the other and defines the political as a peculiar space of translation.

What political talk does

Talk turns to politics when there is doubt about 'the only possible way to do things'. Harold Garfinkel (1967: 50) famously claimed that for social stability to prevail there must be 'a relationship of undoubted correspondence' between what people assume about others, what others assume about them, and what each assumes the other assumes about them'. In the social performance of everyday life, populated by curious and restless subjectivities, such neat correspondences are frequently called into question. People not only disagree with one another but also cast doubt upon the sincerity or competence of those committed to rival perspectives. They question partisan interests, argue about the record and meaning of experience, dispute norms and resist resolution. It is within such moments of disquiet and contention that political talk emerges, confronting the already constituted significations of everyday life with subjective accounts, beliefs, assertions and justifications that throw 'common-sense' perception into crisis. Politics entails a relentless struggle to define social reality and the persistence of political talk stands as an empirical repudiation of the hope that such a contest can ever be finally resolved.

Extensive scholarly research has been devoted to characterizing these moments of interpersonal contention. Such studies have been dominated by a conceptual framework in which the meaning of 'political talk' is taken for granted. Methodologically, researchers have tended to ask people survey questions about how often, with whom and about which topics they talk about politics, assuming that this will mean more or less the same thing to everyone. Findings from these surveys suggest that most people feel safer expressing their disagreements with people they think will share them because they are similar to them (McPherson et al., 2001; Eveland and Kleinman, 2013; Colleoni et al., 2014; Lev-On and Lissitsa, 2015); that most people recall talking about politics with conversation partners with whom they have had a long-standing relationship, such as family members and close friends (Bennett, Flickinger, and Rhine, 2000; Knoke, 1990; Mutz, 2006); that such conversations take place overwhelmingly face to face, though increasingly online (Stromer-Galley et al., 2015; Barnidge, 2017; Chan, 2018); and that people only very rarely change their views as a result of political conversations (Eveland et al., 2011). While such studies have resulted in rich findings, they are limited by a misplaced confidence that when asking respondents questions about political talk they will answer with reference to a single, defined activity. But this is rarely the case. In a fascinating empirical study, Jennifer Fitzgerald (2013) has shown precisely how varied and inconsistent people's responses are when they are asked to classify an event or phenomenon as being 'political'. She notes that 'regular people often disagree with one another over what the term "political" signifies. . . . Some people have broader interpretations of the political sphere than others; that is, some people operate with a sense that very few themes are political while others perceive many as such'. Such semantic pluralism poses a formidable challenge to studies of political talk as a quantifiable activity. Given that survey research has focused on themes deemed to be politically relevant rather than a broader range of situations in which the meaning of social reality is contested, it is hardly surprising to find that there are concerns about its 'relative neglect of important aspects of the interpersonal communication process that we should consider more carefully to enrich our understanding of political conversation' (Eveland et al., 2011).

How, then, should one go about exploring the ways in which people talk about an 'essentially contested concept' (Gallie, 1956) like politics? There are two ways of thinking about this. The first conceives of political talk as a discrete discursive domain. We live in a world in which 'politics' seems to be relentlessly going on around us. Even the most energetically inattentive find it hard to resist its encompassing noise, while the actively interested buy into its headlines, jargon, policies, personalities, events, jokes, slogans, outrages, histories and evasions, thereby perpetuating its semblance of urgent relevance. Political talk in this sense is a mode of cultural acknowledgement – an expressive yielding to a defined object.

A second way of thinking about 'political talk' is as a manner of relating to and intervening in the world. In this sense the embodied act of speaking is itself political, for it constitutes an incipient exercise of agency. Rather than defining political talk with reference to its thematic content (government policies, election campaigns, wars, taxes), it can be read as a gesture of self-disclosure – a mode of announcing that one is actively in the world and not merely a mute spectator. As a tacit, habitual and infraconscious social practice through which people seek to register their public presence, political talk is performative: it makes things happen, even if only by breaking what would otherwise have been an inert silence.

There is a tension between these two conceptions of political talk. According to the first, politics is an object of attention and attachment that suffuses the cultural atmosphere. To recognize and reflect upon this object is a form of acculturation. People inhabit political cultures and learn to express themselves in relation to their norms, narratives and institutions. The mode of such expression is open to normative evaluation, allowing scholars who study political talk to arrive at qualitative assessments based on the extent to which it is civic (oriented towards public rather than selfish ends), civil (conducted with appropriate restraint), propositional (semantically structured with a view to making its implications explicit) and reasonable (weakly conceived in terms of basic coherence, but sometimes strongly appraised in terms of epistemological rigour). Such standards have led political scientists to merge description and appraisal in their accounts of the relationship between types of political culture and qualities of public discourse. For example, Almond and Verba (1963), in their seminal study of 'political cultures' in five nations, argued that the more democratic and tolerant a culture is, the more likely it will be to generate voluminous and pervasive political talk. The more authoritarian and sclerotic a culture is, the more it is likely to be characterized by political reticence. Having asked their survey respondents 'how often they discussed public affairs' and having found that Americans and Britons engaged in such conversations more often than West Germans, Italians and Mexicans (even though a significant number in all countries claimed that they rarely or never did), Almond and Verba concluded that these findings reflected different qualities of 'civic culture', some of which were more conducive to political talk than others. Civic political cultures, they argued, are 'allegiant participant cultures' (1963: 31), characterized by the positive orientation of their members towards their input structures and processes. Building upon this line of theory, Ronald Inglehart (1988: 1220) felt sufficiently confident to assert that 'over half of the variance in the persistence of democratic institutions can be attributed to the effects of political culture alone' and that '[t]he same is true of a given public's rate of political discussion'. Thought of in this way, culture is an immensely powerful independent variable. On the one hand, it possesses active, transmissive agency which makes things happen through socialization and on the other hand, its very survival depends upon strong normative allegiance from socialized actors.

The circularity of this explanation has led more recent social theorists to cast doubt upon the notion that 'culture shapes actions by supplying ultimate ends or values towards which action is directed' (Swidler, 1986: 273; see also Pateman, 1971, 1980; Lane, 1992; Street, 1997; Jepperson and Swidler, 1994; Wedeen, 2002; Couldry, 2004; Jones, 2005; Dahlgren, 2002, 2009; Dalton and Welzel, 2014). In contrast to the cultural determinism of functionalist political science, theorists have suggested that participation in a culture has less to do with allegiance to norms than the exercise of practical intelligence, tried and tested in contingent situations and over time. It is through improvisational and creative social practices that people navigate and negotiate their way through the world – and speaking is one such practice.

To characterize political talk as social practice, as I do in this book, is to acknowledge that it is an animate way of being in, and acting upon, the world – of declaring a capacity to affirm, question or potentially unsettle established narratives of reality. When a group of people at a rock concert begin to sway collectively to the beat of a band and, perhaps, join in with the chorus of a song, they do so on the basis of a number of implicitly shared understandings about what a rock concert is; what it means to be part of a crowd at such an event; how to recognize when the collective mood is attuned to moving en masse; how to differentiate an all-join-in chorus from the lyrics of a subtle ballad; what the words of the chorus are; and what they mean. People do not calculate the right moment to sway their bodies or deliberate about the best way to interpret or join in with the chorus. It just happens on the basis of practical reason that seems to make sense at the time. If pressed to say why, most people would say that they know how to perform in certain situations and what such performances mean by drawing upon their awareness of how similar actions were performed in comparable contexts.

This is not to say that practices are merely handed down as ready-made performances, but that the improvisational and re-interpretive aspects of social practice draw upon a range and mix of cultural symbols, stories, memories and codes. As Ann Swidler (1986: 13) reminds us, 'people know much more of their culture than they use'. The fact that one lives in a market economy does not mean that one will subscribe to the norms and practices of commercial competition. Some people will be deeply attracted to such practices (even though, in some instances, they might be weakly positioned in relation to market power) and others will find such practices shallow, frustrating or immoral. Even within individual lives, some ways of behaving make sense within one social circle, but not within another; some high principles serve well in certain situations, but cannot be sustained in others; some arguments rely upon beliefs, narratives and references which will be jettisoned at a later moment (sometimes a matter of seconds later) when a different argument – or part of the same argument – needs to be justified. In short, people use cultural resources pragmatically. 'We must think of culture less as a great stream in which we are all immersed', argues Swidler (1986: 24), 'and more as a bag of tricks or an oddly assorted toolkit . . . containing implements of varying shapes that fit the hand more or less well, are not always easy to use, and only sometimes do the job.' The idea of practices as exploratory gestures that are contingently appropriated, revised, combined and discarded captures the difference between the notion of culture as a comprehensive normative agent and a much more improvisational sense of cultural agency.

The performance of social practices assumes shared understanding. In a crowded restaurant where it is not immediately obvious who is a waiter and who is a customer, waiters need to enact practices that will be recognized by others. They might stand still next to the table with their hands behind their backs or hold out a menu or pull out a chair. Performing a practice that only makes sense to them – sitting under the table humming a tune or distributing leaflets about a carpet sale or sitting on the chair in order to warm it up for the customer – will be regarded as an idiosyncrasy rather than a meaningful social practice. To be effective, social practices must be communicatively intelligible. They depend, therefore, upon felicitous interaction – the performance encompasses feedback as well as enactment.

To say, then, that political talk is a social practice is to make five basic claims: First, it entails an attempt to make meaning, but not necessarily (or usually) in the formal fashion associated with systematic philosophical inquiry. Political talk tends to rely upon what Russell Hardin (2002: 165) calls 'street-level epistemology . . . which is not about what counts as knowledge in say, physics, but rather about what counts as your knowledge, my knowledge, the ordinary person's knowledge'. Unlike formal knowledge, street-level epistemology is concerned with establishing the usefulness and consequences of what is said. The validity of useful and consequential political meaning depends less on tests of internal rationality than upon its fit with experience. People ask themselves the practical question, 'Is what is being said to me helpful in making sense of my standing in a complex world'?

Second, identifying the practice of political talk entails more than a search for discrete moments or periods of activity. Political talk 'comes up' and is 'dropped', leaving traces that range from the vividly imprinted to the barely discernible. Rarely confined to intentional declarations or coherent flows of argumentation, political talk lingers longer than the echo of a specific moment of disagreement, often preceding it within other strands of conversation and hovering around it as an enveloping mood. The task of understanding what is really being said within political talk often calls for insight into the biographies, motives and insecurities of the speakers.

Third, the practice of political talk relies upon a range of proficiencies which are more likely to be tacitly acquired than consciously learned. Such practices entail knowing how more than knowing that. Just as people joining in with a chorus at a rock concert might not recall having learned the words or know that their voice is moving to a different key or recognize consciously the synchronicity of the swaying of their bodies with those around them, people often find themselves contributing to a policy debate without knowing that there is a policy to debate or performing being hurt by a social injustice without feeling able to articulate the depth or cause of that hurt or the precise nature of that injustice.

Fourth, political talk draws upon a range of cultural references that 'establish associations among things that count' (Boltanski and Thévenot, 2006: 22). In short, such references serve to effect social connections and forge discursive cohesion. As Bakhtin (1986: 93) points out:

> The topic of the speaker's speech, regardless of what this topic may be, does not become the object of speech for the first time in any given utterance: a given speaker is not the first to speak about it. The object, as it were, has already been articulated, disputed, elucidated and evaluated in various ways. Various viewpoints, world views, and trends cross, converge and diverge in it.

Practices of political talk incorporate stock phrases, textual references and citational tones, gestures and facial expressions. Such somatic, gestural and intonational signals are often registered before 'the topic of the speaker's speech' is ever comprehended. It is as if the form is conspicuous prior to the content.

Fifth, political talk practices are geared towards communicative legibility. A contention that nobody recognizes as a contention might just as well be a nod of agreement. Making sense of political talk calls for a sensitivity towards the ways in which people's expressive actions generate shareable meaning and the extent to which there is a correspondence between performance and reception. Making oneself intelligible entails more than semantic accuracy or clear-cut diction. It is through practice that communicators learn to make themselves not only clear but also accountable and esteemed.

The messy fragmentation and indecipherability of political talk calls for attention to the formidable exertion involved in producing intersubjectively recognizable political meaning. Following George Steiner's (1975: 45) important insights, I want to consider this task as one of translation, for

> Any model of communication is at the same time a model of trans-lation, of a vertical or horizontal transfer of significance. No two historical epochs, no two social classes, no two localities use words and syntax to signify exactly the same things, to send identical signals of valuation and inference. Neither do two human beings.

Political talk, more than most other forms of communication, is characterized by an impulse to translate – to attract others into one's perspectival orbit. More than just a semantic operation, translation relies upon a broad repertoire of pragmatic cues ranging from intensity of gaze and gestural signalling to pace of delivery and tonal inflection.

The generation of intersubjective meaning within political talk entails three kinds of translatory sensibility, each of which is considered in detail in this chapter. The first involves the delicate work of relating personal experience to public affairs This is not merely a matter of understanding how one's own life challenges relate to broader social forces or how the latter impinge, sometimes imperceptibly, upon what seem to be private sorrows, but of finding a language whereby the intimacies of the particular can be expressed in the impersonal terms of abstract social relations. Second, the performance of political talk depends upon a sensibility towards the protocols of self-presentation – the 'feeling rules' that serve as both conduits and constraints for the expression of passionate beliefs. Third, claims made within political talk do not emerge naturally or randomly, but relate to modes of justification, the intricate genealogies of which frame such claims and position speakers within ideological meshes that are not of their own making.

Of course, we are not referring here to standard linguistic translation, which sets out to establish a correspondence between two texts. Translation, in the sense that Steiner uses the term and I am using it here, is itself a social practice, pointing towards the vulnerability of any attempt to generate unambiguous shared meaning. Political translation reflects back on itself meta-pragmatically, drawing attention to its fragility as a communicative compromise – always a reduced copy of private sensation and complex thought. When people patch together their political talk, frequently peppered with phrases like 'you know', 'I mean' or 'what I'm trying to say is', they are acknowledging that 'no two human beings share an identical associative context' (Steiner, 1975: 170), and therefore 'all communication interprets between privacies' (Steiner, 1975: 198). All political talk, one might say, stretches the personal into the social and the social into the personal.

Making the personal political

The boundary between the embodied consciousness of personal experience and the manifold ties of the social environment is dim and blurred. Everyday talk moves imperceptibly between one and the other, translating between domains of perception. People are neither wholly first-person selves, knowable only through solipsistic introspection, nor sensory sponges, incapable of sensation without social priming. The much-vaunted moral autonomy of the liberal subject is a learned competence, acquired through what the philosopher Charles Taylor (1989: 36) calls 'webs of interlocution'. Speaking subjects are relational beings who know themselves to be themselves through interaction with others (Archer, 2000; Sedikides and Brewer, 2001).

The relational self assumes identity through mundane conversations which veer between the particular and the universal, the immediate and the distant. (Tannen, 1984; Gergen, 1991; Blum-Kulka, 1997; Papacharissi, 2012). Sociolinguists have observed how people's speaking styles change between talk within everyday social relationships and the transmission of messages to a more remotely universal audience. The former is classified as listener-oriented and the latter as message-oriented speech (Brown, 1981). Talk with friends tends to be characterized by listener-oriented flexibility, empathy and assumed mutual understanding. Speaking to a university seminar, an interview panel or a public meeting entails an orientation towards universal comprehension. Message-oriented speech is marked by an absence of intimate nuance and ellipsis because it is routed towards abstract space; the amorphousness of its recipients extends its reach but limits its depth.

The distinction between these contrasting registers is far from being simply stylistic. People do not merely speak, or produce meanings, but they speak to; they have in mind an addressee who will at least hear, and at best respond in some way, to what they are saying. Listener-oriented communication occurs within a context in which the addressee is a known entity. As one speaks, it is possible to anticipate reception. The more distant and indeterminate the addressee, the less confident a speaker can be that there will be a correspondence of perspectives. Political talk between friends and intimates shifts between shared experience and more impersonal propositions, while the kind of political talk that is addressed to a diffuse audience is more prone to abstraction and principle.

Pursuing a related theme, Frederick Erickson (1982: 45–6) points out that 'There are at least three types of production resources available to conversationalists: "immediately local" resources, "local resources once removed" from the immediate scene, and "nonlocal resources"'. It is in local terms that many mundane conversations begin and end. In such cases, the world that is the subject of talk is within the immediate sight and grasp of the speakers:

> an essential aspect of local production is the continual activity of the partners in telling each other what is going on in real time – what time it is, what activity it is now. This telling is done explicitly and implicitly, verbally and nonverbally, by

a host of surface structural means that Gumperz (1977) calls contextualization cues.

What Erickson refers to as 'local resources once removed' are utilized when immediate conversations are extended across time and space to evoke themes that are not directly present but are part of the speakers' shared history:

> Influences on the immediate conversation can come from outside it, across days, weeks, even years, as in the recurring meetings of a committee, in long-standing family disputes ('Oh God, you're not going to bring that up again!'), or in a military attack, in which various subgroups begin an assault simultaneously, the officers having synchronized their watches.

Beyond these directly and indirectly localized conversational references, Erickson refers to 'nonlocal resources' which 'derive from the wider social structure'. These include a vast array of references to common knowledge, official accounts, cultural protocols, geopolitical images and appropriate modes of expression.

Erickson's classifications are particularly relevant to political talk, much of which emerges within the realm of the 'local' or 'local once removed', but in order to be seen to relate to the codes of political culture, they are compelled to draw upon nonlocal resources. Perhaps this is what C. Wright Mills was referring to in the chapter on 'Politics' in his classic study *The Sociological Imagination* (1959: 187), where he identified a fundamental problem facing the inhabitants of contemporary democracies:

> Whether or not they are aware of them, [people] in a mass society are gripped by personal troubles which they are not able to turn into social issues. They do not understand the interplay of these personal troubles of their milieux with problems of social structure.

All too often this 'interplay' is impeded by the abstract formulations through which the social is characterized. Translating between the generalized language of politics and the specificity of personal experience is not easy. Writing about the reported fact that 'the most Googled question during one of the leaders' debates [in the 2015 UK election] was: "What is austerity?"', Owen Jones observed that 'It is an abstract concept to many voters' (*The Guardian*, 14.10.15). Indeed, many economists have concluded that most consumers, including University graduates, lack the 'minimal economic knowledge' required to understand how to participate effectively in economic life (Walstad and Allgood, 1999; Steiner, 2001; Wobker et al., 2012). In a fascinating study exploring how average Americans and US economists differ in their perceptions of the state of the economy, Blendon et al. (1997: 115) note that 'personal experiences may yield a different public perception of economic conditions than that described by official statistics'. They point out that

> when the economy is growing slowly, people may not perceive their financial gains, because they are relatively small increments to family income. During much of the last two decades increases in average families' incomes have often occurred because of spouses working more hours in paid employment. This commonly means lost work in the home and extra expenses such as day care, transportation and the need for paid in-home help. Taking these costs into account may lead the average family to see their net income, after working costs are deducted, as growing at a much slower rate than portrayed by economic statistics.

In the face of this gulf between the aching awareness of concrete effects and the cognitive anxiety produced by estranging terminology, people are compelled to engage in a kind of epistemological translation, decrypting the aggregate quantitative optimism of economists' and politicians' thought and rendering it meaningful in terms of their personal experience.

The pressure to translate between the personal and the social presents a major challenge to people who want to give voice to political feelings but feel daunted by the impersonal abstractness in which 'problems of social structure' are conventionally couched. It is one thing to speak about 'the lousy landlord' who seems interested only in raising the rent and another to talk about the regulation of the housing market. It is one thing to be anxious about the quality of the neighbourhood air and its effects upon your child's asthma and another to enter into a debate about international environmental policies and ways of enforcing them. Many people will talk confidently to their friends and family about how the local school could be improved or traffic controls made more efficient or the rewards for their job made more generous, but when these matters are re-presented to them as 'education policy', 'town planning' or 'just principles for distributing national wealth', they insist that 'politics' is either beyond or beneath them. As Nina Eliasoph (1998: 8) explains in her insightful study of how Americans avoid talking about politics, people seem willing to speak energetically about matters of concern to them within the safe, 'backstage' context of their homes and neighbourhoods, but as soon as such matters begin to be discussed as 'frontstage', public issues, these same people retreat from public discussion, claiming not to be interested in 'politics'. 'Most people', Eliasoph observed, 'did not usually talk about their concerns to an audience larger than one, in a voice louder than a whisper'.

The depiction of social problems as emanating from an abstract social domain is relatively recent. In her admirable study of the rise of the social domain in nineteenth-century Britain, Mary Poovey (1995: 133) illuminates a project which 'privileged normative abstractions and calculations about aggregates, both of which were (supposedly) derived from empirical observation'. The perils of code-switching between the vernacular languages of personal talk (the local whisper) and the official register of political discourse (the appeal to the social) entails a process of subtle translation. When people seek to relate their own narratives, thoughts and feelings, their speech tends to draw upon local resources and be listener-oriented. It is inter-biographical, in the sense that it emanates from personal experience and is oriented towards the common sensibilities of others. Relating such accounts to aggregate entities such as 'the social' or 'the political' calls for a different mode of communication, characterized by the kind of 'rationalizing abstractions' (Poovey: 133) that can often render experience flat and homogeneous. To enter the domain of the social – of which the political is a sub-set – entails an accommodation with forms of abstraction, such as structural relationships, policy cycles, market expansions and contractions, class formations and global crises. 'The political' as a social domain comprises a series of repetitious and replicable patterns of human intercourse that constitute the abstract relations of power. In seeking to stretch the relevance of their personal experiences beyond themselves, people are compelled to engage with such impersonal terminology, speaking of the merits or otherwise of 'austerity', the records of the 'left' and 'right', the health of 'the economy' or the best ways to 'defend the West'. Valuable as these abstractions might sometimes be as heuristic signposts, their effect is to distance the political – to render it flat and inhuman. In the personal accounts of political talk discussed in subsequent chapters, we shall see how commonly political conversations are blighted by an inability to infuse the abstractly social with the pulsating presence of the experiential.

From feel to speak

Erasmus famously asserted that 'all the emotions belong to Folly, and this is what marks the wise man off from the fool; he is ruled by reason, the fool by his emotions'. A crude split between expression emanating from 'the heart', conceived as flowing from passionate and uncontrollable urges 'within', and sober utterances emerging from 'the mind', filtered through the purifying screen of rationality, has resulted in an arid notion of cognition and an obtuse account of feeling.

Modernist thought has been characterized by a disjunctive contrast between reason and emotion, intellect and affect, and mind and body. Speaking from the heart has traditionally been considered to be emotionally charged, impulsive and feminized, while those who speak from or to the mind are more likely to be regarded as reflective, calculating, serious men of the world. Kuklinski et al. (1991: 1) embrace this normative dichotomy when they assert that 'In a democratic society, reasonable decisions are preferable to unreasonable ones; considered thought leads to the former, emotions to the latter'.

When affective speech is either devalorized as little more than a verbal grunt or feared as a force likely to overpower cognitive composure, producing political meaning becomes a project of protecting Aristotelian logos from contamination by unruly pathos (Coleman, 2015). At best, appeals to emotion are demoted to the function of reinforcing rational discourse (one of the most popular published guides to 'effective speaking' advises its readers that 'emotional appeals supplement logic' (Verderber, 7th edition, 1994: 262) and at worst, any deviation from dispassionate talk is regarded as 'hollow and void' infelicity (Austin, 1962: 22).

In recent decades, this dualism has been called into question, both normatively and empirically. Feminist scholars, such as Iris Marion Young (1985: 382), have argued for 'a conception of normative reason that does not oppose reason to desire and affectivity'. She argues that

> Impartial civilized reason characterizes the virtue of the republican man who rises above passion and desire. Instead of cutting bourgeois man entirely off from the body and affectivity, however, this culture of the rational public confines them to the domestic sphere which also confines women's passions and provides emotional solace to men and children. Indeed, within the domestic realm sentiments can flower, and each individual can recognize and affirm his particularity. Because virtues of impartiality and universality define the public realm, it precisely ought not to attend to our particularity. Modern normative reason and its political expression in the idea of the civic public, then, has unity and coherence by its expulsion and confinement of everything that would threaten to invade the polity with differentiation: the specificity of women's bodies and desire, the difference of race and culture, the variability and heterogeneity of the needs, the goals and desires of each individual, the ambiguity and changeability of feeling. (Young, 1985: 390)

The empirical reality is that people engage in political talk as embodied, sentient beings. Before words are ever spoken, affects simmer and surge. Before enunciation ever happens, sensations and images, each with its own textures, intensities and circuits of memory, animate the expressive urge. The idea that emotional speech somehow undermines or embarrasses serious meaning completely misses the sense in which '[i]nstinct and feeling . . . everywhere intrude to influence what is said – just as the things which come to be said intrude back upon feeling' (Soper, 1990: 11). The feeling that there is something wrong or unfair about the way things are not only precedes verbalized contention but also shapes its expression (Campbell, 1997). To be left speechless by anger in response to injustice is not to be quiescent or dumb, but to be replete with feelings that cannot yet be organized into a coherent utterance. To find appropriate words of disagreement that can be spoken is not to transcend feeling, but to combine linguistic expression with a range of tonal, gestural and somatic signs with a view to communicating deep meaning.

Recent empirical findings in the fields of psychobiology and neuroscience have caught up with this dialectical understanding of the entanglement between what is felt and what is said. Researchers have identified a much more complex relationship between cognition and affect than had been acknowledged by those who considered 'basic emotions' to be genetically evolved and independently operating priming triggers. Rather than thinking of affects as universal phenomena that impose upon thought, current research points to an intricate patterning and splicing of affective sensations, dialectically inseparable from cognitive appraisal (Davidson et al., 2003; Probyn, 2005; Ringrose, 2011; Wetherell, 2012; Blackman, 2012).

In responding to this new thinking about the relationship between cognition and affect, scholars have mainly focused upon its implications for individual intentionality. Some have drawn the radical conclusion that, because affectivity operates below the threshold of cognition, accounts of human behaviour that emphasize conscious intentionality are exaggerated – that much of what people think, say and do is motivated by precognitive and proprioceptive factors that precede and shape their intentions. Adhering to a position that 'valorises those processes that operate before . . . conscious, reflective thought' (McCormack, 2005: 122), so-called non-representational theorists, such as Brian Massumi (2002), William Connolly (2002), Nigel Thrift (2008) and Teresa Brennan (2004), are suspicious of accounts of human action that overestimate premeditation. They argue that much of what passes for intentionality amounts to rational conceit – that individuals cannot but collude with affective surges that overwhelm their conscious reason.

Critics of non-representational theory argue that, while dualistic neglect of affectivity has historically circumscribed positivist origins, a radical turn to neuropolitical explanation merely reverses the previous error by giving conceptual priority to affect over cognition in ways that diminish scope for deliberate action (Barnett, 2008; Leys, 2011).

Both non-representational theorists and their critics seem to have in mind the figure of a lone individual, balanced precariously between cognitive purposefulness and affective turbulence. In thinking about social practices, such as political talk, these binary distinctions seem misplaced. As Margaret Wetherell (2012: 73) puts it,

> speech acts formulating reasons and thoughts ('cognitives'), or action plans and goals ('motives'), will be as important as speech acts forming emotions ('emotives'). Affective-discursive action is probably most frequently accomplished seamlessly through all three where it is more or less impossible to establish credible analytic distinctions between them.

Thought of in this way, the practical relationship between cognition and affect entails not so much a competition between qualitatively discordant forces as an ongoing process of translation between different ways of arriving at and executing a social performance. William Reddy's (2001: 80) conception of the disaggregated self, rendered integral by means of tacit translation, is particularly illuminating in this respect. Reddy argues that translation is

> something that goes on not just between languages and between individuals, but among sensory modalities, procedural habits and linguistic structures. This idea points not to a reconstitution of a Cartesian type of subjectivity, but toward the conception of the individual as a site where messages arrive in many different languages or codes, and where some of the messages are successfully translated into other codes, while others are not.

At the most basic level, this kind of translation entails coordination, at the levels of both attention and action, between different ways of responding to the world. As will become clear when we turn in subsequent chapters to people's accounts of political arguments, disagreement often stems not from anything that has been stated explicitly, but from assumptions about values and intentions that frame ongoing interpretation. Unspoken motives often become detectable through micro-observation of a speaker's non-verbal behaviour. While what is being 'said' is non-verbal, communication is still taking place and can be read as if it were enunciated in words (Beattie, 2003; Kendon, 2004; Kostic and Chadee, 2015). Political disagreements are typically infused with affective tensions which are appraised in real time, as interactants attempt to discern consistency or incongruity between explicit expression and tacit feeling. Appraising each of these communicative modes (saying and feeling) involves different sensory resources and it is only through tacit translation that people can feel convinced that there is a correspondence between signals and their meanings. Such cross-sensory translation will rarely be conscious or explicit. As Margaret Wetherell (2012: 79) explains: 'Because we engage in affective practice all the time, every member of society possesses a wide-ranging, inarticulate, utilitarian knowledge about affective performance: how to enact it, how to categorise it and how to assign moral and social significance to affective displays.' This understanding of affective social practice is particularly relevant to political talk, the success of which seems to depend upon an attunement to rules of apposite social performance.

Of course, all effective self-presentation relies to some extent upon a sensibility towards rules of the game. But political talkers seem to focus on these rules in a self-conscious manner, working constantly at the task of translating between the motivating rationale for their performance and its affective as well as cognitive impact upon interlocutors. Given its typically message-oriented character, political talk often entails a way of speaking that puts itself on display – that is performed with particular sensitivity to the judgement of its audience. To 'pull off' this special kind of social performance, three kinds of translatory challenges have to be faced.

First, there is the quest for what we might call 'proper expression'. Cultural expectations regarding appropriate terms, tones, times and places for expressing contention play a crucial role in determining who speaks, how they speak and whether they should be taken seriously. These expectations are rarely codified or even made explicit. They inhere within the infraconsciousness of social practice. Typically, they become conspicuous only when they are breached, and they change between and within cultures, often in accordance with what some have called 'emotional fashions' (Stearns and Stearns, 1985; Craib, 1990; Reddy, 2001). For example, the Churchillian mode of performing authority was regarded as admirable in an era of late patrician politics, but by the early days of television, the post-deferential cultural turn and new technologies of close-up observation left such performances seeming increasingly ridiculous (Churchill famously disliked appearing on the small screen; see Cockerell, 1989; Lawrence, 2009). Expectations regarding lay political talk have also changed: consider, for example, the stylistic contrast between the typically clipped and deferential responses to 1950s' vox pop interviews and the prevalent volubility and self-assurance of callers to contemporary radio talk-shows. Assumptions about what constitutes 'proper expression' change, but expectations continue to mark off the sayable and serious from their unsettling opposites.

Arlie Hochschild (1979: 566) describes such expectations as 'feeling rules': 'guidelines for the assessment of fits and misfits between feeling and situation'. The flight attendants about whom Hochschild (1983) wrote were compelled to suppress their private emotions for the sake of producing smooth performances of cheerful servility. Such performances constitute a form of 'emotional labour' whereby the expression of feeling is sold to an employer (and thereby alienated from the embodied self) in much the same way that physical labour is exchanged for money. More recent scholars have investigated other forms of commodified emotional labour that depend upon the maintenance of highly managed affective displays (Smith, 1992; Ashforth and Humphrey, 1993; Isenbarger and Zembylas, 2006; Grandey, 2015).

Emotional regulation is not confined to the workplace or to paid occupations. Affective display rules apply to unpaid social activities, such as political talk. Failure to adhere to protocols of expressive propriety can doom a political utterance to scorn or disregard. Politicians are under pressure to perform in ways that make them look and sound like politicians. An important part of the social performance of being a political activist entails managing an affective balance between commitment and fanaticism. Even being a political onlooker or outsider, 'engaged' in the modes of avoidance described by Eliasoph (1998), calls for a certain sensibility towards self-positioning that does not emerge by default. These tacit protocols of affective practice are picked up – and dropped – along the way as people form and modify their political identities.

As will become clear in subsequent chapters, the feeling rules that surround political talk are far less commonly spoken about in academic or 'insider' accounts of political discourse than in lay reflections of what it feels like to talk about politics with other people. On the ground, politics occupies a discursive soundscape in which the risks and frustrations of expressive impropriety can often be discerned at the hazy level of pre-linguistic intonation. People sense when it is dangerous to talk about politics, even if they cannot always explain the source or consequences of the risks they are apprehending. Parents pass on political feeling rules to their children and, as with many other rules, some faithfully internalize them, while others choose to experiment at the boundaries. Certain institutional settings, such as A-level Politics classes, university political groups, political parties and debating clubs, specialize in adjusting people to feeling rules, often at the same time as they encourage the illusory belief that politics is a purely cognitive game (Rowbotham et al., 1979; Jasper, 1998; Zembylas, 2006).

Burdened by emotions that exceed the available terms and tones of political vocabulary, and verbal repertoires that offer the hope of expressive propriety at the cost of authentic self-representation, deciding whether, when or how to express a political feeling becomes a task of everyday translation. Is this the right moment to speak? Could my words reveal more about what is on my mind than I want to share? Could the unruly tone of my voice or movement of my body undermine the constrained propriety of my utterance? Might my speech be smothered by my feelings? (And who is to say that it should not be? Who sets the rules of discursive propriety?) Translation fluctuates between technical and normative interpretation, turning the framing of political discourse into an act of discursive politics.

Second, political talk involves translation between subjective inclinations and dispositions that people have internalized (the way they have come to see themselves and their potential) and the objective vagaries that they encounter by simply being in the world (their responses to social forces and structures). Feelings of inadequacy and vulnerability are routinely internalized: people ask themselves 'How can someone who speaks like me take on the received wisdom of those who are in the know? How will I feel if I state my view, only to have it refuted by incontrovertible statistics? What if I'm shown up as an angry, opinionated person? Why should I commit myself to this public encounter when I can be left in peace with my unexpressed disagreements?'

Subjective dispositions towards the world and one's position within it play an important part in determining whether and when it feels right to speak. But such dispositions constitute a much more intractable barrier to political articulation for some people than for others. Those who have grown used to the expectation of being heard; who have been schooled to believe that their voices will probably count; and who fall into the narrow social category from which members of the political elite tend to be recruited are least likely to experience awkward, shameful or immobilizing dissonance between how they feel and how they speak. The terms of admissible political talk seem designed to reflect their ways of feeling the world. The very pitch, pace and volume of their speech declare a belief that how they feel should be made known. Others are much less comfortable engaging in the kind of message-oriented speech in which political beliefs are conventionally couched. They are often unconfident about translating their feelings – commonly judged to be raw, vulgar, fickle and unmanageable –

into words, fearing that the latter might expose or betray them. Just as 'proper expression' is a mark of political distinction (to use Bourdieu's term), the risk of being exposed as improper leads some people to adopt strategies of self-exclusion from the political sphere, while others – most notably populists – refuse to engage in inter-discursive translation, believing, instead, in the efficacy of collective rage as an end in itself.

Faced with an urge to speak out, complain, contest claims or put things right, people are frequently compelled to translate between their conditioned sense of weakness in the face of greater powers and an imagined sense of themselves as articulate beings, capable of translating their affective impulses into socially appreciated utterances. Quite often such putative translation is played out in silent, counterfactual thought: 'This is what I would say if I were to say it. This is how I would say it if I were to be able to say it that way'. Much political talk takes place within these voiceless rehearsal spaces of the mind, in which free expression is unmediated by explicit social judgement.

Third, because political talk is by definition a social interaction, those who engage in it are compelled to orient themselves towards the cultural atmosphere within which they speak. This entails reading the social mood; having an idea about what seems to matter to other people; possessing a sense of how public events, trends and emotions seem to connect to one another; distinguishing between commonplace, controversial and outlandish values; knowing where to find like-minded thinkers; being able to tell the difference between the vital and the incidental. The notion of social mood 'provides a way to articulate the shaping and structuring effect of historical context on our affective attachments' (Flatley, 2009: 19; Highmore, 2013).

Mood has emerged as a key feature of late-modern politics. Political statements that used to open with 'I think that' (or 'believe that') increasingly start with 'I feel like' (Worthen, 2016). What does the term 'mood' mean? Charles Altieri (2003: 2) describes moods as 'modes of feeling where the sense of subjectivity becomes diffuse and sensation merges into something close to atmosphere, something that seems to define an entire scene or situation'. This captures the sense in which moods are not possessed by subjects as discrete representations, but are mediated by socially shared, aesthetic forms of representation. Moods are felt – we are in them and they constitute an affective lens through which experience is felt. Caught up in something 'ambient, vague, diffuse, hazy, and intangible' (Felski and Fraiman, 2012) that discloses the world to them in non-propositional terms, people find themselves riding 'the wave of collectively recycled affective knowledge' (Berlant, 2010: 8). Moods are pre-conceptual rather than representational objects which trigger evaluative responses to complex intersubjective experiences. They can disturb, block, overcast, distract, paralyse and unleash – among many other effects – inflecting political agency in countless ways.

In a mass-mediated society, acts of translation between personal disposition and social mood depend more than ever upon a capacity to stay in touch with and read accurately the authoritative signalling of what constitutes social significance. As Silverstone (2007: 30) argues, 'Increasingly, what passes for public life . . . takes place, more or less exclusively, on the screen.' What becomes visible frames the social mood. Political talk is not only about issues – which typically bear a striking resemblance to the order of the media news agenda (Kim et al., 1999; McCombs, 2013; Ponder and Haridakis, 2015) – but also occurs against the backdrop of a highly mediated cultural ambience. Crises generate crisis-talk; moments of national celebration and solidarity open up space for more apolitical consensus talk; war permits modes of aggressive talk that would seem pathological in peacetime; election campaigns often descend into horse-race talk. Talking the wrong kind of talk at any of these moments can result in embarrassment. Affective translation calls for sensitive accommodation to the social mood.

But not everyone has time to spend on deciphering the inflection of the social mood. As Lauren Berlant (2008: 6) points out, 'most of social life happens in . . . modes of lower case drama, as we follow out pulsations of habituated patterning that make possible getting through the day (the relationships, the job, the life) while the brain chatters on, assessing things in focused and unfocused ways'. Caught up in the parochial soap opera of everyday life, most people's attention to global political drama tends to be intermittent. When people do not engage with capital-P politics it is not because they are apathetic (from the Greek 'without feeling'), but because their lives are crowded by pressures to simply keep going and, when they do have time to reflect, they are unsure what to do with the torrent of feelings that emanate from their being in the world. As we shall see in the chapters that follow, much of what happens in political talk has less to do with structuring arguments and choosing the right words than finding appropriate ways to express feelings, manage memories and adjust oneself to the affective inequalities of interpersonal dynamics.

From disagreement to justification

Despite the fact that many people go to great lengths to avoid engaging in any form of public political disagreement (Price et al., 2002; Brundidge, 2010; Morey et al., 2012; Cowan and Baldassarri, 2018), the agonistic spirit remains remarkably tenacious and pervasive. This is because, even at the most basic ontological level, people experience and make sense of social reality in different ways. People argue not only about what things mean but also about what they are; not only about how to respond to a situation but also to what is going on. What for one group of people might look like a flourishing entrepreneurial economy will seem to others like a system of ruthless, unbridled exploitation. Cosmopolitan cities might be experienced as vibrant places by the socially mobile, but to some indigenous communities they can feel ominously disorientating. For some people, the social order can be described in terms of what Richard Rorty (1989) calls a 'final vocabulary' (a set of terms that are incontrovertibly indexed to reality), while for others, who are perhaps more sensitive to historical contingency, everything remains open to incessant redescription.

Only in an imagined world of consensual accord, in which the manifest felicity of the social order is beyond dispute, could politics ever be rendered superfluous. For the residents of literary utopias there is quite simply 'nothing left to argue about' (Goodwin and Taylor, 1982: 34). Structural injustices having been eradicated and social solidarity having become the norm, any aberrant disagreements that do occur are so inconsequential that there is no need for adversaries to justify their positions to one another. In Chapter 26 of William Morris's *News from Nowhere* (1890), Guest, who has spent several days observing the new social order with unbounded astonishment and admiration, comes across a group of builders who have fallen out with the rest of the community. Referred to as 'the Obstinate Refusers', this dissenting group is committed to spending its time building a stone house, even though the majority of their fellows are openly sceptical about giving priority to such an objective. This being utopia, the conflict is quickly passed over as 'friendly bickering'. Why would anyone want to argue about social priorities in a community where harmony depends upon the absence of any need for justification?

But for those of us who are yet to reach the shores of Utopia, there remains a lot left to argue about, and it only rarely takes the form of 'friendly bickering'. From considered critiques to rants; from sullen grouches to viral memes; from parliamentary deliberations to street demonstrations, expressions of political contention surface and circulate. Broadly speaking, there are three approaches that individuals and groups can adopt when they find themselves in disagreement with the political status quo: grumbling, expressive speaking and constitutive rhetoric.

First, people can give expression to their objections without proposing any way of reconstructing the conditions of their dissent. Colloquially, this is usually referred to as 'grumbling', the dictionary definition of which is illuminating. In its first sense, to grumble is to produce 'a low rumbling sound'. It is a pre-lingual gurgitation that points to the futility of language. Grumbling in this sense is a sort of onomatopoeic groan – a vocal register of fated inefficacy. In its other sense, to grumble is to complain in a way that places greater emphasis upon expression than reception. The grumbler invests everything in the articulation of dissent and little in the expectation of considered attention. (The much-discussed negative emotional condition of *ressentiment*, in which hopeless grumbling in the face of seemingly inevitable inefficacy becomes a politically masochistic habit, is relevant here – Jameson, 1976; Meltzer and Musoff, 2002; Sloterdijk, 2012.)

Much of what passes for political talk in contemporary democracies amounts to little more than a stream of low-level grumbling – fragmentary content engulfed by negative form. This has led many normatively inclined democrats – and especially deliberative theorists and practitioners – to lament the absence of a public sphere in which considered judgements are made on the basis of meaningful argumentation (Fishkin, 1991; Dryzek, 2000; Parkinson and Mansbridge, 2012; Coleman et al, 2015). They argue that while a democracy of active grumblers meets one key democratic norm of free speech (literally, the right to state one's views), it diminishes civic agency by confining expression to the reiteration of original positions rather than any kind of search for intersubjective understanding. Stated in less normative terms, grumbling can be characterized as a failure of translation, resulting in a communicative impasse whereby political talk seems to be devoid of addressivity. Bakhtin (1986: 95) notes that speech is not only directed to others but also shaped by expectations regarding how likely others are to receive it respectfully:

> I try to act in accordance with the response I anticipate, so this anticipated response, in turn, exerts an active influence on my utterance. . . . When speaking I always take into account the apperceptive background of the addressee's perception of my speech: the extent to which he is familiar with the situation, whether he has special knowledge of the given cultural area of communication, his views and convictions, his prejudices (from my viewpoint), his sympathies and antipathies – because all this will determine his active responsive understanding of my utterance.

Addressivity calls for a willingness to invest in a search for shared meaning. Abandoning hope for such responsive understanding, grumblers retreat into soliloquy. They become their own audience, perhaps overheard by others, but without expectation of communicative reciprocity.

For political talk to amount to more than mere grumbling, speakers need to be 'in audience'. That is to say, they must go beyond the simple reiteration of an objection and offer some kind of justification intended to make others sympathetic to its validity. Moving from objection to justification entails translation between personal motives and public understanding.

Modes of translation differ. Some people attempt to justify their positions by focusing simply upon the validity of their own perspective. Others are more focused upon affecting the perspective of listeners. Barbara O'Keefe and Steven McCornack (1987: 71) refer to the former 'message design logic' as 'expressive':

> Characteristically, message producers who use an expressive logic fail to distinguish between thought and expression; in producing messages, they essentially 'dump' their current mental state – the thoughts and feelings the situation provokes in them are simply expressed – and they assume that that is the way others produce messages too. Within an expressive design system, expression is not systematically altered in the service of achieving effects, and message interpreters relying on an expressive design logic seldom find anything other than 'literal and direct' meaning in incoming messages.

In some respects, O'Keefe and McCornack's expressive argumentation resembles Brown's (1981) message-oriented speech, discussed earlier in this chapter. Expressive speakers assert what they believe to be the simple facts of the matter without editing their utterances for the benefit of their listeners. Ideologues and dogmatists are exemplary expressive speakers; so convinced are they by the truth of their own thoughts that they assume that only those who are incapable of or unwilling to pay attention to them could possibly disagree.

By contrast, rhetorical speakers devote their energies to generating a consensus between themselves and their listeners regarding the nature of social reality. Assuming from the outset that relating private motives to public concerns involves translatory effort, they seek to engage listeners in a shared drama:

> Rather than seeing selves and situations as given in a conventional system of rules and rather than seeing meaning as fixed in messages by their form and context, instead all meaning is treated as a matter of social negotiation. The potential of language to evoke roles and to structure context is exploited through the manipulation of stylistic variation in language and explicit contextualizing elaborations of messages. The same attention to the details of message construction is devoted to message interpretation, leading to more careful listening and deeper interpretation of intentions, motives, and character. (O'Keefe and McCornack, 1987: 72)

The task of rhetorical talk is not simply to express what is on the speaker's mind but also to address this message to others with a view to changing the way that they see themselves positioned within the drama of social reality. Raymond Williams (1974: 15) referred to this as 'the dramatization of consciousness' – a process that lays the groundwork for intersubjective understanding in which there is potential for co-orientation. Being able to put forward what seems like a 'good argument' is of limited value unless those hearing it can be persuaded that it responds to dilemmas or deficits in their own social reality. This is an enterprise of constitutive rhetoric whereby 'representations of the world . . . are engaged in constructing the world, in shaping the realities of social reality, and in accommodating their writers, performers, readers and audiences to multiple and shifting subject positions within the world they both constitute and inhabit' (Montrose, 1989: 16).

The notion of constitutive rhetoric turns on its head the conventional assumption that persuasion is at best an inveigling supplement to meaning, summoned in defence of firm conviction. Rather than taking beliefs as the principal object of study, the rhetorical analysis of political talk regards beliefs as outcomes of the ways in which social reality is framed. As Alan Finlayson (2007: 554) puts it:

> Within the rhetorical situation an argument takes place. But what an argument concerns is not always clear. . . . The point of a dispute, the 'bone of contention' is established by the act of arguing itself and the side that succeeds in fixing it secures great advantage.

Thinking of the most persistent political controversies of our age, they are seldom discussed by people as if they were logicians trying to establish the objective truth of propositions, but as contingencies that need to be appropriately framed. Before clear preferences are ever declared, narrativized plots and images, each with its own textures and intensities, and emanating from its own circuits of memory, animate the expressive urge and shape reception. Wars are fought between rival stories about who 'we' are and how 'they' constitute an existential threat; policy debates about poverty are couched in a language of moral judgement in reference to contested accounts of the causes of deprivation (Asen, 2010); elections become storytelling contests in which leaders compete to offer a choice between more or less plausible accounts of who 'the people' are and what 'the public' needs (Coleman, 2013, 2015); racial categorizations are loaded with semiotic virulence (Yanow, 2015); even claims to political and economic expertise are constructed narratively (McCloskey, 1998; Hajer, 2009; Elgie,

2015). In the search for tangible preferences, these rhetorical allusions, plots and metaphors are often dismissed as mere ideological undergrowth. But as Jeffrey Alexander (2010: 285) has provocatively stated,

> the factual status of 'issues' – what is rationally ascertainable about social problems and the policies proposed to solve them – is relatively insignificant. . . . Problems and policies are ostensible referents. What students of social power miss is the symbolic language within which issues are framed and claims for legitimacy made.

Translation between 'ostensible referents' and symbolic frames is central to both the performance and the comprehension of political talk. For speakers, a capacity to narrativize beliefs and claims is vital if effective political communication is to take place. For those seeking to make sense of political talk, attention to its rhetorical generation is likely to be more fruitful than a narrow focus upon its semantic meaning, for much of what is said in the course of any political argument relies pragmatically upon what remains unsaid – and does not need to be said because its wider meaning is invoked by reference to familiar and credible frames of meta-justification. In such contexts, the force of an argument depends upon clusters of associations and values that are not necessarily relevant to the immediate situation but serve as translatory mnemonics capable of connecting the situation to others in which similar principles are or have been at stake. It is to these frames – or orders – of justification that Luc Boltanski and Laurent Thévenot (2006) refer when they speak of 'higher common principles' to which people turn in order to legitimize their complaints and disputes. Such orders of justification are rather like the character summaries and stage directions that actors use in order to give meaning to their roles and their intentions. But, as Alexander (2011: 57) points out, there is a difference between the function performed by the dramaturgical directions given to actors in a stage play and those adopted by everyday actors within the social drama of everyday life:

> If script is meaning primed to performance, in theatrical drama this priming is usually, though not always, sketched out beforehand. In social drama, by contrast, scripts more often are inferred by actors. In a meaning-searching process that stretches from the more intuitive to the more witting, actors and audiences reflect on the performance in the process of its unfolding, gleaning a script upon which the performance 'must have' been based.

Mundane political talk tends to entail performance without any obvious script. Even though it often appears to be the case that interactants are locked into fixed roles, the interruptive potential of spontaneous dialogue confounds the predictability of any given performance. Even though much of what is said is borrowed, speakers rarely know where it was borrowed from. Even though we can often tell when speakers have gone off-script, being in-script feels much more like improvisation than rote performance. The rhetorical work of political talk amounts to more than simply finding one's proper place on the stage or adhering to a script that sustains the momentum of an agreed plot. When people talk about politics, they are not simply responding to the world around them but attempting to constitute it in the minds of others through acts of reflexive extemporization. As Lloyd Bitzer (1968: 4) puts it in his seminal paper on 'The Rhetorical Situation', rhetoric is 'a mode of altering reality, not by the direct application of energy to objects, but by the creation of discourse which changes reality through the mediation of thought and action'. To engage in political talk is not only to speak from a particular position on the social stage but also to raise questions about how different positions relate to one another as well as the horizons and constraints of the social space that the stage comprises.

As we turn to people's memories and stories of political talk in subsequent chapters, the significance of rhetorical staging will become palpable. People do not simply 'have an argument'. They argue about what it is they are arguing about. They argue about what constitutes a justifiable position. They argue about whether they should be arguing, and in these disagreements about disagreement politics emerges, reminding people that the political is not an object, but an act.

Exploring political talk as generic accomplishment

It is one thing to produce a theoretical outline of political talk as translatory social practice, but quite another to understand the ways in which the experience of political talk and its attendant feelings are incorporated into embodied routines, memories and sensibilities. Rather than being taught explicitly, the art of 'proper' or 'acceptable' political expression is absorbed by watching, reading, imitating, posturing and being corrected for behaving inappropriately. Through a series of rehearsals, people practise combinations of words, sounds, bodily gestures, ways of standing and walking, strategies of affective release and disguise, and protocols of shutting up and giving way.

This book explores how people come to learn the language, grammar and prosody of political expression; how some people become veritable rhetorical artists, while others learn to live with the permanent blush of political evasiveness; how people sense when their conversations are approaching political and civic issues; how they understand the difference between 'speaking like a politician' and 'speaking politically'; and the extent to which they believe that what they say can make even the slightest difference to the world around them. These are matters of tacit pedagogy. Just as people learn without consciously remembering learning how to eat 'properly' at a dinner table, how to laugh in ways that avoid accusations of 'madness' or 'vulgarity', how to address others of 'superior' or 'inferior' status and how to perform 'being in love', they also learn how various social situations call for different modes of talk – and how 'political talk' entails a particular set of competencies and sensibilities relating to the performance of personal agency.

As soon as a person opens her mouth (indeed, sooner: the moment she is acknowledged visually or aurally), judgements will be made about whether she is worthy of recognition and how what she says should be evaluated in terms of the genre of talk to which she is contributing. All performances are based upon a series of expectations: that addressees and onlookers possess the capacity to decode the norms of the contextual genre in which the speaker is trying to perform; that they are capable of making judgements about the speaker's position in the social landscape; and that they will understand that much of what is being said or hinted at should not be taken literally, but as tacit signals of deeper meaning. How does this work in the case of political speech?

When people 'talk politics' they perform themselves in particular ways, sometimes drawing upon received scripts, recalled tropes and unconsciously imbibed postures and at other times improvising creatively with a view to combining deep feeling and outward expression. As with any cultural practice, political voice extends across a spectrum from unconscious routine to self-conscious performance; from imperceptible tightening and loosening of bodily muscles to complex reflective states; from deep intentionality to transient time-filling; and from getting it right to screwing it up.

As Bourdieu (1992: 54) puts it:

> To speak is to appropriate one or other of the expressive styles already constituted in and through usage and objectively marked by a position in a hierarchy of styles which expresses the hierarchy of corresponding social groups. These styles, systems of differences which are both classified and classifying, ranked and ranking, mark those who appropriate them.

For many people, apprehension about the inadequacy of their speaking voices engenders an unremitting status anxiety. Racked by internalized feelings that the very sound of their voice betrays an innate vulgarity, it is not uncommon for speakers to affect imitations of acceptable conversability in the hope of avoiding elite disdain. From the clipped repression of 'telephone voices' to the 'staleness of imagery' and 'lack of precision' lamented by George Orwell (1946) in his essay 'Politics and the English Language', mimetic speech tends to be punctuated by hyper-correction and strained by rhythmic dissonance. In trying to speak 'well', speakers find themselves adopting voices that are not their own. In aspiring to be taken as an insider, they are driven to betraying themselves as impostors.

Consider, for example, the famous occasion when the established political interviewer, Jeremy Paxman, interviewed the comedian, Russell Brand, on the BBC *Newsnight* programme. He began by asking him the following question about his guest editorship of a special issue of the political magazine, the *New Statesman*:

Russell Brand, who are you to edit a political magazine?

It is a piercing opening shot, the effect of which is to cast the interviewee as an impostor. Had Brand edited a joke book, a lads' magazine or a documentary about drug addicts, the 'who are you to . . .' formulation would have seemed out of place. With this rhetorical question, Paxman aims to cut Brand down to size and remind the audience that whatever he might subsequently say should be regarded with deep suspicion. Paxman goes on to expose the temerity of Brand's position: 'If you can't be asked to vote, why should we be asked to listen to your political point of view?' Brand's whimsical response to Paxman's relentless questioning of his legitimacy as a political speaker adds further confusion to the exchange: 'I'm a kind of a person with crazy hair, quite a good sense of humour, don't know much about politics – I'm ideal'. By placing himself outside of what is usually regarded as political competence, Brand affirms his eligibility for the subversive role he has taken upon himself; it is his very out-of-placeness as a performer on the political stage that qualifies him to interrupt the scene of the drama.

This interview between an established speaker of the language of politics and an alleged impostor offers a striking illustration of how politics is not simply a subject to be spoken about but a way of speaking about experiences of power, (mis)recognition and justice. Political talk is in this sense a social practice that calls attention to the entwined relationships that always exist between speakers and the world of which they speak. At stake in the Paxman-Brand encounter were questions about whose voices are entitled to be taken seriously. Who has the right to speak about politics without being made to feel that they are paddling in the deep end of a swimming pool that they should never have been allowed into in the first place? The many ways in which the performative force of political speech is routinely dissipated by cultural expectation has been a major focus of Bourdieu's (1992: 111) writings:

> Most of the conditions that have to be fulfilled in order for a performative utterance to succeed come down to the question of the appropriateness of the speaker – or better still, his social function – and of the discourse he utters. A performative utterance is destined to fail each time that it is not pronounced by a . . . speaker who does not have the authority to emit the words that he utters.

To be regarded as someone who is capable of speaking with political authority is a generic accomplishment:

> The competence adequate to produce sentences that are likely to be understood may be quite inadequate to produce sentences that are likely to be listened to, likely to be recognized as acceptable in all the situations in which there is occasion to speak. . . . Speakers lacking the legitimate competence are de facto excluded from the social domains in which this competence is required, or are condemned to silence. (1992: 55)

This observation is particularly apposite to political talk. When people speak about politics, they are expected to provide signals of 'legitimate competence'. Signalling such proficiency entails generic modes of expression: forms of speech that serve to produce fusion between the contingency and exigency of a recurrent situation and culturally patterned forms of responding to them. So, a eulogy is a recognized form of speaking in the presence of a dead body; an examination essay is a mode of conveying competence in situations where prescribed knowledge is being tested; recipe books comprise acknowledged form of instruction for the preparation of food. The political speech is an example of such a genre, but so, less obviously, are political arguments, monologues, complaints, asides, parodies and slogans. We know what they are when we see them coming because they possess forms that constitute typical responses to recurrent encounters with the dynamics of social power.

The legitimacy of political talk depends as much – maybe more – upon fluency in the arcane terms and tones of the genre as upon the originality of what is being said – in short, the form of political speech both mediates and confers authority. Bakhtin's (1986: 80) observation that 'Many people who have an excellent command of a language often feel quite helpless in certain spheres of communication precisely because they do not have a practical command of the generic forms used in the given spheres' chimes with the stories that I heard from many of my interviewees. While feeling perfectly confident when employing other speech genres – ranging from sales talk and doctor–patient interaction to parenting and romantic intimacy – many of them felt 'quite helpless' in situations where politics was on the agenda. This led some interviewees to tell me that they 'don't talk politics', in much the same way as a tourist in Moscow might confess to not speaking Russian. In some cases, this sense of helplessness convinced people that they had nothing to say about politics or that anything they considered politically meaningful was bound to be dismissed as trite or foolish.

This experience of vulnerability in the face of an inherited code of legitimate political expression was by no means shared by everyone. Some of my interviewees considered themselves to be competent, if not fluent, in this formidable genre. They had learned the common references: names, dates, parties, alliances, isms, schisms, policies, records and iconic allusions. They had a feel for the game and would offer their own definitions of winning and losing; principles and tactics; is and ought. They had become attuned to the tonal variations of political speech, recognizing its aural cues while trying their best to dodge its rhetorical traps. Even though core agendas were set and narratives shaped long before they had arrived on the scene, they did not falter as they edged their way into the political fray.

But even here, when citizens are engaging in political discourse as if it were their own, a certain imposture is at work. For, as Bakhtin (1986: 87) points out:

> When we select words in the process of constructing an utterance, we by no means always take them from the systems of language in their neutral, dictionary form. We usually take them from other utterances that are kindred to ours in genre, that is, in theme, composition or style. Consequently, we choose words according to their generic specifications. . . . In the genre the word acquires a particular typical expression. Genres correspond to typical situations of speech communication, typical themes, and, consequently, to particular contacts between the meanings of words and actual concrete reality under certain typical circumstances. Hence also the possibility of certain typical expressions that seem to adhere to words.

In responding to recurrent situations, generic speech relies upon reiterative forms and formulations. Meaning is all too often blunted by cliché. What is being said comes to be evaluated in terms of what had been said before in similar circumstances. Learning to 'speak politics' comes to depend more upon the technical inelegance of the tourist phrase book than the poetics of a felt engagement with the world.

***

Returning to the frustration and disappointment that followed the plebiscitary moment discussed at the beginning of this chapter, perhaps this is best understood as popular acknowledgement of the chasm that stands between the ideal and the experience of democratic discourse. The vision of a 'national conversation' – a whole country forgathered in moot – offered an attractive image of vibrant public debate bringing people together beyond the ritual isolation of the ballot box. It appealed to a popular impulse that, left to themselves, people could explore their differences and arrive at a political settlement which, if not universally shared, might at least reflect a sense of mutual endeavour. But the ebullience of the imagined *agora* was rarely translated into personal experience. At the micro-level, those moments of interpersonal meeting that constitute meaningful political connection remained stubbornly unrealized. The promise of dialogue gave way to simultaneous monologues, with each side in the conflict speaking past the others at intensifying levels of volume.

To the extent that people have come to associate political talk with not being listened to, not being respected, not being understood and not being able to find the right words, the mundane work of being a democratic citizen begins to feel more like a daunting burden than a democratic habit. When people use phrases like 'let's keep politics out of this', 'stop sounding like a politician' and 'I'm not really a political person' they are not indulging in a naïve refusal to acknowledge the necessity of disagreement but hoping to steer interpersonal communication away from what they believe to be an unproductive mode of wrangling. It is not politics that is popularly unattractive, but ways of talking about it that have become unmoored from everyday experience and vernacular expression.

One aim of this book is to understand why the political genre irritates, intimidates and alienates so many people. Such an investigation must start and finish by probing feeling, for it is at the level of sensory responsiveness that the sound, sense, rhythm and integrity of political discourse are most immediately and intensely apprehended. People are not simply convinced by political claims; they are also moved by them. But when they are unmoved, and such dispassion becomes routine, they are left immobilized, facing an impasse in which the political is endured as affective agitation.

Interrogating public feelings is a far from simple matter. In this book I do it by asking a broad range of people to tell me about their memories and experiences of speaking about their political values, disagreements and uncertainties with other people. Eighty interviews were conducted as part of the research reported in this book. Fifty of them took place before the Brexit referendum of 2016. Interviewees were recruited to fit into one of four categories. The first group (sixteen people) comprised people who claimed that they rarely or never talked about politics. I wanted to understand why these people were averse to political talk or, as it transpired in some interviews, why they had been made to feel like outsiders whose political voices were unlikely to be acknowledged. The second group (sixteen people) comprised people who thought of themselves as political talkers. This group ranged from people who spent a lot of time talking about politics to family and friends to activists who talked to much wider social networks. The third group (nine people) were politicians, ranging from Members of Parliament to local councillors. The fourth group (nine people aged eleven to twenty) were young people who were studying politics at school or college. I was interested in how they might have been influenced by institutional notions of appropriate political form (Mertz, 2007). Thirty more interviews were conducted after the Brexit referendum, with an equal split between leavers and remainers.

The conduct of each interview was geared towards uncovering the deep feelings that surround and pervade moments of political talk. (See the Appendix for a detailed account of this approach to research.) The next three chapters comprise reports of my interviews. Each of these chapters explores what I heard from a different perspective. In Chapter 2, the focus is on the biographical sources of political talk. How do people encounter, attune to and remember political talk over the course of their lives? In what sense is political talk always a reflection of personal history? How do people exercise forms of political agency by telling stories about themselves? Chapter 3 considers the ways in which political talk is performed in everyday life, focusing on how some people have a lot to say about politics, while most regard talking about politics as a challenge that they prefer to avoid. What is it that the avoiders are avoiding? How does the political genre make people feel? How do the domains of everyday sociality and political discourse intersect and divide as people weave in and out of them? Chapter 4 focuses on the ways in which people took positions on a particular matter of political controversy: the UK's Brexit referendum. Taking a position entails not simply adopting a political perspective but also speaking from a particular place in the world (Coleman, 2020). How do people use political talk to assert where they stand in the world? How is political argument often a process of putting people in their place? How do the 'deep stories' that frame political talk reveal affective foundations of belief in ways that logical argumentation cannot realize? It is my hope that these three empirical chapters can offer a suggestive stimulus to reflection upon the normative requirements of micro-level democratic intercourse. In Chapter 5, we turn to the vital question of what it means to be an intelligible subject with a voice of one's own. What is implied by the assertion that 'This is me speaking'? How can the exercise of voice go wrong? How have voices been silenced over the course of history? Why are some voices valued, while others are routinely degraded and humiliated? What does it mean to speak of a voice as an instrument of agency? And why does the experience (or fantasy) of vocal agency so often end in disappointment? Chapter 6 begins by exploring contemporary anxieties about toxic public discourse and appeals to the antidote of civility. Proposing that there is more to the invigoration of political discourse than the adoption of good manners and pumped-up civic resilience, the chapter concludes by setting out an evaluative approach to thinking about interpersonal political talk.

2

Biographical feelings

Political conversations are typically transient, experienced less as unified events than relational qualities. Inviting people to talk about them is to steer them towards ephemeral memory, for political talk rarely leaves its mark as coherent chronology. Talking about talk is a metacommunicative enterprise entailing not only the retrieval of words but also the reconstruction of feelings. For this reason, the emphasis of my interviews was upon the ways in which people recalled the socio-affective dynamics of situations when they found themselves in the midst of political talk. What were the trace memories of encounters with power that framed their political identities? What does it mean to inhabit a political life history? How do people go about relating their most privately interiorized selves to the contingencies of the public world?

Once it became clear to my interviewees that I was more interested in hearing from them about their memories of being *in political talk* about contentious issues like Brexit than their attempts to justify their positions and opinions, the connection between us changed. Relieved of the obligation to justify, people began to sound less like interview subjects, dutifully responding to disconnected probes, and more like narrators of their own lives. As Michael Bamberg (2011: 5) observes, narration unites 'two different ways of making sense: a scientific approach according to which events follow each other in a quasi-causal and non-teleological sequence; and a hermeneutic and plot-governed approach from where events gain their meaning quasi-retrospectively owing to the overarching contour in which they configure'. As people started to adopt a more panoramic perspective towards their political biographies, they began to speak of them as dynamic, indeterminate dramas rather than coherent archives.

By framing talk in biographical contexts, specific moments of political interaction were transformed from being seen as singular events into narratively connected episodes. As Margaret Somers (1994: 616) explains,

The connectivity of parts is precisely why narrativity turns 'events' into *episodes*, whether the sequence of episodes is presented or experienced in anything resembling chronological order. This is done through 'emplotment'. It is emplotment that gives significance to independent instances, not their chronological or categorical order. And it is emplotment that translates events into episodes.

Typically, interviewees would situate accounts of declaring a strongly held value, confronting an odious point of view or avoiding a political conflict within a biographical narrative, relating the episode to a longer story of unfolding feelings towards the world and its structures. They used biographical reasoning (Habermas and Bluck, 2000; Habermas and Köber, 2015) to place themselves as consistent characters within an unravelling sequence of related episodes. While the people I interviewed were often prepared to acknowledge changes in their own ideas and behaviour over time, the narrative form served to contextualize episodes of political talk within an 'internalized, evolving and integrative story of the self' (McAdams, 2008: 242). Such stories were often well rehearsed and affectively intense, providing ontological anchorage for intentions and actions: 'I had to speak up at that moment because it's in my nature to abhor injustice'. By recalling episodic political disagreements in the context of enduring moral scripts, it became easier for people to abstract political expression from the ebb and flow of instrumental contingency and explain it in terms of an unfolding life history.

Underlying people's accounts of themselves as subjects of a life story is a strong sense that political talk entails an act of turning oneself towards others with a view to being acknowledged – a bid for recognition as an agentic subject. Few interviewees ever referred directly to the concept of political agency, but most did so indirectly: in almost every interview, people spoke of political talk as if it were a test of subjective efficacy. As Bamberg (2011: 7) states, 'Issues of agency are typically viewed in terms of "who-is-in-control," asking whether it is the person, the I-as-subject, who constructs the world the way it is, or whether the person, the me as undergoer, is constructed by the way the world is, subjected to it'. When interviewees characterized themselves as being 'very persuasive' or 'natural leaders' or 'the type of person who prefers to fade into the background' they were attempting to explain contingent choices in terms of biographical traits. At other times agency emerged as a frustration – a recurrent sense of disconnection between utterance and effect. In all of these instances people were keen to relate their experience of political talk to a sense of themselves as reflexive beings capable of volition and responsibility. Political talk was implicated in intentions to make some kind of difference to the world, if only to the beliefs of an interlocutor.

But difference was rarely interpreted in purely instrumental or cognitive terms. Talk can change moods and atmospheres as well as reasoned viewpoints; it can adjust the affectively delicate balance of relationships as well as the micro-structures of power asymmetry. I was frequently surprised during interviews by the strength and complexity of feeling that memories of political talk evoked. Talk about political talk is an activity coated in raw feeling, rarely recalled with dispassion.

People wanted to speak not only about how political talk made them feel but also about how they felt about having such feelings. Allison Pugh (2013: 51) refers to these as 'meta-feelings' which 'situate emotions culturally, giving a sense for how safe or free or proud (or ashamed or horrified) someone might be to claim a particular feeling, and thus to act upon it'. When interviewees spoke in this way, they were not simply reporting their real-time visceral responses to a given situation but trying to make sense of the distance between how a situation made them feel at the time and how they believed they ought to feel. Recalling the intensity of political disagreements, people often felt a need to explain or even apologize for their emotional displays. Some reported wishing that they had been able to draw upon more evidence or sophisticated language in order to appear more reasonable or authoritative. Others regretted not feeling strong enough to pursue an argument to the bitter end or feeling ashamed of allowing a disagreement about principles to become personal. Several interviewees were intensely proud of the ways in which they had spoken up at critical moments or defended their own or another's dignity when it seemed under attack. These feelings and feelings about feelings were core biographical features of the stories that interviewees told me. Like all biographies, these stories were selective, creative and performative, but it was precisely because the narrators were 'both subject and object of the narration' (Atkinson and Silverman, 1997: 315) that they offered such enormous scope for interpretation. Should people be believed more or less when they are the authors of a story about their own life?

Making sense of biographical accounts and feelings entails an openness to the private meanings that underlie the stories that people tell about themselves. This involves listening beyond the explicit sense of what people say and attending to the patterns of singular signification that emerge as they repeatedly draw upon tropes of self-definition and expressive disclosure. The psychiatrist Donald Spence has suggested that the work of deep listening to people's self-narratives (1982: 112) 'is similar to making a close reading of a poem: it attempts to get "behind" the surface structure of the sentence . . . because language by definition is incomplete'. The theoretical challenge here is not to jump to moral judgements – 'they would say that, wouldn't they' – but to understand how, wittingly or inadvertently, communication corresponds to private meaning. As George Steiner (1975: 172) astutely observes,

> When we speak to others we speak 'at the surface' of ourselves. We normally use a shorthand beneath which there lies a wealth of subconscious, deliberately concealed or declared associations so extensive and intricate that they probably equal the sum and uniqueness of our status as an individual person.

The four stories that follow were selected from dozens that might have been equally illuminating. Their purpose is to show how habits of political expression unfold biographically, disclosing stories of selfhood that hover between coherence and inconsonance.

Moira – a moral script

A 62-year-old grandmother and member of numerous protest groups, Moira was a woman whose moral script was written in capital letters. From the moment she sat down she proceeded to tell me how bothered she was by the numerous social injustices that surrounded her in her daily life. Quiet-spoken, but clearly resolute, she insisted that 'I think you have to see victims of injustice as if you were in their shoes, because I believe very much in humanity and I don't believe that people are unequal and poor for no reason'. Moira regarded her voice as a political weapon, explaining that 'I don't see politics as . . . *politics*. I see it as about our lives. So for me, every – every breath I take is political'.

I asked Moira how it felt to be so driven. 'I'm in a permanent rage. I'm furious,' she answered. But she did not look furious. She came across as a friendly and self-reflective person. I wondered what had made her become so committed to political intervention. It is when people are asked how they have come to think and feel as they do that they tend to turn to biographical narrative. It is as if the best way to explain current feelings is by accessing pre-political attachments out of which future relationships with the world were forged. In Moira's case, the primal source of her moral script was her childhood experience of witnessing parental conflict:

> Right. Um, my mum was Catholic – Irish Catholic. My dad was non-Catholic, Geordie. My mum insisted that we were brought up Catholic . . . and my dad did his very best to enable that. He would be the one: 'Come on, you've got to go to Mass'. You know, that sort of thing. My mum was a Royalist Tory who denied

her Irish background and my dad was a Labour man in his union who went on strike in the 70s. . . . My mum would say to him: 'Get to work; you're lazy'. And I'd say, 'He can't, mum, they're on strike. You know, you can't do that'. So their relationship . . . you know, they were deeply in love clearly and were never ever going to part.

What began as a tale of romantic affection overcoming ideological difference turned into a tragic account of domestic violence. Moira's dad was an alcoholic and would frequently come back from the pub and beat up her mum.

And I used to beg my mum – as I was developing my ideas in the 70s, as you do when you're a teenager – to get a divorce; kick him out; leave him. Ah, and I often used to lock the door so he couldn't get in when he was drunk. You'd hear him coming up the road. The usual story. Oh, God, here he comes. Lock the door. So I wanted her to get a divorce. But she had a very . . . I think a firm set of principles and ideals and she would not have got a divorce. But they wouldn't have split up anyway. So it's complex. . . . I mean, I stood up to my dad quite a lot. And . . . physically as well, when he – I'd plead with my mum to kick him out and get a divorce. Um, but my mum was very quiet, very – I think the word's stoic. Very private. She always worked. She was very well presented. She didn't get involved. And I guess my dad was the character. My dad was the character in the household. A lovely, lovely man. Played the piano, sang songs, but couldn't take drink and had a weakness for gambling, because he wanted to give us more. He didn't gamble for himself; he gambled the wages because he wanted to give us more. . . . And although my father, you know, caused a terrible amount of pain throughout our lives, I actually, um . . . oh dear, um, I looked after him for twelve years before he died. [with tears in her voice] And I do – I did love him. It wasn't about forgiveness; it was just about understanding.

I was struck by the contrast between the single-mindedness of Moira the political activist and the complexity of her teenage attempts to strike a moral balance. Might her current determination to always take the right side be a reaction to the weight of ambiguity she had borne as an adolescent?

As a child, Moira learned to think in very practical ways about the ethical basis of political action. She realized that it was through talking with others about problems that she could work her way towards solutions: 'I enjoyed discussing things at school. I can't believe that we can have a civilized society without talking.' She recalled one experience from her school years that she believed had an enduring effect on her:

I was in a Catholic primary school. . . . So I have a very vivid memory of when I was five we had a school assembly and we were taught by nuns. And in those

days we were also caned by nuns with big sticks [short laugh]. I can laugh about
that now obviously because I've survived. And the nuns wore very heavy habits
. . . and when I was little I thought they were on wheels because their gowns were
so long and the big heavy rosary beads. And a little boy from Biafra was brought
in, which I think is now Nigeria . . . a little boy called Edmund was brought into
the assembly. 'This is Edmund. He's a refugee. We are taking him into our hearts
and our faith.' Tommy, you are going to befriend Edmund. And Tommy said,
'No, I'm not touching him.' And I said [excitedly] 'I will, I will' [short laugh]. I
felt an enormous compassion for this little boy who was the only little black boy
in the whole school of white Catholics. And, ah, we were very good friends for
many years, me and Edmund.

This memory of standing up for an outsider against racist prejudice mattered
deeply to Moira. She followed the story by saying, 'And then I've got memories
of intervening. I always intervene if I see injustice.' It is probably too simplistic
to conclude that this act of speaking up at a very young age determined Moira's
future as an outspoken political activist, but for her the biographical connection
was highly significant. She had come to realize as a child that by using her voice
she could make a difference. Perhaps she found it easier to contribute to social
justice by helping a stranger than by trying to broker peace within the complex
relationships of her own home, but Moira had experimented with a moral script
and the intervention had taught her something about her political agency. She
had initiated a biographical narrative of herself as someone who speaks up at
crucial moments.

Moira become a political activist in her early twenties, once again moving
between biographical influences and structural inequities:

> I was always a Labour voter. My dad was the Labour voter and my mum voted
> Tory. My mum loved Margaret Thatcher. I instinctively did not like Mrs Thatcher.
> So when I was in my early twenties . . . and then I was getting a divorce because
> I had my two babies and he was violent to me and wouldn't work and things like
> that . . . so, I was thrust into this . . . oh God, it was awful . . . but I already knew
> I didn't like racism; I already knew that. And I already knew that I felt oppressed
> as a woman.

Left as a single mother with two children, Moira took a job as a waitress and
used her wages to support herself at a further education college where she took
night classes. She subsequently took an administrative job at a local university
and her interactions with students stimulated her to pursue her own studies.
('I got that itchy thing of "I'm sick of typing other people's ideas; I want to go
and study".') She went to university in her late twenties. It was then that she

found herself involved in the heat of political conversations that shaped her as a political activist. I asked her what she meant when she referred to politics:

> I think that people believe that politics takes place in Westminster. And I think that people believe that it's the learned who should decide for us and what have you. And that's why I'm political, but from the ground.

A well-known political journalist had recently written a piece describing Moira, whom she met at a public meeting, as 'a one-woman riot and a raging grandma'. There was a sense in which Moira felt proud of this characterization, but she was eager to explain that

> I've had to be assertive. Some people may interpret that as aggressive, but I'm very much not an aggressive person. But I am very assertive.

The distinction between assertion and aggression is important. Too often people who express firm views are accused of being too vociferous and strident. Such charges are especially levelled against women, who have been cast by historical prejudice as decorously neutral bystanders, best confined to the domestic dynamics of the private sphere. Aggression is commonly a euphemism for unentitled and uninvited intervention. In not waiting to be asked to speak, Moira was performing a political act. Political talk for her was not merely academic or ideological: 'This is our real lives', she asserted and went on to tell me what she meant by that:

> I have a disabled grandson. He's fifteen. And when he turns sixteen in February they're going to put him on PIP (personal independent payment) instead of his disability money. And make him be an independent adult. So I'm battling with that at the moment. And I feel so protective of him.

She contrasted the seriousness of such human challenges with what she perceived to be the supercilious rhetorical games she witnessed when she watched parliamentary proceedings on television:

> The noise in that place of them jeering and shouting at each other . . . and these are the lawmakers who tell us how to live. It makes me feel quite ill. But I do watch Prime Minister's Question Time – and listen to it. It depends if I'm in my bedroom it's the radio; if I'm in the sitting room it's the TV. Because I want to know what they're saying. I want to know what they've got planned for us next [laughs].

The private meaning of her laughter was significant, for every part of Moira's story pointed towards a refusal to accept what powerful people have planned for her. As with her childhood battles, it was as if the debates taking place in parliament were personal challenges to her. Hers was a narrative of explicit agency based upon unmitigated confidence in the potential efficacy of resistant action. However distant the structures and institutions were from her everyday life, Moira felt that she could speak back to them as if she was engaged in a personal confrontation.

After she left, I began to reflect upon Moira's description of herself being in a 'permanent rage' and the journalist's characterization of her as a 'raging grandma'. I wondered whether it was really rage that animated Moira. Throughout her life she had found it necessary to derive clear conclusions and commitments from morally ambiguous circumstances. Her earliest family relationships put her at odds with a personally flawed father whom she sought to understand and love and an unjustly treated mother whose values she abhorred. She begged her mother to throw her father out of the home, but she did her best to look after him. Situations of conflict do not always lend themselves to simple responses. Again, she was beaten by nuns as a child. But when these nuns called upon her to befriend an African child she excitedly agreed to do so. Moira's political life story had taught her to follow her feelings and to acknowledge that sometimes situations cannot be processed by arid cognition. To be driven by feelings is easily misrepresented as a form of frenzy: hysteria, mania, rage. As a way of speaking about politics it raises questions about the capacity of a speaker to realize 'proper distance' (Silverstone, 2004) and relate to the world with appropriate dispassion. Moira's biographical experience was not conducive to emotional aloofness. What appeared on the surface to be rage was a deeply felt sense that questions of justice are affectively complex.

Terry – a reluctant persuader

A quiet, reflective man who tends to stop and think before he says anything, 46-year-old Terry had spent most of his life keeping his views about the world to himself. As he put it, 'I've always been somebody who's . . . not been as willing or as able to put my own views forward.' He described himself as 'not really being a tub-thumper . . . I'm not somebody who would put myself up in a public meeting and speak, making big deliverances – I think it goes back just to certain social insecurities from youth'. But in recent years Terry had come to be influenced by arguments in favour of 'fair trade' and now believes that 'people could make very small changes in their consumer habits' which would make the world a better place. This belief had motivated him to reluctantly overcome some of his 'insecurities from youth' and attempt to develop a more persuasive voice. He has found this far from easy:

> I don't necessarily see myself as being an obvious leader, but I think, you know, you have an influence by subtler influences. So maybe I use different tactics. I generally like to use written form rather than verbal form to express myself. There's time when I'm slightly frustrated because I know that . . . often the, um, the verbal speakers can often have more impact. You know, the great leaders are associated with . . . standing up and talking about things.

I was interested to learn more about where this reticence came from. Terry was clearly someone who wanted to make a difference to the world, however small and local. But he felt estranged from what he understood to be a certain language and style that characterized political expression. I asked him how it was that he had come to think of himself as someone for whom putting his views forward was a challenge. As with most of my interviewees, he interpreted my question as a prompt to speak about his life story:

> I consider myself to be a guy who grew up in a family that wasn't political at all. In fact, politics was very much rejected as being something other and venal.

Can a family be not 'political at all'? There might be families that tend to ignore politicians or consider them to be 'venal', but could they thereby avoid the political? I asked Terry to tell me more about the interpersonal dynamics of the family in which he grew up:

> It was a manual, working-class family in the north-east of England. So my parents were in a mining community, but, um, they weren't from . . . they weren't miners themselves, although the extended family were. . . . . It was a supportive family. A small family. There was my mother and father, me and my brother. Younger brother who was a little bit headstrong. I mean, he was the headstrong one. I was the kind of studying type. So he took . . . probably took more attention than I did. I'd probably have been a bit more passive. . . . It was very much a busy household insofar as my dad would have come in from work late and my mum might have been going out to work on the evening shift. And my grandmother might have been coming in to do a bit of the childminding as well in the meantime. Father was a socially gregarious person. Quite a grounded, magnanimous kind of guy considering his lack of education. Very much a rapport-builder. My mum tended to be the organizer. My mum particularly lent herself to rejecting things she didn't particularly understand . . . if she didn't understand something she'd reject it and rubbish it – very much rubbish things. The other person in this mix

was my grandmother who was kind of like . . . still alive actually and still a good source of debate and information – learning. And she was coming in often for the childminding. So she brought some of that kind of learning as well into the family. There'd be no reading about politics. Occasional news items, but skirting the surface. You had very few sources of information. I don't think my parents read a newspaper anyway. Whereas I think my dad would have picked up things from conversation. The other person who was kind of on the periphery of this who was perhaps the most political influence . . . my uncle who was a similar age to him, who was actually at that time an NUM miners' union steward up in Durham. He was obviously a . . . an official as well as a worker there. So he had a . . . a mining sort of union background.

Terry became influenced by his uncle's accounts of the unfairness of conditions down the coal mines:

My dad and him used to work together quite a bit, so would . . . my dad would pick up information about things and pass on that information. So it would often be . . . passed on indirectly. But when we were around we'd have conversations about what was going on within the coal industry, which he knew.

Meanwhile, Terry's 'headstrong' younger brother, who was doing a sheet metal apprenticeship, was forging his own biographical trajectory:

He gravitated towards the end of 1980s electronic dance club kind of semi drugs scene that was prevalent back then. It was a kind of subculture, I suppose. It was part of the Madchester kind of scene and the kind of rave culture sort of thing. So I suppose it was . . . an underground . . . kind of anarchic sort of subculture which was almost anti-politics. But it shifted power to some extent. Perhaps they wouldn't articulate it in that way, but it was . . . a little bit rejectionist. It was kind of taking ownership of things by other means.

Terry found himself exposed to two quite different models of political expression. His uncle, as a trade union official, was engaged in a classically industrial battle against the employers. This was the era of Thatcher versus the miners – a time of militant talk and fierce clashes between irreconcilable world views. To become part of this battle involved a commitment to a mode of political combat that was sharply delineated, verbally forthright and intensely tribal. At the same time, Terry's brother had 'gravitated towards' a subcultural opt-out from both the domestic quietism and the political turbulence that surrounded him. Anarchic, rejectionist and escapist in its preference for the immediacy of pleasurable activity over the prolixity of argumentative talk, 'it was kind of taking ownership of things by other means'.

As a studious lad, Terry gained entry to university where he maintained his sense of himself as someone who would rarely speak up:

> I was the first person in my family to go to university. You know, I studied hard. I wasn't particularly brainy, but worked hard and . . . maybe didn't have the sense of entitlement to education. Went along and was just a bit passive . . . always in the background, seeking to absorb things . . . I didn't really feel that confident about projecting . . . whether that was a working-class/middle-class thing or an educational thing or my perception of it or just my lack of skill, I don't know.

While he was at university, and then after graduating, Terry made a point of refusing to get into political discussions. They made him feel flustered and in some sort of danger. I asked him what it was about political talk that made him feel so uneasy. Characteristically, he stopped to reflect for quite a while before he offered this response:

> If something upsets me and I can't get my point across and I feel as though I want to challenge, but it's a bit oppressive or a bit difficult to do so . . . I mean . . . especially in relation to conflict in political debates, I've probably struggled over the years with, sort of . . . fuming from within.

I asked him how it felt to fume from within, while remaining a seemingly calm and quiet person. He paused before elaborating:

> Well, I think that maybe refers to my sense of . . . my perception of my own inarticulacy both to do with verbal skills and being able to hold an audience in a verbal sense as well as lack of knowledge. So any combination of those together would, I think, reduce my ability . . . my confidence to be able to engage in a political discussion or thought process.

For Terry, confidence is a quality of performance. It involves a capacity to put oneself on display and hold an audience's attention. He was too busy holding his own attention: fuming from within; internally shouting out views and releasing feelings that those around him might never suspect he had. Terry's self-characterization was of a man emotionally trapped in a voiceless body.

It was not until he entered his forties that Terry began to develop strong values about fair trade and ethical consumerism. While he remained determined to keep out of the kind of pugnacious arguments that he associated with 'politics', he realized that he was quite good at influencing friends through personal example:

> I was able to be a good role model. I think I made quite a few differences in people in my immediate circles of peers where it was very much a peer influence thing at that time.

Action seemed to speak louder than words. Through his social network, Terry was able to make his presence felt as a force for change:

> I'm probably described as being gregarious. I would say I'm a little bit less gregarious than perhaps people think. I do like my space. I do like to reflect on my own. But I am a bit – I can be a bit buzzy in social situation if I'm inspired by a situation and a thought. I just kind to tend to reverberate off people. People can say I'm a little bit . . . little bit . . . semi-manic in some ways. I have idea showers. But, um, I mean, I do like to connect through events.

In what sense was this approach to political talk biographically shaped? Terry described his early family life as 'busy'. His brother was the 'headstrong' one, demanding from his parents much of the little time they could afford to attend to their children. He was studious and passive, spending a lot of his early life absorbing what was going on around him. Just as his father picked up on local events by talking to Terry's uncle, an official in the miners' union, Terry himself learned to take in his environment – to be good at sensing what mattered to people. While Terry spent his time 'in the background, trying to absorb things', he learned to be a good listener. Terry was embarrassed by his lack of verbal articulacy, but at the same time he was learning the skill of paying deep attention to people and situations. It was not until he was in his forties that he realized how valuable that quality was. Meanwhile, he had two models of political agency to draw upon: his uncle's industrial agonism and his brother's post-industrial, subcultural preference for taking ownership of things by other means. Presented with these options, Terry decided to follow his brother's example of bringing about change through example rather than propositional appeal. He became a listener-oriented political speaker, seeking peer influence rather than the sway of a crowd. At every point Terry was making decisions that fitted with his biographical experience.

Sebastian – from guardedness to disclosure

The Member of Parliament's constituency office looked like a shop that wasn't selling anything. Within its closed glass door sat two women who were clearly busily occupied, but it would be hard for a casual observer to know precisely what they were doing. On the wall was a map of the area, a photo of the prime minister and another of the MP that I was about to meet. I stood for a while, thinking about how these images work together to conjure an impression of political representation.

I was taken to meet with Sebastian in his windowless downstairs office and explained that I was not there to hear about his policies, but to understand what political talk meant to him. He began by telling me about the awkwardness he feels when he encounters recordings of himself speaking in public:

> I can't stand watching myself on television. I'm very self-critical about the speeches I make. I always think they could be better.

It was not only his own performances that unsettled Sebastian. As an elected politician, he believed himself to belong to a group that failed to communicate directly:

> You know, you look at what politicians are saying and how they're saying it, or how they look, and you think it's all a bit manufactured.

If politicians are to be representatives of the people rather than remote managerial figures, such distancing is deeply problematic. According to Sebastian, too many people are left feeling that politics is something that is going on over their heads:

> I think the problem is that people don't see how politics affects them. The amount of people I hear say to me, 'Oh, I don't really understand politics', but then express a view or an opinion on something and actually that *is* politics,

For Sebastian, political talk needs to relate to people's lived experience. He says that the job of being a representative involves talking with people rather than simply directing speeches at them: 'I love meeting people . . . the best part of the job for me is actually being out and about in the constituency . . . and meeting all the different people in their walks of life.' But he has come to believe that the way politicians express themselves alienates and intimidates people:

> I had a young woman come and see me, she was visibly shaking. And I said 'Are you all right?' and she said 'I've never met an MP before'. And I found that quite disturbing because I thought, you know, she had a real issue that really did need sorting, but she was terrified. . . . It was almost like she was going for a job interview; and I think that's a bit worrying.

This gap between the political class and most citizens seemed to genuinely bother Sebastian and led him to conclude that politicians need to present themselves in less scripted and risk-averse ways: 'if you really want people to speak a bit normally so that people get it, then we've got to perhaps just let our guard down a bit.' But what would that entail? How did the guard get there in the first place?

As usual, it was only when we turned to his biographical story that this key theme began to be elucidated. Sebastian had encountered feelings of guardedness long before he ever thought of becoming a professional politician. He was brought up in a quiet, undemonstrative family in which feelings were rarely discussed.

> I grew up on a council estate in North Wales and, you know, my family . . . we didn't have a lot of money. . . . My father worked away an awful lot. We were sort of . . . we would just have our dinner and then leave the table . . . there was no real . . . there was no political discussion or anything no, not at all. The family often wonder where I get my politics from . . . because actually throughout the family there doesn't seem to be that much of an interest in politics.

Political views were a matter of secrecy. Sebastian was never even told how his parents voted:

> No, they never spoke about it. In fact, my mother was particularly, you know, keen on making sure that actually it was a private vote. She always thought that that was very important.

Sebastian described himself as having been 'a bit of a nerd' as a child. There he was living in a not very talkative family on a council estate in rural Wales, taking a detailed interest in the byzantine high-drama of Westminster politics. Declaring his political views and joining the Conservative Party at the age of fourteen was a rare moment of outspokenness for him: 'I think some of my friends were surprised . . . you know, that I sort of joined.' Political expression for Sebastian was a form of safe self-disclosure:

> I always say that in my life I came out twice [laughter]: once as a gay man and once as a Tory. And being a Tory was the hardest bit [laughs].

It is in this context that Sebastian's reference to politicians letting their guard down can be understood. Both the buttoned-up restraint of his upbringing and the highly controlled performances of politicians resulted from a fear of appearing as oneself before others. 'Coming out' has come to refer to the brave act of acknowledging one's sexuality, but people come out in many ways, disclosing themselves to the world in ways that always have repercussions.

Under the tutorship of a local political agent – 'She was a tiny woman and if you met her you would probably just walk past her in the street, but what she didn't know wasn't worth knowing' – Sebastian began the journey to becoming an MP. Unlike many Conservatives of his generation he was not much influenced by Margaret Thatcher – 'She looked like a very posh lady' – but was inspired by 'people who talk about their own background or experience and how that's formed their personal outlook'.

This became relevant when I asked Sebastian whether he had ever felt able to use his position as a legislator to 'come out' in his own political voice. He did not have to think about this for very long:

> For me, it was during the same-sex marriage debate . . . when I was just like 'For God's sake, this is . . . . We're not all going to bring down floods [laughs]. This is about human beings.' It was very difficult. There were people on my side of the Chamber who were vehemently against it. The letters that I was getting in the office were . . . you know, it made you feel like everybody was against it. But I thought, 'No, I'm going to put myself out there and say actually what is wrong with this.' I was frustrated by the tone that had taken place and I was determined to challenge it. The third-reading debate was the one where I think I really expressed how I felt deep down.

Sebastian's political biography involved a movement from a marginal and undemonstrative private realm to a public sphere in which political identity is disclosed through speaking and action before others. Contrasting the character of these two social domains, Arendt (1958: 65) observes that 'the most elementary meaning of the two realms indicates that there are things that need to be hidden and others that need to be displayed publicly if they are to exist at all'. Becoming political entails speaking out – allowing oneself to be witnessed as a bearer of public values. Sometimes it is only through the arbitrary convergence of personal experience and values, and public agenda and debate that guards are dropped and political talk becomes an act of self-expression. Biographically, it was the convergent frustrations generated by a family upbringing in which the problems of the world were never really acknowledged or discussed and a political sphere in which matters of substance were crushed by promotional gestures (both, in their own way, forms of anti-politics) that shaped Sebastian's approach to political talk.

Colin – putting politics behind him

Everything in the biographical narrative of Colin, a forty-year-old trade union official is split into *then* and *now*, with the two segments marked by a crucial emotional break. Colin's story is one of retreating from what he now regards to have been a wasteful commitment to radical political self-expression. It is a rite-of-passage narrative in reverse, with coming of age characterized by mature disenchantment and withdrawal.

Colin grew up in what he described as a politically talkative family:

> It was Thatcher's Britain, I was growing up in a mining area, so it was very much a strongly anti-Tory, lefty, protesty family at the time. Not in any constructive way, I have to say. Looking back, there was the odd protest march about pits closing and these sort of things, but . . . we weren't really politically active, in that sense – we didn't do a lot. A lot of complaining. A lot of shouting at the TV.

It was Colin's father who did most of the shouting at the television, regularly engaging in one-way debates against flashing images of Margaret Thatcher. Colin's mother 'agreed with those complaints, but generally took the view that there was not a lot we could do about it'. Looking back at his early years, Colin felt that 'it's very negative to be around people who are constantly complaining about X, Y and Z . . . it would have been much healthier to have had some outlet for that stuff rather than to be locked into a cycle of complaints – which is what it was'.

Colin's response to this mood of permanent complaint was to find a political outlet – an organizational attachment that would enable him to turn his brooding discontent into a more active intervention in the world. 'Looking back, I was a dreadfully self-absorbed young man,' he reflects. He developed an interest in radical politics. 'It didn't really do me any good in the long run, I would have thought, but it was something to get my teeth into'. This last comment is typical of Colin's biographical reasoning, which seemed to be permanently inflected by a tone of hopes dashed and regret for time misspent. In recalling the frustration, dissent and subjective intentness that led him to become a political activist, he chose to frame such feelings as fundamentally sapping and delusory. Framing seemed to be at least as important as content in Colin's narrative; for every recollection of enthusiasm there followed a chasing siren of ineluctable disappointment.

A key political moment for Colin was when he encountered a small left-wing group and felt motivated by its radical objective:

> I was at a sort of social event, probably my first political gathering, if you like. And the leader of the party at that time came and gave a speech which I thought was extremely . . . invigorating. So that that's when I sort of formalized my membership. Looking back at it, it was probably complete crap, to be honest, but [laughs] it did appear to be very important at the time.

Having joined this group (which he did not name during the interview), Colin became one of its leading activists:

> I took a lot of work on and therefore did play a leading role. I was the central point of a lot of things. It's the way that a lot of centralist organizations work . . . a

lot of the work does get piled on to one particular person . . . I just got lumbered with more and more stuff.

As an activist, political conflict became an inescapable part of Colin's life. His relationship with the external world seemed to be characterized by a relentless struggle between routine justifications of systemic unfairness and ideological counterattacks. Fought out relentlessly within the arena of public discourse, political talk came to be experienced as a permanent battle to assert righteousness in the face of mass delusion or mendacity. For Colin, this meant that even the most mundane exchange of views was loaded with huge political significance, thereby raising the emotional stakes of everyday interaction. In addition to this there were interminable internal conflicts to be pursued within his small political group; few combinations are more disputatious than ones convinced that they are the exclusive guardians of foundational truth. Being so deeply embroiled in contention began to get on Colin's nerves. He recalled the 'precise moment when my view on what I was doing changed'. There was a protracted campaign to nominate and then elect members of the National Executive Committee of his trade union. Colin was his group's candidate:

> The campaign process began several months prior to the election, so we had a long period of politicking and networking and all that. And then there was the election period – a long arduous process. Then there was our national conference. And I remember, I went to book a week's holiday just to soak everything in. But I was elected to the National Executive and meetings were arranged, so I had to cancel my holiday and book it again. So I did book it again.

When he finally returned to work, now as a newly elected union official, Colin found himself instantly caught up in intensely draining internal battles. Most of his long days were spent arguing with people. He found the 'level of tension and anxiety that comes with that degree of confrontation on a daily basis' too much to bear: 'It was a situation I needed to get out of.' These feelings of political exhaustion coincided with a period of individual crisis: 'I had issues in my personal life where I was . . . I was in . . . I was a victim of domestic abuse for two years.' He was heading for a breakdown and needed to make a change:

> I made a conscious decision . . . not to let my political objective get in the way of my quality of life. Not wanting to be on the edge of conflict with people for whatever reason is one of the most conscious choices that I ever made.

However, it was not an easy life-change to carry out. Colin found himself getting involved in a number of verbal confrontations with his erstwhile comrades: 'The period building up to it – maybe over a six-month period before I left – was very difficult, very stressful.'

Having detached himself from the zeal of political commitment, Colin now actively resists the emotional costs of confrontation:

> Disagreement nowadays would make me feel very anxious and stressed . . . I think a lot of it is that I don't want to have the obligation to try to convince people . . . just to have the argument with people about why what they think is wrong . . . I've tended to think life's too short to do that nowadays. I have found myself thinking this more often in recent times . . . that most of the time there are ways of dealing with situations in an adult way, if you like, without necessarily blowing things up into a conflict. So . . . when I'm at home I tend to like there to be a politics-free-zone.

It is not the object of disagreement that had changed for Colin (he retained his critical view of society), but the burden of feeling obligated to engage in the incessant work of public discussion. His father's habit of shouting vainly at the television and his mother's forlorn protests had once seemed to be unhealthily stifling: 'locked into a cycle of complaints'. Radical agency had appealed to him as a more invigorating alternative, pointing towards the hope of social transformation. But when this project too drained his vitality, leaving him worn out by the feeling of being caught in an endless cycle of discordant protestation, his willingness to pay the affective costs faded. As Lauren Berlant (2011: 259) observes, 'The compulsion to repeat a toxic optimism can suture someone or a world to a cramped and unimaginative space of committed replication, *just in case* it will be different.' Indeed, it is Lauren Berlant's notion of 'cruel optimism' that best explains Colin's renunciation of political talk as a mode of agency:

> A relation of cruel optimism exists when something you desire is actually an obstacle to your flourishing. It might involve food, or a kind of love; it might be a fantasy of the good life, or a political project. It might rest on something simpler, too, like a new habit that promises to induce in you an improved way of being. These kinds of optimistic relation are not inherently cruel. They become cruel only when the object that draws your attachment actively impedes the aim that brought you to it initially. All attachment is optimistic, if we describe optimism as the force that moves you out of yourself and into the world in order to bring closer the satisfying something that you cannot generate on your own but sense in the wake of a person, a way of life, an object, project, concept, or scene (Berlant, 2011: 1)

'If I hadn't made that change', Colin explained, 'I probably wouldn't be as well-adjusted as I am now.' The normative manner in which he characterized his new-found political passivity was telling. To be well adjusted is to arrive at a point of psychological equilibrium; to eschew aberrant pressures. By abandoning what he came to think of as the destabilizing and deluding impulse to make a difference, Colin sought to extricate himself from the lure of cruel optimism in the hope that doing so would relieve him of an oppressive tension:

> The first real step is to try to disengage yourself from all these pressures to join something and buy into something that you don't want to be a part of. (Berlant, 2011)

But if the price of psychic relief is political disengagement, what becomes of agency? I speculated for a while about what Colin would say to Moira if he ever met her. What would he say to those who believe that her political voice is their most potent weapon against injustice? He paused thoughtfully and then said,

> I feel their pain . . . I wish them all the best and good luck to them, but . . . I do feel to an extent what they're doing is entirely . . . entirely futile.

At stake here is a conflict of feelings about feelings. Moira inhabited an emotional landscape in which desires, frustrations and expectations were framed in political terms because only by infusing agency with feeling could the courage to seek justice be sustained. As Moira spoke about her experience of political talk, the intensity of her prosodic tone directed the content; her expressive register conveyed her meaning. For Colin, whose speaking voice was marked by a blander, more lugubrious tonality, exuberant political feelings were to be distrusted. The voice itself needed to be tempered, lest it succumb to the imposture of cruel optimism. The futility of trying to translate deep concern into vocal urgency led Colin to feel cheated by the excessive promise of political talk as a mode of agency. Verbal conflict was a trigger for anxiety and stress. As he reflected on the non-cathartic effects of his emotional investment in politics, Colin seemed to embody the injury wrought by emotional over-investment. Where Moira sought to run experience through the filter of feeling and express it through the medium of political speech, Colin sensed that political expression, encumbered by the weight of unwieldy ideology, could never do justice to experiential feeling. Terry, who had only recently felt entitled to assert political values of his own, was unconfident about his capacity to translate them into the language of conventional political debate and preferred to 'have an influence by subtler influences'.

Memories and experiences of political talk are shaped by biographical meta-feelings. Terry's sense that political ideas travel more effectively through example and cultural dissemination than demonstrative verbal display constituted not only a pragmatic strategy but also a feeling about how best to convey feelings. For Terry, an exemplary mode of persuasion felt more genuine than a constant attempt to perform with words. Sebastian's anxiety that the generic performance of political speech by politicians has become dominated by contrived form and that the possibility of authentic expression has been lost represents a feeling about how politicians should respond to their feelings. Trapped by his own sense of ineloquence and the tacit demands of professional display, Sebastian had come to feel that political talking was like playing a clichéd part in an over-rehearsed play. That was until he found himself in a dramatic and personally significant political moment in which, challenged to put himself 'out there' and express how he felt 'deep down', Sebastian allowed himself to follow his own feeling rules.

The people I interviewed were remarkably adroit at recalling significant periods and moments that shaped their sense of political self. While their accounts of being involved in political talk referred frequently to the cognitive and conative aspects of argumentation, they were strikingly replete with references to felt emotions and meta-feelings: feelings about how the experience of political agency *should* feel. It was through such affective appraisal that politics as a social practice came to be recognized and recalled. People had somehow come to learn that speaking and acting 'politically' has as much to do with accomplishing an expressive mode as with the generation of specific categories of content. But how do people learn how to communicate politically? How do they become attuned to the tonal qualities and feeling rules that characterize the world as polity? Answering these questions involves turning to the period of childhood in which people are least likely to know anything about 'politics' but are fast learning to act and speak politically.

The emergent self and political agency

Becoming a political subject entails negotiating a tension between agency and vulnerability, a task that begins at birth. According to Winnicott (1971), the newborn baby imagines itself to be omnipotent. It does not need to seek recognition as an individual part of the world because it is granted the illusion that it is already the centre of the world. The task of the 'good-enough mother' is to create such an illusion by adapting completely to the baby's earliest needs and then, gradually, to 'disillusion' the infant by enabling it to individuate. As the baby moves from a sense of illusory merged omnipotence with its parent and begins to experience the difference between me and not-me, a tacit awareness of political reality emerges. The infant's experience of the vulnerability of not being all-powerful and the agency of being a volitional self constitute a dilemma that will persist throughout its life.

The singular self emanates from social exchange with others. By the age of two months babies can distinguish between people who are speaking to them rather than to others (Trevarthen, 1977; Fonagy, 2018). By seven to eight months they are able to monitor emotional expression in others (Klinnert et al., 1983; Repacholi et al., 2016). By nine months they can participate in simple games and coordinate gestures, as in waving goodbye (Bruner, 1983; Fernald and O'Neill, 1993). During their second year, children begin to pick up signs of distress in others (adults as well as babies) and begin to develop comforting strategies (Zahn-Waxler and Radke-Yarrow, 1990; Spinrad and Eisenberg, 2017). By the end of the second year children are able to talk about their own and others' feelings (Dunn et al., 1991; Davis, 2018). By the age of three most children have 'internalized coherent rules about what to do and what not to do in a variety of situations' and have 'a set of emotional signals to guide wilful action according to what feels right or wrong' (Emde et al., 1991: 251). At around the same time they learn how to make excuses for their actions (Dunn et al., 1995). From their fourth year onwards children are able to recognize and comment upon other people's intentions and beliefs (Perner and Wimmer, 1985; Astington, 2014).

As children acquire these communicative skills they begin to employ reflexive narrative with a view to fashioning an account of their own social reality. Jerome Bruner (1990: 85/6) offers an interesting angle on this:

> Young children often hear accounts of their own interactions from siblings or parents. . . . But the account is given in a form that runs counter to their own interpretation and interest. . . . Narrative accounts under these circumstances are no longer neutral. They have rhetorical aims or illocutionary intentions that are not merely expository but rather partisan, designed to put the case if not adversarially then at least convincingly in behalf of a particular interpretation. . . . The child's task when conflict arises is to balance her own desires against her commitment to others in the family. And she learns very soon that action is not enough to achieve this end. Telling the right story, putting her actions and goals

in a legitimizing light, is just as important. Getting what you want very often means getting the right story.

As children learn to position themselves positively in situations of conflict, they enter the world of political accountability. Lance Bennett (1980: 794) defines political accounts as 'explanations that excuse or justify questionable behavior by proposing a normative status for the behavior'. Between attempts to frame reality through plausible storytelling and uses of tactical speech, children learn to impose moral order upon situations. Narrative expresses moral and political perspective, for, as Hayden White argues (1980: 13–14), 'If every fully realized story . . . is a kind of allegory, points to a moral, or endows events, whether real or imaginary, with a significance that they do not possess as a mere sequence, then it seems possible to conclude that every historical narrative has as its latent or manifest purpose the desire to moralize the events of which it treats'.

Developing a capacity to tell one's own story is a critical feature in the emergence of agency. The child can not only cause things to happen – a ball thrown or caught; a cup smashed; a screech yelled – but can also re-describe what has happened in terms that suit his or her own interests. The child's agency is manifested through techniques of authorship that neither determine his or her own identity nor ascribe final meaning to external reality, but intervene in the relationship between the two, rendering each less vulnerable to the other.

As children approach adolescence they begin to acquire an understanding of abstract concepts (Piaget's [1936] formal operational stage) such as 'confidence', 'popularity' and 'empathy', enabling them to arrive at metacommunicative insights into their performances of self. They are able to speak about their own speaking; reflect upon the performative qualities of others; and distinguish between the kinds of narratives that work for them and the ones that are likely to fail. This is a critical moment of reflexive development in which children are learning to make sense of their experiences of having a voice at home, in school and among their friends. They may at this stage regard the idea of politics as something that is remote, confusing and irrelevant, but as children come to acknowledge their existence within psychic networks of power and efficacy, they are beginning to flex their political muscles.

In conducting my interviews on political talk, I spoke with a number of eleven-year-olds in the hope that they would be close enough to these scenes of emergent agency to recall them experientially. They demonstrated an astute awareness of the relationship between the ways in which they expressed themselves and the social consequences of speaking. Even at this early stage of adolescence a number of assumptions seemed to be widely shared. The children I interviewed attached great importance to being seen to 'be themselves' and the risks associated with inauthentic performances of self. Maraid told me about how she loved to do drama and dance because 'people can see the real me, not just the person who's trying to be like other people'. She told me about her friend:

> When he's around other people he's totally different. He's always like being naughty. But when he's alone with me and my friends he's really sweet. So other people don't get to see the real him.

The notion of 'the real me' refers to a norm 'that one's life, both public and private, reflects one's real self' (George, 1998: 134) in contrast to the artifice of over-performed self-presentation, fakery and bad acting. Adolescent children devote considerable energy to impression management, recognizing the function of agency in determining the ways in which they are seen and valued. Related to this is the importance of 'sticking up for yourself' and 'standing your ground'. These quintessentially political concerns were raised by several of my eleven-year-old interviewees, such as Lilly who spoke about how she had found herself in disagreement with most of her classmates in a discussion about abortion: 'It felt a bit awkward, but I've my own opinion and I'll stick to it.' She went on to tell me about an important influence on her:

> I think my nan's the best speaker in the world. She's really confident. She's not scared of anybody. She's not scared of standing her ground and she's got a kind of really clear speaking voice ... She got this by sticking up for herself when she was younger – because she used to get bullied at school and so she had to stick up for herself.

Several of my interviewees had thought about what it takes to stand your ground. According to Billy:

> You've got to be very loud and put your feelings out there. You can't hide them back and just put on a fake you. You have to be open in yourself.

For these children, authentic talk entailed a degree of emotional intelligence. As Libby put it, 'First, you've got to think about what other people are gonna think and like take theirs into account in what you're gonna say.' George explained that 'I'm good at expressing my emotions and other people's emotions'. Children were also mindful of communicative strategies that are unlikely to work. Valentina told me,

> I don't think shouting really inspires. You can have expression in your voice, but shouting just doesn't work I don't think. I think you need to have a softer

approach when you're like being a leader because I wouldn't respond to shouting. I do resent it when people shout at me.

Her speaking role model was her father who had learned his skills from Valentina's grandmother:

> My grandma lived in Dominica and it was different over there. Like speaking a different language and different words to us – like two words for one word here – like a harder one and a softer one. My dad's mum always used a softer one. And she always used to talk to him about things in a soft way and that's how he learned when he got older.

The emphasis placed by my interviewees upon the normative value of talk as reciprocal exchange rather than mere message transmission accords with Crispin Thurlow's (2001: 222) findings from a study of slightly older adolescents who valued communicative relationships 'that are non-judgemental, trustworthy, and which entail sharing and emotional support'.

Alongside this emerging sense of metacommunicative sensibility, it was clear that even by the age of eleven children are deeply conscious of the potential for talking to result in disesteem and embarrassment. Bridie told me that 'I tend to go quiet if things go a bit wrong'. She gave a very recent example:

> I was at church last night and it was like a prayer group and we had to answer questions. So I was picked to answer and then I got told it was wrong, so I got a bit nervous about answering another one.

Bridie went on to talk about how this kind of incident can lead to more general inhibition:

> Sometimes when you think of something it seems stupid, so you don't really want to say it. So you just keep it to yourself.

Maraid also spoke about feelings of awkwardness when speaking misfires: 'I try and put my words across, but it's sometimes "No it's like this – you said it all wrong."'

These examples of the ways in which children begin to pick up the rules, rhythms and conventions of political talk, often long before they encounter politics as a distinct social field or concept, suggest that political socialization has more to do with the management of relational identities and conflictual situations than the acquisition of regime norms, constitutional structures and issue cleavages. As David Easton (1968) pointed out over half a century ago, functionalist political scientists' preoccupation with political socialization as a process of normative compliance resulting in system-maintenance is narrow and conservative. As they explore the gap between their subjective perspectives and the objective materiality of the social order in which they find themselves, children practise political agency. Such explorative practice often takes the form of playing – including play-acting, fantasy-sharing, identity performances and counterfactual resolution-forming – and its common locus is what Winnicott (1953: 90) refers to as 'potential space': 'an intermediate area of experiencing, to which inner reality and external life both contribute . . . a resting-place for the individual engaged in the perpetual human task of keeping inner and outer reality separate yet inter-related'. It is within this potential space that young adolescents learn how to perform their identities; recognize inauthentic personal accounting; communicate both forcefully and empathetically; and respond to or resist corrective discipline. All of this is a long rehearsal for the looming pressures of adult political engagement – and sometimes a prefatory motive for future political avoidance. As Jane Flax (1993: 344) points out, in order for children to become political subjects 'there must be a self which requires reciprocity, which can acknowledge without terror our interconnectedness and mutual dependence but can also honor and do justice to our separateness, to the distinctiveness and integrity of each other person'. It is precisely through such experimentation with self-presentation and effectiveness in framing their own and others' realities that children and adolescents come to experience political agency.

But this process of experiential discovery is not simply a chronological stage of development – a teleological ante-room to mature agency. Political talk is always a form of social rehearsal – a tentative encounter between the force of subjective thought and feeling and the stubborn existence of structures, ideologies and situations that present objective challenges to autobiographical fulfilment.

3

Performing the political genre

Ours is a lopsided democracy. The relentless chatter of the volubly opinionated and the white noise of the politically disengaged conspire to generate a profound civic imbalance. As Bourdieu (1979) observes:

> On the one side, there are those who admit that politics is not for them and abdicate their formal rights for lack of the means of exercising them; on the other, those who feel entitled to claim a 'personal opinion', or even the authoritative opinion which is the monopoly of the competent.

According to the Hansard Society's 2019 Audit of Political Engagement, almost a third of respondents (30 per cent) reported that they never talked about politics to anyone face to face, over the phone or via social media, while one in ten (10 per cent) claimed that they talked politics almost every day. Who are these people who never talk about politics? Is their silence a reflection of contentment or frustration? What would need to happen for them to speak up? And what motivates the small minority of frequent political talkers? Do they know something of which the other 90 per cent are unaware? What makes them so eager to perform as vocal political actors?

While empirically focused macro-level studies explore how commonly people talk about politics, what they talk about and how long their conversations last, my aim here is to explore what people think they are doing when they speak about politics. Understanding this entails reflecting upon the split seconds in which agentic energy is either unleashed through risky speech or smothered by overwhelming unease; the indistinct hesitations within which people gauge the power dynamics of their surrounding environment and calculate the consequences of risking a public utterance; the enduring embarrassments that follow mundane failures of political enunciation; and the misfirings and mishearings through which political discourses are translated into anything from aggressive noise to the banality of tired cliché. The pauses and stammers which mark everyday public discourse matter – and may, indeed, offer important clues as to the roots of a malaise that seems to be blighting contemporary political democracies. Zygmunt Bauman (1999: 65) diagnosed what he saw in somewhat despairing terms as a hollowing out of the public domain:

> The 'public' has been emptied of its own separate contents; it has been left with no agenda of its own – it is now but an agglomeration of private troubles, worries and problems. It is patched together of the individual cravings for assistance in making sense of private, as yet inarticulate, emotions and states of mind, for instruction about how to talk about such emotions in a language which others would comprehend, and for advice about how to deal with the flow of experience which the individuals find so difficult to cope with.

If, as Bauman suggests, a public language of shared political feeling has been lost and citizens locked into a seemingly infinite loop of repeated sounds and gestures of ever-reducing meaning, what hope is there for democratic politics? When political voice is confined to the crafted performances of elites and the privatized moans of the subdued, celebratory references to 'free speech' begin to seem rather hollow. The atrophy of mutual intelligibility is not the same, however, as the absence of weighty public feelings, values and intentions. It is upon the gap between political affect and articulacy that I want to focus. I am interested in what goes on in people's minds and bodies when they find themselves performing political talk. How do people know political talk when they encounter it? What is it about political talk that so commonly evokes feelings of strangeness, anxiety and confusion? How often do fears about political miscommunication beget the stutterings and mutterings of the seemingly unengaged? Upon which cultural sources do people draw when they come to formulate the words and sounds of political enunciation? How do people come to know about the stipulative conditions of 'acceptable' political speech and go on to erect ramparts against the shame of verbal and gestural impropriety? What images do people have in their minds when they say that someone sounds like a politician? What images do politicians have in their minds when they address people who they believe will never speak the language of politics with any fluency? Where might one go to learn the coded inflections of authoritative political speech? And how might one go about forgetting and unlearning the bromidic conventions through which political commitments are routinely reduced to performative cliché?

In asking these awkward questions, I am casting doubt upon one of the most taken-for-granted claims of democratic politics: that the right to speak belongs equally to everyone. For, not all mouths open with the same ease or to the same effect. Indeed, it might be argued that the most commonly used medium of political communication – the human voice – is an unevenly distributed cultural resource.

Making a point by not talking

Asked whether she ever discussed political matters with her friends, Sue, a 24-year-old trainee GP, chuckled and then placed great emphasis upon her answer: '*No – never*'. She elaborated: 'I just feel like it's this far off kind of thing.' This was a revealing metaphor: far off; spatially, temporally and emotionally beyond immediate reach; the opposite of the kind of 'hands on' that characterizes the everyday practice of being a GP. Sue felt most confident within what the sociologist Alfred Schutz (1964: 125) refers to as 'the world within reach' (*erreichbar*): the familiar domain in which people and objects can be grasped directly. Sue experienced politics as a remote, impersonal domain that could only be penetrated with extraordinary effort. As she put it,

> I feel like sometimes . . . to get into current affairs now would be a massive effort because I feel like I'd need to go back in time and learn everything that's happened. (Sue, trainee GP, 24)

This sense of politics as an elusive, historicized drama was telling. What Sue thinks of as being 'far off' are the sinuous genealogies of discord that underlie generic political discourse. To be politically engaged is to subscribe to a history and language of contentiousness, replete with nuanced ideological distinctions, seminal battles, opaque institutional arrangements and star characters. It is not unlike beginning to 'follow' a soap opera that has been running for many years; one can get a sense of the latest developments, but feel unsettlingly estranged from the framing dynamics of the action. When my interviewees claimed to be confused by the complexity of politics they were not admitting to some kind of cognitive inferiority, but expressing a sense of cultural disorientation. For example, Lucy, a 37-year-old college administrator, spoke of her losing battle to catch up with the political narrative and her frustration at feeling so behind with the plot:

> I've attempted to make an effort to be interested in it, but I don't think you can really push yourself if it's not natural. Like, when the um campaigns have been on, I've wanted to read about what's going on and who's fighting for which side, but I find it really complicated and then I just don't give it the time.

But what is this 'it' to which Lucy stopped giving her time? It is tempting to assume that, lacking subjective efficacy, she had become indifferent to the dynamics and outcomes of the stirring disagreements that form the plot of the surrounding political drama. But choosing not to talk about something is not the same as not caring about it. Non-talkers in my interviews rarely gave me the impression that they were incurious or disinterested. Asked whether she followed the political news, Milly, a fifty-year-old charity worker, responded instantly: 'I *should*. I feel guilty that I should do more of it.' But more of what exactly? For Milly, sidestepping what she thought of as an act of civic duty was a way of protecting herself from becoming caught up in a bewildering and mendacious game:

> Politics is . . . it's not straightforward is it? It's . . . I don't know, maybe I'm talking rubbish, but the trouble is you get cynical and you think 'Well yeah, you're saying that, but that's not actually what you believe in, you just . . . .' So sometimes I think politics is just mirrors and . . . what do they call it, smoke and mirrors . . . smoke and mirrors really.

Eddie, who was forty-two and unemployed, was similarly discomfited by this unnerving sense of being ensnared by political talk:

> I sometimes find people who are very politically driven to be either a bit intimidating or a bit boring, if that makes sense . . . like a bit, you know . . . I've met a lot of people who have kind of pet political ideologies and if you disagree with them then they can be quite dogmatic and it's . . . it's off-putting.

Non-talkers referred repeatedly to the predictable tonalities of the quintessential political voice, which they heard as a way of speaking *at* people, of invoking abstraction and ideology as a substitute for direct engagement with raw experience. They experienced the politically loquacious as message-oriented rather than listener-oriented speakers (Brown and Yule, 1983) who were good at clearing their throats and delivering categorical messages, but less adept at registering other voices. It was this habitual mode of generic expression that turned them off. As Gary, a 37-year-old engineer put it, political talk seemed to have an almost mesmeric effect: 'There's kind of like a drone of politics jargon. . . . It's just a feeling, but I'm less interested in conversing with them if you like.' In the face of this monological hum, non-political talkers felt inclined to disengage, not because they had nothing to say, but because they had more to express than they expected to be acknowledged. Their silence was less a listless retreat than a tacit disavowal of the rules of the political game.

Above all, they saw the political genre as characterized by signifying markers that separate insiders from outsiders. Insiders were regarded as a *cognoscente*, fluent in a semi-secret social language that mystified outsiders. Mia, a sixteen-year-old school student, described what she thought of as a typical political insider:

> It's the sort of person that knows everything about a certain topic. Like, the people that I know that are like this, they know the manifestos, they know each little session of every conflict . . . they know all of what Gove has done like off by heart, everything.

What might seem like performative competence to insiders is often experienced as condescension by outsiders:

> In their eyes, we're classed as nobodies. . . . They live in nice houses and there's people like me and my family or my friends or people that are on benefits or neighbours that have got severe disabilities that can't do nothing, so they just win and we get looked down on. (Lucy)

The same sense of unyielding communicative distance was expressed by Kelly, a 36-year-old dinner lady, who spoke of how the politically opinionated appeared to speak over people's heads:

> They need to speak English basically instead of just all these big words. Because there's people out there that might be interested in it, but just can't understand what they're saying. Sometimes they say things that just go straight over top of your head.

For several non-political talkers, comprehending the jargon of politics presented a critical barrier. They preferred to avoid interactions in which they might be embarrassed by references and terminology that would be meaningless to them. They wanted the politically well-informed to offer heuristic concessions to the uninitiated:

> I think obviously there's stuff that they're saying that's important, but I feel like it can be condensed down to be easier to take in. (Sue)

> There's various people out there that have got difficulties or just can't understand what they're saying, so they have to put it in . . . not so much dumb terms, but so people can understand. (Lucy)

Alongside this desire for a more accessible political language was a strong suspicion that 'speaking politically' might be *intentionally* opaque; that obfuscation was, in fact, a generic accomplishment. Non-political talkers returned frequently to a Machiavellian image of the politically outspoken as devious operators, capable of exploiting language to bamboozle the uninitiated. Matt, a forty-year-old lorry driver spoke of political talkers as people skilled in a certain kind of verbal cunning:

> Someone will hit them with a brilliant question and you kind of put your hands together [claps] thinking 'Great, how's he going to answer that?' and he somehow squirms his way out of it . . . whether by changing the subject or basically kind of completely ignoring the question, going off . . . off to a complete tangent and making the person who asked completely forget about it.

I asked Mia how she would feel if she were described by her friends as an effective political talker:

> If you're ever described as a politician it means you're doing it wrong because if you're genuinely a politician no one would be able to realize that you're being a manipulative, nasty so-and-so. No one would realize . . . it's only if you're a bad politician that people describe you as one.

As non-talkers described their ambivalent attitudes towards politics – affected by its material consequences, but suspicious of its rhetorical techniques – it became clear that to be a political outsider was to repudiate a *style* of communication rather than its content. Their silence amounted less to an absence of interest than a quiet act of moral defiance in response to a communicative genre that would probably exclude them anyway. In the face of disacknowledgement, silence can assume a retaliatory eloquence. Political theorists such as Dahl (1998), who argue that 'Silent citizens may be perfect subjects for an authoritarian ruler', but 'they would be a disaster for democracy', have possibly underestimated the relational expectations upon which felicitous democratic interaction depends. When the choice between voice and silence is in reality between the drone of *other* voices and a refusal to engage with them, silence should not be bluntly interpreted as dereliction of civic duty, but rather as a demand for a more equal form of communicative exchange. Challenging the conventional assumption of democratic theorists who have equated silence with inertia, Sean Gray (2015: 2) suggests that 'Silent citizenship reflects a *decision* when citizens actively choose silence from among their available political options, instead of voice'.

Two radically different conceptions of communication are at stake here. According to one, the act of communicating is primarily about transmitting messages and generating effects. According to this fundamentally cybernetic notion of information processing, speakers transmit messages, listeners are somehow touched by them, and failure to produce such effects amounts to a communicative malfunction. In the context of political communication, the task of speakers is to transmit signals with a minimum of distortion by extraneous noise and the task of receivers is to hear and decode the message. A quite different way of thinking about communication is as an intersubjective process:

> . . . not so much as a series of discrete acts or products of acts, but as a flow of activity between people. In this refashioning, we do not have a speaker (actual or metaphoric) 'voicing' and then a listener 'hearing' (actual or metaphoric) as a set of separate acts. Instead, as participants, we are speaking and listening co-temporaneously – or at least the possibility of this. Speakers and listeners are never separate people in the communicative arena, but, rather, speaking and listening are things we jointly do in that arena (Penman and Turnbull, 2012: 64)

The contrast between speaking with a view to generating effects and intersubjective communication with a view to establishing shared meaning reflects the important theoretical distinction made by Jürgen Habermas (1984) in *The Theory of Communicative Action* between communicative action, which is oriented towards realizing common understanding, and strategic action, which is oriented to achieving success in influencing the decisions of other actors. When partaking in the former, people engage in 'the cooperative negotiation of common definitions of the situation' in which they find themselves, while strategic action is characteristic of 'those interactions in which at least one of the participants wants with his speech acts to produce perlocutionary effects on his opposite number'. (Habermas, 1984: 295)

These two conceptions of communication account not only for how and why people speak but also for how and why they listen. Those engaged in strategic action are driven by an instrumental wish to shape effects and are therefore inclined to adopt whatever calculative or manipulative means are necessary to ensure that recipients hear messages on the speaker's terms. Those who are engaged in communicative action are interested in more than simply registering an effect; they are mindful of the relational dynamics of communication in which listening comprises more than mere message reception. Communicative action entails a sensibility to the presence of others within an encounter – a sensibility that non-talkers often found to be lacking in the political talk genre, which seemed to be geared towards utilitarian transmission rather than intersubjective understanding. Asked what the politically talkative would need to do to bring her into their conversations, Kelly was emphatic in her response:

> Actually sit down and take people's views in instead of just standing up and giving all that gobbledygook they give. Just put it plain and simple and take people's views in instead of just not listening.

In one sense this demand to be listened to seemed strange when made by people who say that they do not want to be part of the political conversation. Surely, it is only possible to 'take people's views in' if such views are uttered. In a deeper sense, though, Kelly and the many other non-talkers who complained about not being listened to were referring to routine inattention to the protocols of two-way communication that seemed to them to be inherent to the political genre. This was put clearly by Kieran, a 36-year-old chef, who was one of several non-political talkers to speak about the conspicuous absence of attentiveness in political conversation. He compared the political domain to a kitchen in which productive cooperation depends upon everyone listening out for what others need them to do. In contrast to such a collaborative ethos, political talk seemed to Kieran to be replete with unfinished thoughts, broken actions and unsettling reversals:

> Interrupting. That's what all politics is like. . . . They can't talk in a room singularly. They constantly interrupt each other. . . . You can't afford to be inefficient . . . you can't be interrupted if you're cooking a very important dish, for example. . . . Well, it's a lack of respect and if you're asking for people's trust, but you can't respect the people around you, then why should they trust you? If I came to this interview and I interrupted every question with an answer before you finished the question . . . it would probably feel like I'm trying to be too forceful.

Again, the focus here is upon a style of communicating rather than its content. Kieran's preference for a non-interruptive mode of political dialogue is based on his experience of realizing an objective (cooking) through cooperation. For him, the obtrusive punctuation of political bluster was not only disrespectful but also inefficient.

The premium placed by non-talkers upon listening referred to something more than simply being heard. It comprised an ethical commitment to openness – to making time to take in as well as send out. This speaks to Martin Buber's (1947: 202) insistence that 'The fundamental fact of human existence is . . . rooted in one being turning to another as another, as this particular other being, in order to communicate with it in a sphere which is common to them but which reaches out beyond the special sphere of each'. Calvin, a 63-year-old retired youth worker, described himself as a good listener:

> I just listen and let people say what they want to actually say. I listen to what they want to say . . . Like, all my mates, anyone who knows me, knows that I can be a very vocal person. Talk about things, blah blah, don't care what it is, you know. And another time . . . you going through that moment when you want to just

learn and just listen. Cos sometimes we have to stand back or sit back and listen to things before we can actually start to give an opinion. I'm not saying it's gonna be the right or the wrong one, you know. But if you don't listen you ain't gonna know what the next person is thinking about. Like . . . when I went on a course, right, people used to say 'Are you gonna ask a question?' and stuff, and I'd say 'No' – 'Why?' – 'Cos it ain't the proper time'. When I think that I need to know a bit more, then I'll ask the question.

Calvin is reflecting here upon the propriety of vocal intervention. As 'a very vocal person' he might be expected to have something to say about everything. And sometimes he does: 'blah blah, don't care what it is'. But there are other situations in which he prefers 'to stand back or sit back' and this entails a sensibility to the zone of in-betweenness in which meaning is neither simply spoken nor simply heard, but emerges within a dynamic of communicative exchange. To be fully present within a social situation, the stillness of quiet vigilance is sometimes just as productive as the animated hum of the politically ebullient. It is in this sense that listening seemed to serve as a metaphor for attunement to mutual communication.

'A certain way of speaking'

Unsurprisingly, those who described themselves as frequent political talkers were much more loquacious in their responses to my interview questions than the non-talkers. Many of them were keen to reflect upon the desirable qualities of effective political performance, rather like actors evaluating the techniques of their craft. These were people who spent a lot of their time listening to themselves speak, self-monitoring their performances, subjecting their habits of expression to generic scrutiny. Reflexivity in this context entailed thinking of themselves as being simultaneously producers of meaningful utterances and self-auditors of the performative effects of such production. A sense of this performative reflexivity was conveyed by Steve, a Liberal Democrat member of a major British city government, who offered the following critical observations on his own political voice:

When you sort of hear yourself speaking you um . . . you almost . . . there is a certain way of speaking, a certain way of phrasing which just . . . just becomes part of the way that you communicate. And it's not particularly . . . it's not helpful, I don't think . . . . It is using phrases . . . using phrases that in some way make you sound less than honest . . . shifty . . . where maybe you are trying to hedge something. . . . It's a skill that you learn and that you adopt, but I don't think it's particularly helpful for members of the public and . . . they pick up on that straight away . . . . You do tend to use a language that puts up barriers or makes people feel that you are not being completely honest. . . . I don't know how you change that, but I think it's a problem.

While non-talkers bemoaned the absence of political listening, frequent talkers were keen to express their commitment to the fundamental importance of listening. (Indeed, it was a principle that many of them were prepared to speak about at great length.) When asked about the qualities of an effective political communicator, Sebastian, a Conservative Member of the British Parliament, said, 'I do try my best to listen to other people's views and opinions . . . . I think that's what a good debate is about – listening to what other people have to say.' Mark, a Labour member of a major British city government, regarded himself as a good listener:

I think I try to be very attentive to what people are saying. I try to understand the point people are making. If people aren't making a point very clearly, I try and sort of tease out of them what it is they're trying to say. Or if people present themselves in a very, very angry way, or a very, very upset way, I try to sort of . . . not dismiss them as somebody that's come to rant and rave, but I try and actually understand what their problem is.

Arthur, a Conservative Member of Parliament, was very clear about his commitment to hearing the people he represents: 'You spend the vast majority of your time doing one very simple thing and that's listening.' He elaborated:

So the question is, are you good at listening to people and feeding that back into your argument . . . or are you good at listening to the people who pander to your own thoughts in the first place and shutting out everything else?

Likewise Liberal Democrat councillor, Steve said:

There's the need to listen to people . . . to listen to the concerns . . . listen to whatever the issue is that they particularly want to get across . . . and to withhold judgement or to suspend judgement on that for a certain point of time to allow people to express themselves.

Asked to describe her qualities as a communicator, Moira, a 62-year-old community activist, said:

I like people. I always try to find the thing that will unite us rather than divide us. And I listen all the time.

Rodrigo, a full-time campaigner who described himself as someone whom 'people seem to listen to and take seriously', was of the view that

> I have I believe a natural inclination to working with people and telling them what I think and listening to them . . . and then in the end there is some form of mutual understanding in our conversations.

Given that frequent political talkers placed such emphasis upon the value of listening and spoke of themselves as good listeners, why were they so often characterized by others as being monological, uncooperative and insensitive to other voices? A clue to this glaring contrast lies in a fundamental motivation for political speech. The aim of political talkers is not merely to speak, but to persuade, convince, edify or inspire. As *political* talkers they are not simply passing the time but are engaged in performative work: they seek to make things happen by speaking. The performative imperative of political talk compels speakers to sacrifice the open-endedness of dialogical communication for the strategic objective of convincing their addressees to buy into a particular perception of reality. An irreconcilable tension exists between the kind of free-flowing conversation that eschews predetermined goals and the motivated expressiveness of the performative operator. It is this tension that is perceived when people refer to the inherent slipperiness and opacity that so often frames and inflects political talk.

Are political talkers being cynical or disingenuous then, when they speak of their commitment to listening as well as proclaiming and persuading? Or are they expressing an awareness of the double bind between communicative and strategic action that is inherent to the political genre? It was remarkable how frequently political talkers moved on swiftly from speaking about the importance of listening to explaining its pitfalls and limitations. As Member of Parliament, Arthur put it: 'Rule number one in politics is "Never waste your time in an argument that you're not going to win."' Steve, the local councillor was equally sure that listening to the views of others had its limits:

> There comes a point in time when you then have to say, 'Right, okay, I've heard what people's views are on this . . . what it is that's concerning them.' But now we have to think about what it is we can do to sort it out. What can we do to solve the problem? What can we do to take things further? . . . At that point you have to stop listening and actually start deciding.

Conservative MP Sebastian spoke eloquently about how listening made him an effective representative, but went on to say:

> I think the problem is that you can never make everybody happy . . . You know, if you make a decision that doesn't go with everybody then it can be interpreted

that you're not listening. And it's not that you're not listening, it's that you've actually come to a different conclusion. And I think that's probably why people think that we don't listen.

Lenny, a senior official in the local government of a major British city, put it this way:

> Politicians act in a certain way. They often ponder very carefully what they're going to say and therefore yes, they will listen but . . . in getting the message over . . . listening is probably the least important bit. They concentrate more on communicating the message.

Even Rodrigo, whose experience as a civic campaigner led him to become keenly alert to the importance of listening to people, presented an ambivalent balance between communicative and strategic action – performance and performativity – when describing his capacity as an effective communicator:

> I have I believe a natural inclination to working with people and, um, telling them what I think . . . and listening to them. I try to communicate in a way that, um, comes across as being able to let them know what I think.

Here lies a troubling dilemma for practitioners of the political genre. As a communicative actor, Rodrigo wanted to be seen to listen to others in a spirit of dialogical reciprocity, but as a strategic actor he needed to let his listeners know what he thought with a view to eliciting from them forms of behaviour consistent with his instrumental goals. Could it be that popular suspicion of the political genre reflects a wariness of the artful contrivances through which the goal-seeking imperatives of strategic talk are realized? If political talk never seems to be candid, but forever implicated in charges of disingenuity and duplicity, must it inevitably jar with the unforced cadences of ordinary social interaction? Can political talk never sound innocent?

Socializing the political persona

Even the most enthusiastic and incessant political talkers do not spend all or even most of their time speaking as if they were in a debate. It is within the more relaxed social realms of friendship, family relations, workplace and leisure activities that most political conversation takes place, often in an intermittent and fragmented form. As my interviews proceeded, I began to notice a contrast between the ways in which people spoke about being expressive within explicitly 'political' contexts and within less generically constrained spaces of sociability.

Steve, the local government councillor, seemed almost proud to tell me that there was more to him than his explicitly political persona:

> I've just been for lunch with a friend actually and I think, um, I don't think politics came up once. I don't think my role as a councillor came up once. We talked about other things.

Several interviewees spoke of recognizing a conspicuous difference between the tones and rhythms of everyday social talk and of the political genre. They were able to spot when they were caught up in a political setting, describing such situations as being almost like atmospheric disturbances in which they were exposed to unsettling layers of concealed intention and bullheaded assertiveness. Speaking of the latter, Eric, a 44-year-old office worker referred to 'a sound that . . . people don't feel as if they can challenge'. Political enthusiasts 'do come across as a bit pompous really' said charity worker, Milly. Speaking about the politicians he sees on television, Rod, who is aged thirty-seven and unemployed, observed that 'They look like businessmen; they look like people who are not representing my interests; they don't look or sound at all like anyone I know'. Simon, a 41-year-old solicitor, described how he thought of typical political representatives:

> You have to hit all the popular points. You have to fit in all of the key soundbites that signify to group X and group Y that you speak their language . . . And it's not inspiring.

The relentless negativity of these characterizations contrast with the ways in which people tend to value interpersonal communication, regarding it as 'close, supportive, flexible speech, which functions as the "work" necessary to self-definition and interpersonal bonding' (Katriel and Philipsen, 1981). The task of balancing political self-expression (value-heavy, goal-oriented, loquacious) and conversational congeniality (shared, fragmented, unbounded) within everyday sociability entails sensitive application. Several interviewees spoke about their struggle to manage their political personas across these boundaries, few more forcefully than 31-year-old environmental campaigner, Gabby.

For Gabby the political and the personal seemed to coexist in a strained fashion, challenging her sense of a coherent self. In her personal life she spent a lot of her time trying to fix other people's problems:

> I definitely listen a lot to people. People come to me with their problems. It's actually one of my biggest problems in life . . . people come to me with problems

and I listen to them a lot and then I give a lot of probably very unhelpful advice.
I can't listen and then not give advice.

But she had come to realize that some problems are beyond personal solution; they are both particular and political and Gabby's search was for a language that could bridge both spheres. 'As a child I was quite dismayed by society . . . very aware of society's problems'. This led her to engage in various political campaigns in which she found herself playing an increasingly passionate and voluble part. 'When pressed about my values and what needs to change I do get very emotional about it,' she explained. She felt that such emotive force often seemed out of place within 'serious' political talk, which struck her as being characterized by an over-rationalistic depreciation of feelings:

> Sometimes they're not able to feel the concept . . . and I think that sometimes people feel the need to restrain themselves in that sort of aggressive 'don't defy me' way. . . . I remember going to a court hearing for a friend, an asylum seeker friend, and having a big argument with a friend who was also there supporting him. He had just a sort of aggressive approach to any sort of immigration law . . . to the point where it was like scary to talk to him because I thought I wouldn't dare have an opinion on this. . . . So I think it's about owning spaces . . . But essentially there's very little fusion between how I feel and what political thoughts I have.

Gabby's idea of *feeling the concept* raises important questions about what it means to possess and express political values. Can this take a purely intellectual form and if not, what is the necessary relationship between cognition and affect? This question led Gabby to reflect upon the disjuncture between the rigidity of the beliefs and flexibility of the feelings that combined to constitute her political commitments. Her passions and beliefs often proceeded in lines that were, if not divergent, uneven. The root of this imbalance lay not in normative inconsistency but in the ambivalence of political talk as a generic mode of expression. Gabby heard in this genre 'a sort of confidence . . . which often feels quite male'. She found this intimidating and wanted to reclaim the space of political communication so that she and others like her could feel comfortable within it. Much as she wanted to be politically eloquent, she was often irritated by the tones and traits of the generic political voice. Talking about politics often felt to her as if she were entering hostile territory. Over the years she had attended lots of political meetings, but found them repeatedly dispiriting:

> The more names you could throw about people in Westminster, the more cred you had. And I would sometimes go to the toilet in the middle of a meeting and just feel terrified about expressing myself in the only way I know how.

This sense of not quite knowing the insider lingo nagged at her, leaving her feeling somehow under-qualified and vulnerable:

> Sometimes I do struggle with expressing myself . . . if I feel that there's any limit to my vocabulary. . . . For example, at work sometimes I don't speak like other people in my office. I come at my job with a passion and I just care about this so much that I have a 'let's do it' perspective rather than a very intellectual perspective. So sometimes I'll swear in the office.

Gabby found it hard to understand why being taken seriously was so dependent upon the adoption of an insiders' code:

> I have a slightly guilty conscience about not being able . . . . Well, for a start, I can't really store that much information, like facts and things like that. I don't know names and stuff like that. It takes me years to learn politicians' names. And in a professional capacity, like sometimes I'm slightly ashamed that I don't know more: who's this or what's that in parliament . . . because it's quite an egotistical environment to work in. There's a lot of like geeks throwing around political concepts and social change models and things like that. And often I don't have the time to get really intellectualized about it . . . because it's not what floats my boat really.

In contrast with this sense of unease in the company of the politically engaged, Gabby had carved out a social life that was well insulated from the communicative norms surrounding her political commitments. She described her social life as being spontaneous and vivacious, replete with effusive self-expression in which she feels under no pressure to rein in her passions. Occasionally (and usually unsuccessfully) she had tried to bring together the separate parts of her life:

> I have two very distinct groups of friends. Some are very apathetic . . . lots of drinking and smoking . . . you know you go out and you have fun and you party and you behave like a kid. Great fun! But then I have very political active friends where if you talk about makeup or anything like that . . . you've like automatically crossed the line. You're oppressing them by suggesting that this sort of stuff has to be in their lives . . . . I mediate between these two groups and I've had friends at parties come up to me from my apathetic end (laughs) . . . and say 'You need to stop trying to mix these groups. This isn't fun for us. We don't want to listen to folk music sitting down.' I was quite upset by that, but I was also quite refreshed . . . because I do spend a lot of my time trying to merge cultures that don't necessarily want to merge at all.

The cultural irreconcilability of these two groups suggests something about the challenges of mediating between the everyday social and the generically political.

Faced with deep-rooted incongruity between the austere intensity of political talk and the inclusive congeniality of everyday sociability, Gabby found herself mediating between two preconditions for democratic intercourse: commitment and inclusion. As Steve the local politician acknowledged after telling me about his lunch with a friend in which politics was hardly discussed, the divergence of the political and social spheres spells trouble for democratic politics:

> I suppose you could say that the friends you have outside politics are closer to the normal electorate. So the fact that you are not talking politics to those people is a bit of a worry because it's more important to talk politics to them in a way than it is to talk politics to your other political friends . . . because it's just a little club and you are just perpetuating something.

Left only to the politically committed, confident and articulate, democracy is at risk of becoming a game for a minority who know and like its arcane expressive rules. Avoiding such a fate would entail abandoning many of the generic features that estrange politics from popular social communication. Gabby had internalized this dilemma. Much as she found the political genre unsettling, she found herself adopting it when speaking to her non-political friends:

> Now I think about it . . . with some friends, in order to preserve a friendship, I don't cross certain lines. I've crossed them before . . . just questioning them to the point where they kind of just hate you and think you're being (laughs) oppressive and trying to, you know, preach to them. And that just never works . . . . I think that there are some friends that I know, we're always going to get to that sticking point, but with other people I try sort of different sort of tactics and I can be quite feisty and opinionated. I make very big statements all the time and use the words 'amazing' or 'terrible' a lot.

Gabby manages her political persona by being a resistance fighter among insiders, refusing to engage in what she sees as their name-dropping and hyper-rational intellectualizing, and an assertive preacher ('I can be quite narky and opinionated . . . I have a fiery temper, so often . . . not often, but occasionally . . . I find myself in a situation having just snapped at somebody') towards outsiders whom she realizes she is alienating by adopting the very tones that irritate her. Talking politics feels to Gabby like a lose-lose game, leaving her longing for her insider friends to appear more human and her politically disengaged friends to succumb to the incontrovertible wisdom of her passions. Her enthusiasm to change the world is constrained by the intense frustration of being a committed political talker for whom political talk feels routinely disappointing.

Ronald, a forty-year-old assistant hotel manager, was rather more sanguine about his capacity to blend the political and the social. With a broad smile, he told me, 'I have certain things which I strongly believe in and yes, I have come to blows with quite a few people in debating the issues.' He regards himself as a persuasive person: 'I suppose I tend to get my own way most of the time.'

Growing up, Ronald felt quite socially isolated:

I was a swot and I got picked on. I was very nerdy with big glasses . . . big massive glasses, about this big, with crappy hair and I mostly hung around with girls, probably because I was a gay, I suppose. And I was picked on for being gay, even though I didn't know that categorically I was until I came out when I left school . . . and I was like 'Oh, I am now, so there we go'. But yes, I didn't enjoy school. I hated school.

He came out as gay when he was eighteen:

So that's going back twenty-two years. Oh Jesus. (laughs) Because I'm forty this year. So it was a completely different world then than it is now. I mean, when I first came out I was eighteen. The legal age was twenty-one, so technically what I was doing was against the law. And I think, um, people's attitudes were different then as well.

He moved a few years ago to a large industrial city in the north of England and, although he is a chatty person – 'I never had a problem talking to everybody, anybody, about anything really to be honest' – he does not have many close local friends. Partly with the intention of making like-minded friends, but also as an opportunity to exercise his political voice, Ronald decided to join the Conservative Party:

The people I work with . . . they know I'm politically active now. But I suppose I'm quite a laid-back person . . . I'm not, I'm not a radical. I'm quite a moderate Conservative. I wouldn't say I was a very right-wing Conservative. I would say I was middle of the road, you know, I happen to agree with the majority of the Conservative values. A lot of my friends think I shouldn't have joined the Conservative party because of their gay issues, but quite frankly that's ridiculous . . . that doesn't really make any difference when you are running a country, does it really? You know what I mean? If people aren't voting for a particular party because they haven't got very good gay issues, that's a bit stupid in my mind. Because if you agree with all the policies but you don't vote for them purely because of that, then that's just ridiculous. It's just cutting your nose off to spite your face.

As Ronald talked about his involvement with the Conservative Party it became clear that the political and the social had become delicately intertwined in his lifeworld – that his sense of being political was as much rooted in feelings of affinity and belonging as in abstract ideology:

> I am part of something that's bigger than me and I think that's kind of good because, you know. . . I am being part of something. I am helping a party which I believe in to get into power and that's a good thing I think. I like that feeling because it is a party. It is a family in lots of ways. . . . And there is a social aspect to it and a lot of the time you're hanging around with people who have the same beliefs as you do.

In seeking to merge the political and the social, Ronald drew upon feelings of nostalgia for a lost ideal of community:

> In my mother's day she was a Young Conservative and they used to do all sorts of things, dances and things and all sorts. And that's kind of gone by the by a bit now. I mean, to be honest with you, in my local Conservative Club . . . the majority of the people probably go and vote Labour, I reckon. . . . It's got billiard tables. It's got a cheap bar. It's got like a function room.

For Ronald, the reality of political discourse often fails to live up to its cultural promise. He described how he felt when he attended a regional party meeting for the first time:

> I was sat there and there was probably about six of us who were below the age of forty. There were a few toffs there. Do you know what I mean? A few typical Tory you-knows, but there were a lot of people who weren't. And I think that's the problem with the Tory party in general. I think they are perceived as being toffs. They are perceived as being rich. They are perceived as being arrogant . . . not caring. Do you know what I mean? And that's the problem. Even the Conservatives themselves know this.

In his social life Ronald refuses to allow his political views to interfere with friendships. He spoke with great affection about his close friend Adam, whose political views are quite different from his:

> My best friend, Adam . . . he's very left of my opinions on political issues so we have feisty discussions a lot of the time. He's very pro-European and I'm not. . . . Adam is very intelligent and on things he knows about he is very articulate. On things he doesn't know about he's not so articulate, to be honest. He shuts up very quickly. But he's a total Europhile. He loves the EU. . . . He's studying languages. He wants to go and work for the EU. . . . I don't believe we should

devolve too much power to the EU. I think the EU wastes a lot of money. So yes, so we have these debates . . . I don't know . . . I don't actually know why they happen. They just happen I think. I usually lose when it comes to the EU with him because he knows all about it and I only know certain things about the EU.

Indeed, Adam's objection to Ronald's party affiliation came close to putting their friendship at risk:

His exact words were, 'The Conservative Party is evil.' I was, 'So you're calling me evil, are you?' And I must say that did piss me off actually . . . I did say, 'You can't say a party is evil. You know, Adolf Hitler was evil.' But I mean as I say, yeah, and I mean, I think evil is a very, very strong word.

Maintaining their friendship in the face of these differences entailed hard work:

Well, we talk about politics still, but we don't talk about what I'm doing in the Conservative Party. He doesn't want to know. It's really weird actually. . . . No, we just don't talk about it. We still talk about politics, but we don't discuss what I'm doing in the party.

Ronald seemed to be adept at drawing clear lines between his political and social personae. Not talking about his political loyalties became a way of preserving his social connections:

I think life's too short to be arguing about politics. Politics is politics, you know what I mean? People always have their own opinions on things. And I still respect [Adam's] views even though I think they are a load of crap. I still respect (laughs) that they are his views. Do you see what I mean? . . . That's the trouble with politics . . . there's never a right answer. There's always someone else's opinions.

Both Gabby and Roland were struggling with the practical work of fusing their social and political personae. As they moved between the solidarity-sustaining social ties of their personal lifeworlds and the generic norms of the political sphere they felt compelled to change cultural gear – to translate between different expressive modes. In her illuminating study of the ways in which Americans avoid political talk, Nina Eliasoph (1998) observed a tendency for local volunteers and activists to be desperate to cultivate a public image of themselves as merely parochially minded, non-political folk, while, in the intimacy of private conversation many of them were quite open about the political significance of their commitments and actions. By confining their political personae to the Goffmanesque 'backstage' – that hidden, whispered out-of-the spotlight region of conversational privacy and peripherality – they felt more like 'everyday citizens' and less like political actors whose motives and actions would be open to public accountability and debate.

Eliasoph observed (1998: 7) 'a strange process of political evaporation' whereby 'what was announced aloud was less open to debate, less aimed at expressing connections to the wider world, less public-spirited, more insistently selfish, than what was whispered'. By couching talk of social change in a language of pre-political motivation, Eliasoph's volunteers and activists were able to retreat to safe spaces of intimacy and shared values, while shunning the public domain as a zone of danger, dominated by a forbidding generic code. They were at pains to avoid the strategic games and over-authoritative claims that they associated with politics, but in doing so they diminished their capacity to move beyond their own fragmented and bounded life-spheres.

Florence Passy and Marco Giugni (2000: 121) define life-spheres as 'distinct though interrelated "regions" in the life of an individual, each one with its own borders, logic, and dynamic'. While life-spheres often overlap within individual lives, moving between them entails agile discretion. It was clear from Gabby and Roland's accounts that negotiating between life-spheres can be a delicate operation. How one speaks – and what one speaks about – in one life-sphere might lead to problems when repeated in another. As they move between different areas of their lives people are required to become 'plural actors' and 'each new situation experienced by the actor plays an important role as a filter, selector or trigger and is the occasion for an application or suspension, a flourishing or an inhibition of this or that part of the embodied dispositions' (Lahire, 2011: xii). Perhaps this is what Mead (1932) had in mind in making the astute observation that 'sociality is the capacity of being several things at once'.

It is easy to disparage such adaptive dexterity in the face of different audiences as a characteristic of the political chameleon who is 'all things to all men'. But that is surely to miss the point that what defines political talk is its reference to public issues, problems and disagreements that cannot be resolved by like-minded people talking among themselves. Politics is a product of engagement across heterogeneous social and discursive networks. Political talk is a vocal appeal to universal intelligibility in the face of palpable difference. As Michael Warner states:

> Public discourse, in the nature of its address, abandons the security of its positive, given audience. It promises to address anybody. It commits itself in principle to the possible participation of any stranger. It therefore puts at risk the concrete world that is its given condition of possibility.

Political talk that could only be communicated to people who share a common sense of belonging, an identical set of values and a wholly comprehensible way of speaking about them would be so invulnerable to risk – either of misunderstanding or disagreement – as to be a mere ritual affirmation of collective solidarity.

The challenge facing people who talk about politics is to be able to speak to the experiential specificity of life-spheres while transcending their borders and addressing the potential energy of a universal public. To do only the former risks creating homophilic enclaves in which people are charmed and bolstered by their own echoes. To do only the latter would be to unfasten the political from its social moorings, thereby confining it to an exotic domain of abstraction. It is the common failure of this delicate act of cultural versatility that has given political talk such a bad name.

Political talk as pragmatic performance

As I listened to people speaking about their experiences of and attitudes towards political talk it became clear that the most adroit political talkers are flexible performers who possess the capacity to switch cultural codes in order to relate to diverse audiences. As pragmatic cultural brokers, they are capable of transcending their biographical histories and the normative conventions of local social orders. Possessing the dexterity to vary 'the scope of their engagement, shifting along a scale between greater or lesser generality' (Thévenot, 2005: 66), they manage to relate the conjecturally political to the contingencies of the social.

To describe someone as an effective political talker, then, has less to do with their ability to speak ardently or knowledgably about 'politics' than their capacity to mediate between social groups while managing to seem relevant to the subjective identities of diverse addressees. But it is precisely this capacity for pragmatic translation that arouses suspicion in people who feel alienated by what they regard as the artifice of political talk. As we have seen in this chapter, they sense that when communication turns political speakers are motivated by rhetorical strategies that would not be tolerated in other genres of everyday discourse. When the local politician Steve reflects with considerable candour upon his 'certain way of speaking' which involves 'using phrases that in some way make you sound less than honest . . . shifty . . . where maybe you are trying to hedge something' he captures an image that is widely associated with the political mode of expression. Milly's depiction of political talk as 'smoke and mirrors' is based on her belief that 'you're saying that, but that's not actually what you believe in'. In everyday conversation that would amount to a damning allegation; a fundamental questioning of another's authentic identity. In the context of political talk this passes as an unremarkable observation. Mia's description of the archetypal political enthusiast as 'a manipulative, nasty so-and-so' is expressed as if that is a taken-for-granted definition. She reflects that when someone carries off a political performance well 'no one would be able to realize' that they're being political. Political talk begins to feel like a form of subterfuge, luring its mark into a false sense of assurance.

As a generic mode of *social performance*, political talk arouses suspicions that are commonly associated with acting. To perform is to work to create an impression – to realize intentions through expressive strategies. As performative speech, political talk seeks on the one hand to convey a convincing account of social reality, while on the other hand creating realities that did not exist before they were constituted through utterance. In the terminology of J. L. Austin's (1962: 101) theory of speech acts, political talk can be regarded as possessing illocutionary force when it makes something happen (as in the case of a national leader declaring that a country is now at war) and perlocutionary force when it is intended to 'produce certain consequential effects upon the feelings, thoughts or actions of other persons'. John Searle (1969: 25) expands helpfully upon Austin's notion of perlocution:

> by arguing I may *persuade* or *convince* someone, by warning him I may *scare* or *alarm* him, by making a request I may get him to do something, by informing him I may *convince* him, *enlighten*, *edify*, *inspire* him (get him to *realize*). The italicized expressions above denote perlocutionary acts.

The key term here is 'may'; perlocutionary performances offer no guarantees. Their efficacy depends upon the willingness of listeners to accept that what is being said is meaningful and worthy of being acted upon. Just as sellers can only 'make a sale' if buyers can be persuaded to make a purchase, political speakers can do their best to persuade, convince, scare, alarm, enlighten, edify or inspire, but such perlocutionary consequences will only transpire if citizens 'take up' the messages that are directed to them. When this happens the message is characterized (in Austinian terms) as being 'felicitous' – the performance achieves its effect. The risk entailed in all communicative performances, however, is that they will fail – the unrousing call to arms; the witty comment made at the wrong moment; the catalogue of facts that generate tedium rather than evidence; authority unmasked as pomposity; anodyne demands that lack salience or exigency; stuttering expressions of confidence. Perhaps it is not performance, but infelicitous performance that gives political talk such a bad reputation. That is the thrust of Gabby's concern about the language of her fellow activists. Her observation that 'they're not able to feel the concept' and resort to a 'sort of aggressive "don't defy me" way' speaks to a flawed mode of performance that lacks affective force.

This may well be what interviewees were getting at when they focused upon the importance and problematics of listening. To be seen to listen is to exhibit an ethical sensitivity to the possibility that communication entails more than uptake. What at first appears to be a simple empirical division between people who like talking about politics and people who would rather talk about almost anything else turns out to be a rather more complex disagreement about the nature of interpersonal communication. On the one side is a generic commitment to political voice as a monological tool of persuasion:

> monologue depends on both erasure – the flattening of language to make people, their actions and their voices disappear – and creative performance that attempts to unify speakers in a way that might be called the 'repeat after me' phenomenon. Shutting people up and refusing to recognize their voices may be a precondition of monologue but it is never sufficient; monologue also requires a creative act of discursive displacement or overwriting, an insistence that the voice you are about to hear is the only one – with the implication that the only possible forms of uptake are either perfect assent or faithful repetition (Tomlinson, 2017: 3)

This version of the political genre is so fixated upon communicative output that it fails in its transmissive urgency to acknowledge the presence of listeners, their experiential filters and their role as potential dialogical actors. On the other side is a conception of political talk that is pragmatically adapted to the dynamics of situated reception. As Bakhtin (1986: 95) states:

> Both the composition and, particularly, the style of the utterance depend on those to whom the utterance is addressed, how the speaker . . . senses and imagines his addressees, and the force of their effect upon the utterance. Each speech genre . . . has its own typical conception of the addressee, and this defines it as a genre.

To be addressed politically is to be defined as a certain kind of person, be it an object of representation, partnership, persuasion or manipulation. The gap between how speakers imagine their addressees and how addressees feel defined is bound to generate unsettled feelings. Misunderstood addressees invoke routine strategies of resistance in order to avoid the moral injuries resulting from communicative violation, making addressors even more rhetorically desperate in their attempts to animate imagined relationships. Both strategies depend upon determined non-listening. When Kelly urges political talkers to 'actually sit down and take people's views in' and Calvin observes that 'sometimes we have to stand back or sit back and listen to things before we can actually start to give an opinion', the emphasis is not simply upon listening, but *sitting down* and *standing back*. These are relaxed postures, associated with experiences of bodily ease, pliancy and readjustment. They represent embodied contrasts to images of rising to orate, finger-pointing and putting questioners in their place. Such performances of rhetorical bombast have become metaphorically bracketed with quintessential political speechifying, reducing the genre to an overwrought and uninviting routine. There is a sense here in which the political genre arrives as a tainted good. Its most enthusiastic practitioners – caricatured variously as loud, intrusive tub-thumpers or slick, calculating politicians – seem to have forgotten how to sit down or stand back. The political desire to impose meanings upon situations, events and processes is easily interpreted as a coarse demand for assentive attention.

4

Taking positions on Brexit

My husband shouted up when I woke up and said 'We're out,' and I said, 'I don't believe you, I don't believe it. I don't believe you.' I jumped for joy at the top of my stairs. (Kath, 43-year-old palliative healthcare worker)

On polling day I voted to remain and on the Friday morning there was a lot of tears. . . . I was actually at Glastonbury the day the vote came out . . . and I cried even more and my mum was texting me, saying 'Don't worry, it's for the best'. (Sian, 24-year-old teaching assistant)

How can we make sense of these highly charged responses to the same event? How was it that this great public moment resonated so differently with Kath and Sian's personal experience, evoking such discrepant and mutually insensitive feelings? What were the deep sources of these convulsive emotions? On exploring the conversations that had preceded and surrounded these intense reactions, it became clear that there was more going on in the Brexit referendum than could be gleaned from the predictable and prosaic narratives of the mainstream news agenda.

There was no lack of cues telling people what to say about Brexit. Politicians and journalists were on hand to frame the issues in ways that made it almost impossible to think about notions such as 'ever closer union', 'the single market' and 'free movement' without evoking fears and fantasies. Long before the referendum campaign began, coverage of the European Union in most British newspapers had been relentlessly hostile. Media coverage during the campaign did little to promote calm reflection. 'The campaign leading up to the vote to remain or leave the EU on 23 June 2016 was the UK's most divisive, hostile, negative and fear-provoking of the 21st century,' concluded Martin Moore and Gordon Ramsay (2017: 163) in the most systematic review of what happened. 'This', they argued, 'was partly due to the rhetoric and approaches of the campaigns themselves but was encouraged and enflamed by a highly partisan national media'. It is hard to imagine how the campaign could have been other than crabby and intolerant, given Moore and Ramsay's observation that

> The rancorous, bitter way in which the referendum campaign was fought was both reflected in, and enhanced by, the media coverage. The majority of media organisations that could take sides . . . did so, often uncompromisingly. Their partisanship was then played out in much of their coverage – both in their selection and framing of news and in their editorials, leader columns and their choice of front-page stories. Eventually the campaign became framed as us-versus-them, pro-Establishment versus anti-Establishment, pro-immigration versus antiimmigration, nationalist versus internationalist. Rather than seek to provide a public space in which each side could fairly challenge the other, many news outlets encouraged and stoked the partisanship.

In their analysis of the campaign, the Reuters Institute for the Study of Journalism concluded that

> The relatively narrow range of information sources and voices, when combined with a highly partisan approach, did little to respond to the need of those seeking more high-quality information to make up their minds. (Levy et al., 2017: 35)

The ways in which newspapers framed the EU debate as being about immigration had consequences for interpersonal political talk that will become clear in subsequent chapters. Moore and Ramsay (2017: 165) report that

> There were more leading front pages about immigration during the campaign than about the economy. Six in 10 of these immigration front pages were published by three newspapers, the Daily Express, the Daily Mail, and the Daily Telegraph. . . . Out of 111 articles that expressed a view about Turks, for example, 98% (109) were negative. Out of 90 articles that expressed a view about Albanians, 100% were negative. Three metaphors were dominant in the coverage of migrants: migrants as water ('floodgates', 'waves'), as animals or insects ('flocking', 'swarming') or as an invading force.

Three points should be understood about the relationship between this mass-media priming and interpersonal political talk. First, the media play an important agenda-setting role, but they do not write the script for people when they come to discuss contentious political issues. The mass media do not have the kind of powerful effects attributed to them by those who argue that they simply tell people what to think. The media tell people what to *think about* and perform a strong, often pernicious part in framing the ways that people make sense of issues. For example, if 'Europe' is repeatedly framed in terms of 'interference' and 'loss of control', or 'immigration' is routinely invoked through metaphors of 'flooding' and 'invasion', it becomes more difficult to make common sense beyond these ingrained fields of meaning. Much political talk is about negotiating media frames. Second, when people talk about politics they draw upon their own experiences and the clearer they are about what these experiences are the less vulnerable they are likely to be to propagandist efforts to tell them what or how to think. The media offer people vicarious experience to talk about, but this rarely trumps direct engagement with the world. Third, the rise of social media, which do not on the whole exist to disseminate single messages to mass audiences, has changed the communication ecology. Much of what people talk about they learn from others online. A certain amount of interpersonal talk about politics now happens online. But most happens in face-to-face contexts, or else moves between online and offline exchanges within a process of seamless social interaction. In short, when people talk about turbulent topics in troubled times, they do so within a complex media ecology, but they are not its passive victims.

In the weeks and months preceding the Brexit vote, tens of millions of unrecorded, informal, fragmentary conversations had taken place. Some of them were so transient that they were lost within the flow of mundane chatter; others were deeply reflective. Some followed received scripts, mimetically reproducing well-rehearsed rhetorical tropes. Others were creative and passionate, frequently incapable of fully containing or revealing the feelings that impelled them.

In asking people what they remembered about Brexit-related arguments – how it felt to be engaged in the drama of political talk – it became clear that Brexit talk entailed acts of informal translation between the local and immediate and the nonlocal and mediated. People gave meaning to Brexit by splicing grand political narratives with their own experiences of being in or out of control of their own lives. Filtered through the prism of personal biography, such preoccupations were charged with the affective force of memory. For the lack of a common language for speaking about their own value and efficacy as social actors, politics served as a practical surrogate – a space for articulating what it means to possess or lack control over one's position in the world.

As people recalled the ways in which they conversed and argued about the referendum, feelings about speaking out in a world of disparately valued experiences came repeatedly to the surface. To speak in the face of unequally distributed respect is to render oneself vulnerable to the judgement of others. In the precarious moments between opening one's mouth and formulating an utterance, forms of political framing are always at work, calling attention to one's position and value as a social being. The political is experienced in its most elemental form at such moments. For, as Andrew Sayer (2011: 197) notes, 'To be able to speak out, to be listened to and have our views taken seriously rather than mocked or ignored or treated as merely symptomatic of our condition is to have our dignity respected.'

Talking about Brexit evoked a range of highly personal feelings. Narratives of national sovereignty at odds with turbulent globalization competed with locally situated accounts of thwarted personal autonomy, dignity and agency. Never far from the abstract logic of *an argument* lurked the fragile sensitivities of *the arguers*. Wayne Brockriede's (1975: 179) astute observation that 'arguments are not in statements but in people' (see also Hample, 2007) was reinforced as interviewees repeatedly told stories of how they felt *positioned* within political talk in ways that framed and constrained their agency.

What does it mean to be positioned by talk? When people engage in conversation or argument, they do not simply exchange semantic content, as if they were intelligent machines transacting data. Interpersonal talk is inflected by assumptions about who is being addressed and the cognitive, emotional and moral capacities they are deemed capable of bringing to a social interaction. As Bakhtin (1986: 94) recognized, all utterances contain 'dialogic overtones'. They are spoken with a particular kind of addressee in mind: 'This addressee can be an immediate participant-interlocutor in an everyday dialogue, a differentiated collective of specialists in some particular area of cultural communication, a more or less differentiated public, ethnic group, contemporaries, like-minded people, opponents and enemies, a subordinate, a superior, someone who is lower, higher, familiar, foreign, and so forth.' In short, the act of talking to someone else entails a parallel act of evaluation and positioning. Speakers establish a discursive position for themselves, not only by using particular words but also by adopting tones, postures and countenances that announce the terms on which they hope to be recognized. At the same time, speakers offer addressees a position from which to respond to them – not simply an argumentative position of agreement or dissent, but a relational position comprising subjective capacity and moral entitlement. To address persons as if they were 'like-minded' or 'lower' or 'foreign' amounts to a call for them to accept and adopt a subject position – to speak from a metaphorical platform that is appropriate to their status.

While political talk is commonly regarded as speech that takes politics as its object, positioning theorists remind us that the subjective allocation of parts within social interaction always and inevitably engenders political relationships. Theorists, such as Harré (1999), Davies (1990), van Langenhove (1998) and White (2009) argue that communication is inherently political insofar as agency is framed and constrained through modes of interpersonal positioning. To accept a subject position is to take up a fixed moral orientation towards the world and one's place in it:

> A subject position incorporates both a conceptual repertoire and a location for persons within the structure of rights for those that use that repertoire. Once having taken up a particular position as one's own, a person inevitably sees the world from the vantage point of that position and in terms of the particular images, metaphors, story lines and concepts which are made relevant within the particular discursive practice in which they are positioned. (Davies and Harré, 1990: 46)

To refuse a subject position – declaring, for example, that 'You might speak to me as if I'm *just a girl*, but I see myself and wish to be known as a *confident democratic citizen*' – amounts to an act of resistance to moral injury. To disavow unfair categorization is a first step towards the recovery of dignity and should therefore be regarded as a political act. So the questions 'Who are you to say this?' and 'Are you right to say this?' become entangled within the cut and thrust of political contestation. To dismiss consciousness of conversational positioning as if it were mere parochial jostling for competitive status is to miss a fundamental aspect of political sensibility. As we shall see in the two final chapters, denials of and struggles for recognition cut to the root of democracy as a felt condition as opposed to an abstract constitutional label. The ways in which people feel demeaned, constrained and insulted, or affirmed, engaged and buoyed by being positioned within a communicative order are fundamental to the quality of feeling generated by political talk.

As people recounted their Brexit conflicts it became clear that vulnerability to the moral injury of being diminished through derisive addressivity pervaded these stories in ways that gave fresh meaning to calls to 'take back control'.

Kath – on being pushed too far

Kath described herself as a 'down to earth' person who just wanted 'to earn an honest living'. She still lived in the same neighbourhood in the post-industrial north of England that she grew up in. As a child she was very close to her grandparents – 'I did everything with my grandma and my grandfather' – spending much of her time in their house. 'I picked things up about what kind of people they were', she explained, 'and how they'd worked all their lives and how they'd paid their money, and, you know, my grandmother didn't even trust banks . . . there were no money in the bank, it were all stashed around the house.' Kath felt that the political and business leaders who run Britain are insensitive to the struggles and ethos of working-class people like her and her grandparents:

> They've never really lived in that kind of environment where you've had to really earn your money. They're almost from a different setting completely, a different upbringing. To understand the harshness of things you need to be real and down there gritty with it.

'I honestly believe,' said Kath, 'that they've pushed a lot of people in this country too far.' This feeling of being pushed too far framed most of what Kath had to say about her position in the world. It was as if her personal autonomy had been violated by unsympathetic outsiders who wanted to tell her how to live, how to speak and how to vote. This sense of not being in control shaped Kath's attitude to politics:

> I'm not *not* interested. I choose not to get too into politics . . . purely because there's not a lot we can change and there's a lot of frustration around it. And I feel I've got other things in life which worry me more, which are closer to home than worrying about things I can't change.

When offered a chance to vote in the referendum on Britain's membership of the European Union, Kath believed that she was faced with a rare moment of political efficacy. Rather than deciding which one of several unreliable parties should be in power, she sensed that here was a more fundamental opportunity to determine who should be in control. She 'felt that it was time for us to have our freedom back slightly and make our own decisions as a country'. She claimed that she 'didn't listen to any of the political parties whatsoever', but 'listened to what a lot of people had to say' and found that many people she respected shared her sense that Brexit presented a chance to realize a degree of independence and dignity that had been stolen from them over decades of 'the same old politics'.

Having decided that for once her vote might just have a valuable outcome, Kath became irritated by the condescending tone of politicians. Their repeated dire warnings about the extreme danger of leaving the European Union seemed to be trying to scare her into accepting a point of view that would only benefit those already in power:

> Nobody really gave me the real benefits of staying in. They was just saying 'it's the right thing to do. It's the safest thing to do'. But tell me why then. And nobody really did because they were as confused as I were really.

As Kath spoke about Brexit, the affective force of her story was hard to miss. She was much less interested in the finer politico-economic details of Brexit than in a long-felt sense of being diminished and disrespected by a collective 'them' – an amorphous elite that appeared to take her acquiescence for granted. Kath had never met any members of this remote European elite, but she sensed that if she did meet them they would fail to relate to or value the history that made her who she was:

> I grew up with a grandfather and a grandmother that both went to war, you know. . . . Listening to their conversations, when someone's expressing their own feelings about how they got hurt, or how life was for them, it's quite difficult. And when they fought like that for their country, part of that passion carries on through your life doesn't it . . . You feel that . . . I don't know . . . maybe I just . . . you know, I relate to that situation . . . that they fought for this country to be as great as it is.

The language of feeling rarely resembles the hard logic of political argumentation. Memories of conversations overheard in which frustrations were rehearsed at length and loyal passions celebrated with pride do not instantly translate into policy positions. But they linger, playing on vulnerabilities and triggering emotional reflexes. When asked to recall an exchange that she had about the referendum, Kath responded without pausing, pointing out that the conflict she had in mind was not so much about what was said, but how it was said and by whom.

It was a short, public argument about Brexit with a younger work colleague which took place in the office that they shared with three other people.

> He were a young lad at work who's I think's twenty-four, twenty-five. I'd clearly seen that he's had a good upbringing by his parents. He's got himself a degree and all the rest of it – which, you know, that's not anybody can get degrees. But he seemed to be quite sheltered in the real world. And we had a conversation. I don't know how it opened up that we was . . . how were we gonna vote. And his outright conversation was 'We've got to vote "in". We've got to remain in.' And I sort of, cos I like to see what people have got to say, so I just played devil's advocate and said, 'Oh, why do you think that then?' 'Because it's the safest thing to do. We'd be absolutely crazy to go out.' And I just thought it was the way that he'd been brought up by his parents. It was almost like he'd said to me 'Outrage, it's ridiculous that we'd even do anything different' . . . I said, 'Why do you think we should remain in?' I genuinely believed the response was that he just didn't think we were strong enough. And it was all conservative. You could see it in him [mocking his accent]: 'It's ridiculous that we would do anything different.'

You could see that obviously he were a Tory. That shone straight through in his reaction.

In many respects, this might not seem to qualify as a political argument. At no point during it did either Kath or her colleague put forward any reasons for remaining in or leaving the European Union. Almost as soon as her colleague had finished speaking, Kath withdrew from the conversation: 'I didn't raise my voice, but I sort of cut the conversation because I didn't want to talk about it anymore . . . because I knew that I would have lost my temper with him.'

The real conflict here was about the playing out of entitlement. Kath believed that her younger colleague felt entitled to assert his opinion with the confidence that any contrary view must be 'absolutely crazy'. To Kath, the sheltered upbringing, privileged education and predictable political sympathies of this young man 'shone straight through', somehow commanding her to defer to his superior tone. This triggered a feeling in Kath that not only she but also the family and class from which she came were being disrespected. The immediate effect was visceral: 'I started to feel a little bit of fire in my belly just because of his blatant ignorance . . . that bothered me more than anything.'

It bothered her, but she felt unable to take it any further, adding as a seemingly throwaway comment, 'Oh, my father wouldn't have got into that discussion, absolutely not.' Not uncommonly, when talk becomes political there are ghosts in the room – echoes and shadows of formative influences that cry out for discursive recognition. Kath's summoning of her father, whose mute contempt for the arrogance of class entitlement might have concealed both contempt and awe, added force to the ethereal presence of her grandparents, slighted by a young man who had never met or heard of them, but appeared to somehow disparage what they stood for.

Kath believed that she was being positioned by the mode of address adopted by her work colleague and she retaliated by positioning him as someone incapable of understanding 'real people'. An immanent political struggle for recognition was inherent to that exchange which was as truculent in its silences as in its words.

Sian – on feeling shamed

'I babble quite a lot,' Sian tells me, 'and the words don't necessarily come out how I always mean them to sometimes.' Despite this negative self-appraisal,

Sian's voice was measured and her answers to my questions reflective. But the questioning upward inflection at the end of her sentences suggested a certain vulnerability to critical judgement – perhaps her own as much as other people's. Although she had been terribly upset by the referendum outcome, she had at an earlier stage considered voting for Brexit:

> I was actually thinking about voting Leave. I was kind of on the side that said 'Ooh this could be exciting, unknown territory'. . . . So then I started really kind of paying attention to the campaign so that I could make a proper decision. I'd had . . . before the campaigns really kicked off . . . I'd had conversations with people and I was saying 'I'm kind of swaying this way' and then they'd kind of put something forward to me saying 'But my friend's not going to be allowed to stay in the UK possibly – this could happen.' That's when I started thinking 'OK just having a bit of adventure isn't necessarily a good thing'.

On 23 June, Sian was one of the 48 per cent of voters who opted to remain in the European Union. On 24 June, she wept about the result:

> I felt like . . . I felt upset that we were shutting people out, that we'd made this decision . . . I think that was what upset me quite a lot. I didn't want the rest of Europe or anyone else in the world to feel we were putting our walls up basically. Yeah, that quite upset me. I felt like I had to walk around with a sign saying 'I was one of the Remainers'.

It was shame that Sian was describing that a majority of her fellow citizens appeared to be rejecting people from other countries, that she had been incapable of preventing such an outcome, perhaps even that she had quite recently subscribed to the view that was now so noisily triumphant. At a more personal level, Sian's story was rooted in the patterns of her own life story.

She had been brought up for eight years by her mother and father who then split up. Nobody had ever talked to her about the split; as she put it, 'It was just a case of "this is happening" and it happened.' Ten years later her mother entered a relationship with a man she now calls her stepdad. He was a man of strong and oft-stated opinions, few of which Sian much liked. But she was happy that her mother had a partner and learned to keep her reservations about his views to herself. Sunday lunch was an important moment of coming together for the family and her mother asked Sian and her older sister not to get into disagreements with their stepfather on such occasions. They complied.

At the end of May, a few weeks before the referendum, it was Sian's birthday and she decided to invite a group of her friends to join her for a night of celebration in a local pub. She also invited her mother and stepdad – a rare opportunity to bring family and friends together for a night out:

> We were sat outside on benches. And actually half the table were Leavers and the other half were Remainers and it was literally split like. . . . There was my stepdad and my mum, and then it was just friends, and my sister was there as well. So yeah, my stepdad, who is quite opinionated a lot of the time, somehow got onto the Brexit argument. . . . It just got quite nasty to be quite honest. There was a lot of talk about immigrants and that was his main concern. It got to the point where it got so heated a lot of the Remain people just had to walk away. . . . I wasn't actually there when the conversation started, I'd come back from the toilet and they were all, I mean these people had never met before either, so it was first time they'd all met . . . this was the first time they'd met my mum, first time they'd met my stepdad. A few of my friends were so angered that they did walk away and were saying 'I can't speak to these people anymore'. . . . It was upsetting that a few of my friends were thinking, 'Your family are very like, narrow minded' I guess, so that was quite upsetting.

I asked her whether she had been surprised by this turn of events. 'I don't think it was appropriate, but I don't think I was surprised,' she said. Her stepdad's comments had been 'straight up racism' and this, as well as his insensitivity to her friends, was all too predictable. But would *he* have described what he said as racist or insensitive, I asked:

> I think he really believed that people were agreeing with him and I think he'd go down that route because people didn't stand up to him. Only one person stood up to him. So I think he honestly believed that what he was saying people were agreeing with, like I said. He didn't notice people walking away from the table. He didn't notice the kind of the feeling, the energy dropping all of a sudden. . . . He can't read the situation. No, he didn't notice at all. He didn't notice he was angering people. . . . I honestly, I think he believed so much in what he was saying he didn't notice what was going on around.

Her mother's role in the event was one of silent collusion – 'She'll spout kind of quotes that she's heard somewhere; she'll regurgitate them without even knowing, but in a public forum like that she was quite kind of quiet on the subject to be honest.' The only person to stand up to her stepdad was Sian's boyfriend:

> I think everyone else was . . . it was more him talking . . . and everyone else feeling very uncomfortable. No one necessarily called him up on it, apart from my boyfriend, and that's when people . . . . It was probably maybe twenty

minutes, half an hour that it went on for, and people started leaving the table, slowly moving away.

At the core of Sian's story was a profound feeling of shame about a situation that she was unable to control. Just as she was to feel ashamed by her compatriots' display of inhospitality in the referendum vote, her account of her birthday night-out evoked feelings of wounded humiliation. In both situations, Sian was confronted by a deep sense of personal inefficacy. How, I wondered, could she have taken back control and stopped her stepdad from engendering such bad feeling? Her response veered between the apologetic and the counterfactual:

> I wasn't fully engaged in the argument because I was trying to entertain my friends and have a nice time. So I was just kind of hooking in and out and listening to certain snippets and most of it was kind of people coming up to me afterwards and saying 'This was said' and I said 'yeah'. I kind of heard it, but I just didn't feel part of it, so yeah, I wish I'd have said something, but I think . . . I just would have told him how he was wrong. I think that I was a bit kind of down by that point . . . I was just like, I'd given up at that point. Because I'd had so many arguments with my mum previously, and I just was tired I think. I was like 'This is not the time, I don't really want to get involved. I'll stay out of it'.

Sian's story was not only about political talk but also about political silence and withdrawal. The droning chauvinism of her stepdad constituted a conspicuous political provocation, but no less political were the muted retreat from his table of her closest friends, the tight-lipped complicity of her mother and, at least to some extent, Sian's own exhausted resignation in the face of predictable prejudice. Unless we can account for these voiceless disengagements, we are in danger of reducing political talk to the distorting signals of confident utterance and missing the relational dynamics through which they inevitably travel.

One of those relational dynamics was closely linked to a deep experience of being positioned: as a child of parents who felt it necessary to give her only the most cursory information about their break-up; of being thrown into a relationship with a man she found offensive and then ordered not to contradict him at family gatherings; as a young woman who had come to believe that she was often incapable of expressing what she really thinks; and as a centre of a network of friends and family that became literally uncontrollable. Taking on any of those subject positions called for a degree of political tenacity that Sian believed was beyond her.

Rita – on the fear of being judged

Rita, a forty-year-old clerical officer working for a northern English city council, was emphatic in her insistence that she was being stifled: 'I think people are too frightened to say owt or do owt, that's what it is.' Moving from the general to the personal, she explained that 'I couldn't have my opinion at work' because she felt 'a bit racist, if you like, at work'.

Rita and her one close friend in the council office where she works share a first name:

> I call her black Rita and she calls me white Rita . . . and we did an online survey and it said you can't call people black. It's just silly. To me it's just silly.

Both Ritas voted for Brexit, but they felt that they had to keep quiet at work about their reasons for doing so. 'A lot of them in my office are young,' she explained and 'they all seem to think that we voted "out" because of the immigration'. The simmering silence in her office lasted for a while:

> I kept quiet until it sort of bothered me. We just spoke about it yesterday or the day before and I tried to get my opinion across best way I could, without them thinking I was thinking this way when I really wasn't. So I'm in my office, my colleague Eileen's at this side of me – similar age to me – then at side of her there's this young Asian guy and opposite him is Kevin. So we were all chatting and I were telling them about my daughter-in-law being at the hospital. I were fuming because they'd sent her home. And I were worrying . . . . And my friend said, 'This is something to do with Brexit' or whatever she said. And then Kevin were saying 'Well that won't make a difference . . . not everyone comes to this country to claim benefits.' So I said, 'No, but when they do come in they're allowed to go on NHS and claim anything they want like we do, but when there's nowt being put in the pot it's so stretched, something's gonna have to give and it's NHS, so something needs to be done.' So he's saying 'Well, you mean, it's the Tory party blah blah that needs to be changed' and I just said 'Well, people should be able to live where they want to live as long as they know they've got to earn a living. I do understand people want to go to a better place and not everybody can do that, but you can't just have so many people being put in one place.' And that were just my overall view. Then it went quiet and tense. It always does with stuff like that. Yeah, my colleague sat next to me and she went 'This is why I can't say owt because they think it's because I'm racist'.

Acutely aware that to speak is to make a public appearance, but that how one appears can never be entirely under one's own control, Rita felt herself to be silenced by the judgements of others. She presented herself as someone worn down by the interference of impalpable authorities, but at the same time courageous in her refusal to adhere to an official script. She particularly objected to compulsory courses at work promoting principles of equality and diversity, reflecting that 'we're like kids when we have to go on those courses':

> They keep introducing new stuff and things we've got to learn, this e-Learning and stuff like that . . . and how people can take offence to certain stuff. I could overhear someone speaking and find it offensive and then go register with management that I found it offensive. I don't know, sometimes I'm sure it's only tit and tat, or words don't mean much, which I know they do, but that's sort of . . . because I wouldn't say something nasty to hurt somebody . . . I always say when I come out, 'That was a waste of time that.'

And yet, as she stumbled between 'words don't mean much' and 'I know they do', she revealed an uncertainty in her thinking that confounded her apparent self-assurance. This uncertainty added nuance to Rita's seemingly unequivocal stance, unsettling her sanguine assertion that 'as long as you respect a person, whoever you're having a joke with, and it's not in a malicious way, no harm will come of it'. Rita's qualms about the illocutionary power of words drew her in to the very debate about the consequences of speech that she wanted to decry as intrusive and futile. While Kath and Sian felt themselves to have been unjustly positioned by others, Rita yearned for a world in which vulnerability to the interpretive judgement of others could be somehow eliminated. If her claim that 'words don't mean much' raised the possibility of escaping from expressive responsibility, her concession that 'I know they do' compelled her to think about what it might mean to 'say something nasty' or 'hurt somebody'.

Rita seemed to be caught within the normative compulsion of what James Scott (1990) refers to as a 'public transcript': a symbolic performance that is required of subordinates in order to demonstrate that they are beholden to a superior social actor. Unlike forms of tyrannical authority that required slaves and peasants to cow-tow to their masters, liberal authority demands performative adherence to norms of global cultural commensurability. For Rita, finding herself positioned as an object of moral disapproval raised fundamental political questions. Who is authorized to determine such disapproval? To whom are these arbiters accountable? Should comments be judged in terms of a speaker's intentions or the tangible consequences of their utterance? To which authority can one appeal if misjudged? These questions remained tacit, shaping the tone of Rita's resentment, while leaving her uncertain about the nature of the symbolic contest in which she was embroiled. As Scott (1990: 138) astutely observes:

> What we confront . . . in the public transcript is a strange kind of ideological debate about justice and dignity in which one party has a severe speech impediment induced by power relations. If we wish to hear this side of the dialogue we shall have to learn its dialect and codes.

Decoding the idiolects that people bring to ideological debate cannot be accomplished solely at the semantic level. As Raymond Williams (1977: 134) reminded us, political feelings are often experienced 'at the very edge of semantic availability', comprising more or less than words can say. Identifying the tonal and gestural energies that give contingent and historical meaning to utterances; the stammers and silences that punctuate the unsayable; the associative ordering of points that disclose underlying structures of belief and commitment are all part of the act of decoding – or translation. When Rita declared that 'people are too frightened to say owt or do owt', did she mean all people or only those worthy of being rhetorically cast as 'the people'? What would happen if the vernacular 'owt' (anything) were replaced by a specific verb? What are the actions that 'people' would like to perform, but are prevented from pursuing through fear? And what is the source of this fear? What would happen if 'frightened' were replaced by 'sensitive'? As George Steiner (1975: 172/3) puts it:

> When we speak to others we speak 'at the surface' of ourselves. We normally use a shorthand beneath which there lies a wealth of sub-conscious, deliberately concealed or declared associations so extensive and intricate that they probably equal the sum and uniqueness of our status as an individual person.

The work of translating political meaning is twofold: in live interaction between speakers there is ongoing evaluation and negotiation not only about the connotations of what is being said but also about the moral right and capacity of interactants to say it; and retrospectively, as disagreements are narrativized, reported and interpreted, such accounts are rarely innocent, but replete with rhetorical allusions to subject positioning. Rita's account of being silenced relies heavily upon a framing narrative in which veiled and asymmetrical power relations precede and prescribe political discourse, shaping and constraining scope for comprehensive moral agency.

Mia – on friendly fire

When Mia came to see me, she brought along her friend Zoe. They had recently completed their GCSE exams and were now preparing to study for their A-levels. Their confidence and openness were striking. It was Mia who answered my questions, with Zoe intervening occasionally to add detail and emphasis. Mia explained that 'a lot of the time I'm quite eloquent and I can articulate what I'm saying', but at other times 'I'll just be like . . . I'll know what I'm thinking, but I'll struggle to say it. So I'll just listen'. Sometimes, she thinks, 'just due to personalities, you can't go as far into a debate because it just becomes more of an argument'. When I asked her whether she considered herself to be someone with an interest in politics Mia said, 'I'd say I'm rather interested. I know some people that are very extreme and they're passionate and I'd say I'm very interested, but I wouldn't say politics is my overall passion.' For Mia, the political is an interpersonal phenomenon, most vividly experienced in relationships between friends and peer groups rather than through the spectatorial drama of state politics:

> I'd say that it comes down to personal interactions with people and how power is done in a specific group, . . . how people interact and how people try and manipulate one another, and I'd say you could call that politics.

I asked her about the kind of people who succeed in interpersonal politics:

> Basically, people who from day one, as soon as they get into a social situation, people that naturally just came to the fore. Like, those people naturally have a certain, I'll call it magnetism, let's say, that makes people follow them and makes people do what they ask . . . I think it's a personal trait that you either have or you don't have. But then I'd say there's another group of people that can kind of . . . they're not naturally magnetic, but they can influence people by . . . in a way that they've learned to do.

She recalled the first political news story that had ever grabbed her attention: the election of Obama as US president. She remembered thinking at the time 'There's an actual person of colour that's actually leading the country' and feeling immensely proud and hopeful about what this might mean for her as a black British girl. As she grew older (she is now seventeen) Mia began to feel increasingly confident about her own political views:

> When I was younger I definitely agreed with everything my parents said. As I'm getting older, I agree less so. So it's kind of like, usually my parents are of the

same political mind, and a lot of the time, a lot of the time . . . but I think going on to other issues, I think I'm differing from them a bit more.

I wanted to know whether Mia could recall any discussion she was involved in during the lead-up to the Brexit referendum. Both she and Zoe exchanged knowing smiles. The story they had to tell me was fresh, evoking the kind of raw feelings that made its telling urgent and animated. It was a tale of friendly disagreement alongside strategic conflict.

What happens when friends disagree about basic values? This was the dilemma that Mia and Zoe faced when their friend, Danny, gave voice to a view that threatened their rapport. Mia explained:

> There's a guy in my year, Danny, who, um, bizarre as it may be, supports UKIP . . .
> We're good friends with him. So it wasn't . . . he's not a racist. He just believes that
> UKIP's not racist . . . but they are.

It was a complex narrative opening, bursting with contradictions. Danny was a friend, but he was an opponent. He was not a racist, but he supported the United Kingdom Independence Party (UKIP). He did not consider UKIP to be racist, but it was. As Mia began to explain what happened it became clear that this was less like a bounded event than a drama in several acts:

> There was about four different rounds, four different debates. I had one with
> him, she [pointing to Zoe] had one with him and she [Zoe] had another one
> with him and I had another one with him . . . It was kind of sprawled out in
> different settings, like . . . The thing about this debate was that a lot of . . . some
> of . . . the girls – like, obviously the nasty ones – don't like Danny, so they kind
> of used it as an excuse to rip into him. And like, I think they started a chat
> group, like 'Destroy Danny's Life' and they made a picture of him as Hitler and
> all sorts like . . .

The introduction into the drama of the 'nasty' girls pointed to complex motivational tension. Personal dislike for Danny led 'the nasty girls' to side with Mia and Zoe, who *did* like Danny, but felt compelled to challenge his 'bizarre' support for UKIP. The opening round of the disagreement involved the identification of clear binaries:

> It was kind of like we were walking home and there were UKIP posters and I
> said they should be taken down surely, and obviously he's like 'no, actually, a lot
> of people are ignorant, here's what I've got to say about UKIP' and obviously I
> listened, and obviously I disagreed, and then it went on . . .

A few days later the debate moved to a new level:

> It was before an exam, like a couple of hours before, and we were just doing like our last-minute revision, and . . . . This argument lasted a lot. We had about half an hour to get ready for the exam. By the time we'd finished, it was like one and a half hours, just constantly . . . . So there was other people in school who started chatting online about Danny's recent revelations. Apparently, some guys had knocked down these UKIP signs and he'd gone behind them putting them all back in place. And we were discussing this. We were like 'Hoohoo, no' . . . . So when he came to school I was like, 'Danny, here, now' and we were having this discussion . . . . I think he was kind of anticipating it, cos I'd set to him before like, 'We have to have this debate', so it was kind of like already agreed. And we basically had this discussion. He was like, 'It's not a racist party. There's racists in all the parties.' And I was like 'Yeah, but the amount that comes from UKIP is ridiculous and far outweighs any other party, so would you really feel safe and happy with a government knowing that this amount of the members are individually racist? Like how are you gonna be happy with that . . . that's gonna skew the whole system, rah rah rah' . . . . And basically I just like won. But loads of other people got involved with this as well. It wasn't just us two, other people were there, like throwing their two penny in.

Danny's strategic response was to attempt to divide his opponents. He told Mia that 'at least when I'm talking to you you know what you're saying', but then turned on the girls who were supporting Mia and said 'you're just ignorant, you're just uninformed'. Mia found herself in agreement with Danny on this point:

> It's true. They just copy loads of memes from Twitter and are just like 'And UKIP does this and they do that and they do that and you're a racist and homophobic person and we don't like you any more'. So I think, although argument-wise I was aligned with the girls, I think me and Danny . . . like I say, we are good friends . . . he knew that I wasn't aligned with those guys. So even though, like, content-wise, like, we're both on the same side, he knew that we weren't on the same . . . so, it's kind of like I was far closer to the girls and far closer to Danny than either of them two were to each other, as opposed to being distanced from both.

Zoe added to Mia's assessment: 'He said afterwards that he enjoyed the debates with me and you because they were debates and not a gang attack on him.' This led Mia to explain that 'I think you can disagree with what someone believes without hating them as a person.' 'He's a foolish boy,' sighed Zoe. 'He's oblivious,' added Mia, smirking. 'He has views that we disagree with. We did tell him. But we're still friends,' explained Zoe.

As I listened to Mia's story, I was struck by its diffuse spread across time and space: online and offline; planned and accidental; instantaneous and drawn out. Political talk is often regarded as an episodic phenomenon, bounded in time and analysable as discrete interaction. But listening to Kath, Sian, Rita and Mia's accounts of Brexit talk, moments of political conflict seemed more like surges of affective energy that brought into focus enduring patterns of relational disquiet. The ostensible grounds of immediate discord had become entangled with layered patterns of accumulated distrust, often leaving disputants barely aware of their motives for entering the fray. Political talk commonly entails angry exchanges with echoes of past wrongs, immanent within the drama of the present moment, but never quite articulated. Elizabeth Grosz (2004: 250) reminds us that

> Although the present does not contain the past, they coexist. They function simultaneously. This coexistence of present and past, the way the past grows and augments itself with every present, the virtual potential the past brings to each present, provides it with a capacity to enrich the present through resonances that are not themselves present.

Political talk can seem to be inspired by a single feeling, but within that feeling are many currents that are not always consonant with one another. An important function of political talk is to disambiguate these currents – to attune the austere premises of *logos* to the nuanced resonances of *pathos*. On the face of it, Mia's conflict with Danny was about the veracity of rival interpretations of UKIP. But more than that was going on. Mia's pleasure at the end of the interaction was not only because she believed that she had exposed the error of Danny's claims but also because it was an expression of satisfaction at being recognized by Danny as a person worthy of respect. Mia regarded the girls who supported her argument as ill-informed and disingenuous and wanted to distance herself from their discursive style.

The politics of Mia's story emanated from her efforts to frame its meaning by artfully positioning its protagonists. Rather than seeking to describe an authentic experience, Mia sought to organize the disparate affective flows within a sequence of incommensurate exchanges into a coherent moral story. In seeking to ascribe subject positions to her cast of characters, Mia was constructing a rhetorical narrative, fashioning its 'semblance of meaning and order for experience' (Gubrium and Holsten, 1998: 166).

The social life of deep stories

In the accounts considered above we never get the whole story – there is no such thing as a 'whole' or definitive narrative – but we find ourselves in the presence of deep stories that transcend the minutiae of claim and counter-claim and cut to the lurking feelings that flavour disagreement. Infused with private meanings and acute sensations, the deep story

> is a feel-as-if story – it's the story feelings tell, in the language of symbols. It removes judgment. It removes fact. It tells us how things feel. (Hochschild, 2016: 135)

Deep stories are translatory devices through which the relational effects of power are incorporated into personal dramas of everyday life. They attach the micro-experience of subjectivity to the macro-order of political structure. The work of socially positioning classes, communities and individuals is performative, its effects enacted and registered at the level of locally situated experience. Unless it can be realized within contingent contexts, political power remains a mere aspiration, for power is not a substance that can be held, weighed, allocated or divided up, but a relational effect of social interaction. (See Allen, 2011, for a persuasive development of this argument.)

Every one of the accounts of political disagreement about Brexit that interviewees related to me incorporated deep stories about their personal positions in the world. The tellers of these stories differed in their socio-economic classifications as well as their ideological perspectives on Brexit. Some used more typically political language, while others refused to engage with it. But all seemed eager to reflect, often with considerable passion and insight, upon what it feels like to be caught within, or struggling to resist, a structure of rights associated with an ascribed social position.

In Kath's account of feeling patronized by a work colleague, the narrative timbre was there long before either of them entered the immediate scene of the conflict. Her belief that people like him were 'from a different setting completely, a different upbringing' and could never 'understand the harshness of things' in her world had led her to position him in terms of emotional capacity, just as she sensed that he was seeking to position her in terms of intellectual capacity. Both addressed moral targets that exceeded what was ever actually said, but which had long lurked suggestively in the mood history of class inequality. The deep story here was about the supposedly reckless disrespect of the over-entitled.

Sian's deep story spoke of politics as a pretext for pushing people around. It reflected profound feelings of being excluded or responsible for the social exclusion of others. Her response to the Brexit referendum result was to feel 'upset that we were shutting people out'. She wanted to carry a sign around saying that she was not part of this iniquitous decision. She knew what it felt like to be excluded, having been brought up in a family where major decisions were taken without her ever being consulted. Her account of a disastrous birthday gathering at which her insensitive stepfather sounded off to the point that 'a lot of the Remain people just had to walk away' was a shaming culmination of a pattern of feeling at the mercy of the loudest mouths – the most pushy but unwarranted influences. This was not only about being pushed around but also about the shame of not feeling able to resist.

Rita told a deep story in which she cast herself as a gagged and censored victim of liberal intolerance. 'I can't say owt' and 'people are too frightened to say owt or do owt' were the running motifs. As she made herself heard she told the story of not being able to make herself heard. It was a deep story of resistance against a public transcript that is rigged against common-sense expression. But within this blunt certainty lay a discreet hesitancy: 'words don't mean much, *which I know they do*'. Perhaps this was the deeper narrative beneath the bluster of victimhood: a story about the unintended consequences of seemingly plain talk.

In Mia's case, the surface story of fierce, but playful conflict was embedded within a deeper story about intelligence and the accordance of respect. While the surface narrative referred to a simple clash of opinions, fought out through logical argumentation, Mia's deeper concern was about the right to be taken seriously. Paradoxically, she accorded this right to her political opponent and denied it to her chorus of supporters. Politics for Mia was more than a matter of strategic or opportunist alliances. The deep story here is about conferring and receiving respect.

The overarching narrative to which my interviewees turned again and again as they recalled their discussions in the lead-up to the Brexit vote was about control: maintaining control; losing control; being controlled; not trusting those perceived to be in control; seeking to restore some kind of self-control. The polysemously interpreted Brexit campaign slogan, 'Take Back Control', hit a nerve that sparked complex affective reverberations, playing out quite differently in the context of distinctive deep stories.

While surface narratives tend to adhere to a relatively narrow range of syntactical conventions referring to temporal structure and thematic connexity

(Labov, 1972; Frank, 2010), deep stories take a more transcendent form, making them available for interpretation in more symbolic and visceral terms. Arlie Hochschild (2016: 297; f.135) suggests that 'the deep story crystallizes pre-existing feeling' by generating 'a metaphor in motion'. This metaphor might, for example, depict a political order in which 'ordinary people' are in a permanent state of fear in the face of the harsh strictures of 'political correctness'; or embroiled in an unwinnable battle by the affable and unassuming against the overbearing stridency and coarseness of the socially insensitive; or engaged in a comedic playground farce in which only certain players understand their lines. Such 'metaphors in motion' point, however subtly, towards moralizing judgement, hinting at the propriety of felt reactions. Indeed, Hochschild (2017: 190) has suggested in a recent interview that deep stories allow people caught up in situations 'to detach him or herself from the idea that they feel the "wrong" thing'. In this sense, they provide a framework for affective reflexivity. They make it possible to refer to the contextual mood that surrounds political disagreement, not with a view to exorcizing it as distracting pathos, but in order to confront it as a key element of the agonistic condition for, beyond the terms of logical contention, discord is invariably marked by affective inflection. Every political argument has its own volume, pitch and pace through which its motives are registered at the level of raw feeling. Deep stories allow such intense feelings to be acknowledged and justified. Argumentative moods are replete with unspoken thoughts, bodily estrangements and barely masked hostile gazes. Adversaries 'pick up' such moods before they comprehend arguments, sensing emotive drifts that can never be adequately reduced to common logic. Within the precognitive moments in which emanant conflicts smoulder, traces of historical grievance are tacitly registered and sometimes challenged.

As well as calling attention to the constellation of feelings that shape political talk, deep stories can also be used as a means of evading and discounting aspects of experience that get in the way of their framing ambitions. As Hochschild (2016: 297; f.135) puts it, 'every deep story implies an area of amnesia, non-story, non-self'. It was striking to observe how often people recalling their political disagreements were eager to make it clear that 'I'm not that kind of person' or 'I didn't know what they were talking about – they seemed to be living in a different universe' (both are verbatim quotes). It was as if any attempt to position people, either personally or socially, in divergence from their self-conception could be interpreted as a political violation and disowned. The disparate deep stories that constituted 'the Brexit debate' in everyday talk not only consisted of attempts to promote framing metaphors but also consisted of stubborn refusals to acknowledge data, sensations or conjectures that might endanger the plausibility of a particular narrative. Forgetting – or pragmatic amnesia – is a vital element of political consistency.

Deep stories lead a double life. They are a way of framing disagreement in real time as political talk happens and they are a means of recording and making sense of feelings surrounding conflict after it has taken place. Deep stories address the psychological tension between what a person felt at the time of a disagreement and the counterfactual version in which their currently processed feelings and framings take precedence over the past tense. Arguably, it is within this gap between live feeling and subsequent interpretation that political agency is put to some of its most complex work, editing out moral nuances and communicative glitches in order for the original disagreement to be rendered fit for vindicatory narration. In this sense, deep stories open up a space for political repair work in which there is an opportunity to ascribe weight and value to the elements of a conflictive event. Ricoeur's (2004: 21) observation that 'testimony constitutes the fundamental transitional structure between memory and history' reminds us that political effects are rarely unambiguous, but typically enmeshed in the rhetorical artefacts of narrative.

5

Unintelligible subjects

The promise of democracy is haunted by the vulnerable figure of the speaking subject whose acute primary need is to be heard, acknowledged and respected amid the amplified voices of the privileged and confident. In the absence of such recognition, ideological commitments, material aspirations and passionate yearnings amount to very little, for the voice that enunciates them is rendered indistinct and inaudible. As lurking, ethereal figures, too often consigned to an indistinct chorus of background noise – opinion polls, vox pops, protest chants, political mood music – citizens seem doomed to evanescence. The aim of this chapter is to examine the ways by which substantial sections of the public in most Western democracies have come to feel scarcely registered in the circulating murmur that constitutes political discourse.

Conscious of the casual misrecognition through which their voices are discounted, many of the interviewees reported in the preceding chapters had come to think of political talk as a bruising experience. As they recalled past political disagreements, they re-experienced the disagreeableness of reciprocity unrealized. Made to feel like impostors in an alien domain, some of them had come to believe that 'no one listens to you, you never have the floor, or else, when you have the courage to seize it, your speech is quickly erased by the more garrulous and fully relaxed talk of the community' (Kristeva, 1991: 20). To be speechless, inaudible or unintelligible is to become politically absent or muted in a world where enunciation is the political currency. As Hannah Arendt (1959: 158–9) put it,

> Speechless action would no longer be action because there would no longer be an actor, and an actor, the doer of deeds, is possible only if he is at the same time the speaker of words . . . though his deed can be perceived in its brute appearance without verbal accompaniment, it becomes relevant only through the spoken word in which he identifies himself as an actor, announcing what he does, has done, and intends to do.

Though certainly a material force, political voice is not a natural phenomenon, but a social practice that is learned, worked on and played with long before sounds are ever emitted or words formed. When people 'talk politics' they perform themselves in particular ways, sometimes drawing upon received scripts, recalled tropes and unconsciously imbibed postures and at other times improvising creatively with a view to combining deep feeling and outward expression. Political voice emerges when people's subjective sensations of power are made to reverberate across various planes of signification, from the phonic to the semantic. It comprises speeches, rants, asides, corrections, jokes, grumbles, grunts and gestures. It can appear every day or once every few years. As with any social practice, political voice extends across a spectrum from unconscious routine to self-conscious performance; from imperceptible tightening and loosening of bodily muscles to complex reflective states; from deep intentionality to transient time-filling; and from getting it right to screwing it up.

In its most material sense, voice entails complex, but unconscious, physiological and neurological coordination:

> Under normal circumstances, voice is produced when airflow from the lungs is converted to acoustic energy by vibration of the vocal folds, which are located within the larynx. These patterns of vibration are then shaped (or filtered) acoustically when the sound passes through the vocal tract above the larynx. The respiratory system serves as a source of power for phonation, by setting air in motion through the vocal tract. The larynx acts as an oscillator to convert this aerodynamic power to acoustic energy, and thus is often referred to as the acoustic voice source. Finally, the vocal tract above the larynx – the pharynx, mouth and nasal cavities – filters the sound. Changes in the way the vocal folds vibrate, or changes in the configuration of the vocal tract above the larynx via movements of the tongue, jaw, soft palate and lips, will change the sound produced. (Kreiman and Sidtis, 2011: 25)

In short, 'the voice' is not a discrete organ, like the ear or the eye, but a bodily process, dependent for its success upon the complex choreography of several organs. The sonic dance that is voice is more than a mere bodily function. It is an indelible cultural marker of identity in its many manifestations within a single body.

To think of *a* voice as a political medium is to be drawn towards imaginaries of *the* voice. The normative frames through which voices are found, performed, trained, heard and evaluated reflect imaginaries of ideal voice. Imaginaries are pre-theoretical forms of implicit knowledge – assumptions and expectations that comprise an 'unstructured and inarticulate understanding' of a phenomenon or situation (Taylor, 2002: 107). These have tended to conform to three dominant frames. First, there is the metaphysical figure of voice as discarnate conduit between endogenous identity and embodied disclosure to the world. Occupying a liminal space between the hidden domain of sensate, cerebral interiority and the performative declaration of identity, the voice is imagined as a naked and inescapable display of self – a window to the deep personal core. As Mladen Dolar (2006: 37) puts it, 'The voice offered the illusion that one could get immediate access to an unalloyed presence, an origin not tarnished by externality.' For Adriana Cavarero (2005: 173), voice is the guarantor of a unique identity:

> The sphere of the vocal implies the ontological plane and anchors it to the existence of singular beings who invoke one another contextually. From the maternal scene onward, the voice manifests the unique being of each human being, and his or her spontaneous self-communication according to the rhythms of a sonorous relation. In this sense, the ontological horizon that is disclosed by the voice or what we want to call a vocal ontology of uniqueness stands in contrast to the various ontologies of fictitious entities that the philosophical tradition, over the course of its historical development, designates with names like man, subject, individual.

In this sense, voice becomes the key testing ground for claims to authenticity. Its congruity with intentions and drives underwrites credibility, while any evidence of incongruence between displayed voice, private thought and bodily action can serve to impugn a speaker's sincerity. Most starkly theorized in the Freudian tradition, where 'the talking cure' voice is regarded as the most reliable available translator of subterranean unconscious thought and feeling, the imaginary of voice as the register of integrity has become culturally ubiquitous. The ears, nose or shoulders cannot deceive or betray, but the voice can.

While the imaginary of vocal candour invites us to listen out for artifice, a second conception of the voice as signifier of cultural value serves to justify the subordination of certain groups and individuals. Imagined as an indicator of social worth, the voice is regarded as a conspicuous betrayer of normative deficiencies. The ideological image of 'the proper voice', subscribing to an approved 'standard', condemns vocal inadequacy and difference, classifying them as proofs of cultural inferiority. In allowing some speakers to demand respect because they express themselves in a superior fashion and others to be disparaged because their voices fail the test of propriety, this imaginary performs the politically important symbolic work of justifying social inequality.

The imaginary of 'proper speech' originates in Aristotle's normative distinction between mere animals, which are only capable of producing crude sounds signalling pleasure or pain, and humans, who possess a sophisticated capacity for the expression of reasoned judgement. To classify a voice as 'reasonable' elevates its user to the status of human. The ultimate condemnation of a voice deemed to be unworthy is to suggest that it emanates from 'beings belonging to inferior forms of evolution' (Le Bon, 1895: 16). This was a common strategy among eighteenth and nineteenth-century anti-democrats who sought not merely to silence the majority of people, but also to categorize them as roaring and howling unintelligible beasts (Neocleous, 2004; Howard, 2008) – most memorably, as a 'swinish multitude' (Burke, 1793).

Closely related to this ontological chasm between humans and animals is an intra-species distinction between those who speak 'properly' by conforming to a prescribed standard and those whose voices are considered to be in permanent need of correction (Crowley, 2003; Milroy and Milroy, 2012; Cameron, 2012). Bourdieu (1991: 60) observes that the imaginary of vocal legitimacy is 'sustained by a permanent effort of correction, a task which falls both to institutions specially designed for this purpose and to individual speakers'. Speakers who are deemed to be culturally inferior find themselves caught up in a relentless drill of speech repair – a neurotic performance of linguistic keeping up. Richard Bauman and Charles Briggs (2003: 32) suggest that it was Locke's (1690) *Essay Concerning Human Understanding* that sanctioned such vocal regulation:

> Locke created a new regime that required each individual to closely monitor his or her own linguistic repertoire and each and every utterance. Individuals who had submitted themselves to his linguistic regimen earned the right to regiment the speech of others, to model linguistic precision and constancy and to point out the errors of their fellows.

In its intention to manage the flow of public communication, Locke's regimen amounted to more than a linguistic strategy; it served the political purpose of moderating discourse by shaming disruptive speech. As we have seen in previous chapters, the form and content of disagreement are not easily separable and it is often at the level of communicative form that offence is given and injury sustained. Control vocal form and content is invariably vitiated.

Combined together, voices are imagined as the collective social refrain of an entire population, community, class or group. 'Public voice', as the agency of everyone in general and no one in particular, serves as a foundational democratic metaphor. In her historiographical account of the image of 'the People' in the

French Revolution, Linda Orr (1990: 15–16) grapples with the opacity of this potent metaphor:

> the people implies everyone and no one particular group. . . . So *le peuple* is a metaphor, a metaphor for reference, for the social referent itself. Though a metaphor, it still exists. It circulates in and out of social class, professional and political groups, in and out of official and unofficial power, both the innermost self and the common whole. . . . But everything in which it circulates, contradictory and warring, gives it back the effect of a most physical shape, something thick and consistent, with adamantine desire and a will.

To refer to the voice of the people is to invoke the image of a socio-political 'body' capable of aggregative self-expression. But, as in all aggregations, judgements have to be made about which voices are to be acknowledged, which are to be excluded and the relative weighting of parts (Coleman, 2013). Given that '[i]ndirect exclusions function tacitly through discursive norms and practices that prescribe particular ways of interacting in public forums' (Asen, 2002: 345), the realization of democratic justice is crucially dependent on which voices are imagined to be acknowledgeable (Fraser, 1995, 2000; Honneth, 1996; Taylor, 1997; Markell, 2009; Benjamin, 2017). Historically, cultural demands for recognition and respect have provided an affective framework for more materially tangible struggles for social justice.

It is according to a third imaginary, of voice as agency, that acts of speaking assume their greatest potency, but are also at the greatest risk of being nullified. Voice is thought of in this context as a tool for making things happen. Possessing voice, giving voice, raising voice, demanding a voice, making a voice heard – these are conceived as elemental gestures of democratic action. To be denied a voice is to be rendered politically impotent, but to have one is to possess the potential to make oneself and other social forces and relations visible within a perceptual order. As Nick Couldry (2010: 8) states, the notion of the voice as a force for agency assumes that

> The exchangeable narratives that constitute our voices are not random babblings that emerge unaccountably from our mouths, hands and gestures . . . the act of voice involves taking responsibility for the stories one tells. . . . Such a view of voice does not commit us, however, to a naïve view of agency, only to the view that we cannot understand voice except by linking it . . . to what 'individuals', 'persons' or social movements might want or be able *to do* in the world.

Agentive voices enable their users to intervene in the indeterminacy of historical drama – to improvise and thereby make a difference. This imaginary of voice as a robust force for efficacy provides a tangible linking mechanism between individual bodies and vast social orders. It is at the conjuncture between the articulate body and the sensed environment that voices perform their most political interventions. The effects of such interventions have been widely studied, with appropriate attention paid to the sociological variables that limit them. Rather less commonly is the voice as political actor explored phenomenologically. What does vocal agency feel like? What is its abiding tone? In what ways are its absence registered? These are questions that we have edged towards in the preceding chapters, as we have excavated memories of political talk as a felt experience. It is now time to theorize about these phenomenological accounts. What is going on when talk turns to politics? How does it feel to be caught between the intimacy of self-expression and the worldliness of political action? If political speech is supposed to unleash the exhilaration of agency, why is it so often surrounded by the oppressive strain of disappointment?

This chapter proceeds in three stages, beginning with the disguises and divulgences of vocal form, moving on to the genealogical traces that have shaped the significance and efficacy of political voices and concluding by considering some contemporary problematics and potentialities of vocal agency.

The grain of the political voice

Let us begin with the imaginary of voice as a primary signal of identity – an oral signature. More than a mere instrument for transmitting messages or a figurative term to describe the abstract will of the public, voice is a signifier of selfhood – a material rather than metaphorical connector of bodily feeling, vocal sound and cultural meaning. Mladen Dolar (2006: 22) suggests that 'We can almost unfailingly identify a person by the voice, the particular individual timbre, resonance, pitch, cadence, melody, the peculiar way of pronouncing certain sounds'. There is, indeed, a sense in which we cannot move away from our voices, for, as Brandon LaBelle (2014: 5) points out, 'The voice does not move away from my body, but rather it carries it forward – the voice stretches me; it drags me along, as a body bound to its politics and poetics, its accents and dialectics, its grammars, as well as its handicaps'. Before we hear the words of a political speaker we have already listened out for its sound: the tonal signals of not only the spoken but also of the unsaid. Indeed, meaning is sometimes the very last element to be evaluated when we encounter the sound of political talk.

Most commonly, attention is focused upon the production of speech: the semantic, syntactical ordering of words that point towards meaning. Most accounts of voice focus upon this phonological end-product, dismissing pre-linguistic emissions of vocality as mere noise. In the context of political voice it is common to assume that structured speech is all that matters because it is the source of rational meaning. But that is to overlook the vocal sounds that produce meanings 'beyond or in addition to the syntactical and semantic meaning of a spoken text' (Mills, 2009: 391). Roland Barthes (1975: 66–7) urged his readers to think of vocality as comprising 'the pulsional incidents, the language lined with flesh, a text where we can hear the grain of the throat, the patina of consonants, the voluptuousness of vowels, a whole carnal stereophony: the articulation of the body, of the tongue, not that of meaning, of language'. By attending to vocal expression that exceeds the linguistic order and resists semantic classification, one can begin to recognize the underlying timbre, pitch and cadence that reach the ear before words are even formed; to detect the communicative strategies by which intentions are masked and hesitations disciplined into apparent fluency; to sense the conscious and unconscious ways by which the body signals the idiosyncrasies of the self; and to reflect upon why it is that some words seem to be coming out of the wrong mouths, borrowed from culture and rendered implausible through discordant reiteration.

How can the sound of a voice before words are even spoken raise doubts as to the integrity of a speaker? On what grounds does vocal resonance give rise to political critique? How is it that some voices undermine the professed intentions of speech? Such questions are best answered with reference to specific instances.

On 14 March 2010 the then British prime minister's wife, Samantha Cameron, appeared on a television programme about her husband. It was hardly a controversial performance, but, according to one critic, it was in every sense a *performance*. Samantha Cameron, claimed *Daily Mail* journalist Peter Hitchens (27.3.10), was not 'being herself' – and the evidence for that was the artificiality of her voice. Under the headline, 'Leave it aht, Samanfa. . . Mrs Cameron's Estuary English typifies a society that mistrusts aspiration and mocks excellence', Hitchens accused the prime minister's wife of adopting a vocal sound that was not 'her own':

> I . . . think that it is enormously interesting and significant that the Tory leader's wife, daughter of a land-owning baronet, brought up on broad acres, educated at a genteel private girls' academy and then at one of the great Public Schools, and now running a business that caters to London's dwindling but unflinching cut-glass classes, should speak Estuary English.

By appearing to adopt vocal characteristics that disguise her class privilege, the prime minister's wife stood accused of cultural betrayal. The 'enormous' interest and significance of this act of vocal distortion, according to Hitchens, lay in what it said about contemporary British culture, where 'aspiration' and 'excellence' are indicated by the sound of a person's voice. Although Hitchens seemed to be deriding Mrs Cameron with his condescending 'Leave it aht, Samanfa' (a phrase that caricatures the non-aspirational mediocrity of the speaker's tone), his real target was 'a society' that forces the 'cut-glass classes' to speak as if they were just like everyone else. For Hitchens, the advantaged genealogy of the speaker ought to be reflected in her voice, thereby asserting an implicit entitlement to be heard with special respect. By disavowing such entitlement and adopting the tone of Estuary Everywoman, Cameron stands accused of succumbing to the expressive egalitarianism of the democratic agora.

Two years later Hitchens found himself embroiled in another conflict about the meaning of vocal tone. On 29 July 2012 he published an article comparing the Opening Ceremony of the London Olympic Games to past May Day displays in Soviet Russia. An excerpt from this article was selected for quotation on the long-running BBC radio review, *What the Papers Say*. The standard format of this programme is for an actor to read out selected passages from newspapers, usually aiming to capture the flavour of the piece in their vocal rendition. Hitchens submitted a formal complaint to the BBC and the media regulator Ofcom, stating that the quotation from his article had been read by an actor 'in an absurdly exaggerated and hostile caricature of his voice'. This, he argued, constituted a deliberate attempt to humiliate him. Airing his sense of hurt in the *Mail Online* blog (31 July 2012), Hitchens wrote:

> My voice has been described as a plummy baritone, and it certainly isn't Estuary English, but I don't think that I or any living Englishman, speaks as I was portrayed as speaking on that programme. It was the sort of voice used in 1960s satire programmes to denote the thoughts and opinions of a ludicrous tweedy old buffer. It might do for a very old-fashioned butler in a provincial Agatha Christie stage production. And I was the only individual writer singled out for this caricature.

What was it about this vocal parody that so incensed Hitchens? His reaction was hardly exceptional. After all, few affronts are more likely to wound and diminish an enemy than the mockery of their voice, for voice is intimately bound up with identity. As Steven Connor (2000: 7) has observed: 'Nothing else about me defines me so intimately as my voice, precisely because there is no other feature of my self whose nature it is thus to move from me to the world, and to move me into the world.' When a voice is distorted through simulation, its subject loses temporary control of their identity. A journalist whose self-representation as a 'plummy baritone', rather over-defensively distanced from the vulgarities of 'Estuary English', is turned without his consent into a theatrical butler or a 'tweedy old buffer' with a voice that would not be claimed by any 'living Englishman'. In his eagerness to emphasize that the tone ascribed to him by a BBC actor was inconsistent with his true identity, Hitchens was yielding to a widespread cultural belief that a person's genuine character is reflected in the nuances of their voice. The voice serves as a unique identifier – 'This is me speaking'.

To be a morally autonomous (and thereby potentially political) being is to have an identity that can be recognized, both by oneself and by others. 'This is me speaking' cannot be an ambivalent claim. If identity is to remain intact, so must the voice of the subject. It matters greatly to people that there is a perceived congruence between what they say and how they say it, not only in terms of words but also in terms of tone, gesture and comportment. People who cannot enunciate in their own voice cannot be taken seriously; they are destined to be regarded as individuals at odds with their individuality or dummies who have fallen victim to the degradation of bad ventriloquism. This is the accusation that the journalist Steve Richards levelled against the former Labour Party leader, Ed Miliband, in an article in *The Guardian* newspaper on 24 July 2013:

> His failure to discover a fully developed public voice manifests itself in a curious way. Often in public he chooses to speak like Tony Blair and adopt the former leader's mannerisms.

The charge against Miliband is that he mimicked Blair in the vain hope of reproducing the latter's charisma. According to Richards, however, Miliband's impersonation has the opposite effect: of highlighting the difference between the original and its awkward citation. His advice to Miliband is to find his own voice: 'the need to hit upon an authentic public voice is not trivial. Indeed, the recent past suggests that authenticity is a pre-condition to winning elections'. Richards was by no means alone in taking this close interest in the sound of Miliband's voice. *The Guardian* newspaper devoted a four-page spread to the matter (2 April 2014), inviting performers and spin doctors to offer Miliband advice on how to sound less 'weird'. The prosaic conclusion offered by one of them that 'He's at his best when he's himself' serves as a reminder that few of us are ever at our best when we don't sound like the person we claim to be.

To find one's own voice entails more than simply saying what one means. Speaking in one's own voice calls for a consistency of self-presentation that affirms the presence of a cohesive being, not only in the words spoken, but also in the breath that precedes them, the gaps in between them and the life that will be lived after they are spoken. The embodied voice roots enunciation in the ineluctable integrity of the speaker.

While affectation calls attention to the incongruence between the original and its copy, affective vocal release points to a visceral nub that resists the semantic arrangements of contrived speech. Examples of involuntary affective emission are discussed by Joshua Gunn (2010) in one of the few studies of political rhetoric to pay serious attention to non-verbal acoustic expression (see also Hart et al., 2013.). Writing about the infamous 'Dean Scream' which emanated from one of the leading candidates for the Democratic presidential nomination in 2004, shortly after he finished in third place in the Iowa caucuses, Gunn attempts to make sense of 'that pure sound of expressive vocality that doesn't simply carry meaning, but also bodies forth the body in feeling in a manner that cannot be signified' (Gunn, 2010: 187). British election-watchers will recall a similar lyrical eruption in June 2001, when Peter Mandelson defied those who believed his career was over by being re-elected to Parliament and convulsively declaring that 'I am a fighter, not a quitter'. Mandelson's vociferation was remarkable because it seemed to emerge from a somatic depth not usually associated with the banality of political speech. It was as if it were a feeling being exhaled. Of course, all speech is breath interrupted by the articulation of vowels and consonants, but some vocal emissions are breathier than others. When breath takes the form of – or is punctuated by – screams, gasps, grunts, cackles and giggles, affect is laid bare. Cultivated speech entails an attempt to control or repress such leakage. In the cases of Dean and Mandelson, what they had hoped to give out verbally was overwhelmed by what they gave off expressively.

The common thread running through these instances of phonic self-betrayal is a casting of doubt upon the claim that 'This is me speaking'. In such situations, whether emanating from the alleged mendacity of impersonation or involuntary somatic discharge, the authenticity of voice is compromised, calling attention to its form rather than its content. Such ambiguities of vocal identity cast doubt upon the simplistic notion that communication is about the transmission of meaningful messages and lead us to think about the ways in which meanings are generated through the impulses of the embodied voice. This points to Adriana Cavarero's (2005: 11) penetrating account of the voice as 'the register of an economy of drives that is bound to the rhythms of the body in a way that destabilizes the rational register on which the system of speech is built'. The voice makes speech happen, but in its pre-semantic form it transcends the linguistic code and emits signals about the speaker that exceed descriptive language.

Recent sociolinguistic and neuropsychological research has explored how listeners perceive speakers' social characteristics by making tacit sense of Barthes's 'grain of the voice'. People hear sounds and pauses before they read the messages of speech and from these phonetic modulations and variations they piece together the kind of person they are hearing; they make assumptions about the nature of the semantically and syntactically constructed messages that they are about to hear; they prepare themselves, often subliminally, to be addressed on certain terms. As they listen to sounds that they associate through memory with particular moods, personality types, status positions or subject genres, people are primed for hearing the world around them. Intriguing experiments have been conducted in which the same words have been enunciated with marked phonetic variants and listeners have arrived at significantly consistent judgement about traits such as the authority or likeableness of different speakers (Addington, 1968; Preston, 1999; Bayard, 2000; Campbell-Kibler, 2007; Drager, 2010; Chen et al., 2017). Prosodic voice quality has the effect of both shaping the meaning of speech content (by, for example, distinguishing between ironic, sarcastic and descriptive statements) and of characterizing the speaker. Goldinger et al.'s (1999: 328) observation that 'spoken words lead "double lives", serving both as perceptual objects (with unique voice characteristics) and as gateways to linguistic representations' captures the sense in which speech emanates from the voice, but is far from being the sole dimension of vocal expression. The poet Ruth Padel (2008: 40) refers to the 'unconsciously heard notes' in music that we would 'miss if they weren't there', even though we 'don't realise we are hearing them'. Like these opaque harmonic notes, Padel argues, words 'hold unheard resonances of sense as well as sound'. And the same can be argued even more forcefully for the pre-semantic tones of the voice. They evoke identities by enacting particular sound plays. A political speaker might be described as 'Churchillian', even though the theme of his or her speech has nothing to do with war, patriotism or conservative ideology; another might be described as being 'one of us', even though we have never met the person and he or she has yet to say anything to show that he or she shares our experience; yet another might be called 'pompous' simply on the basis of a particular manner of clearing the throat and appearing to command rather than attract attention. As Celia Hunt and Fiona Sampson (2006: 30) astutely observe,

> The tone of the voice . . . is closely bound up with the body. It is the indicator of a bodily self-presence underlying and informing the language we use.

Rarely is this tonal underlay more conspicuous than in political talk. As many of the interviewees quoted in the previous chapters testify, the distinctive vibrations of political interaction are audibly conspicuous, marking them out from ordinary communication before one even hears the meaning of what is being said. Political speeches have familiar tunes, increasingly narrow in their melodic range as the practice becomes ever more professionalized, citational and risk-aversive. A political argument in a living room, bar or workplace has a rhythm that suggests immediately that this is not a joke being told, a holiday tip being shared or a group of friends exchanging gossip. People can hear the political coming towards them, beckoning them to join in by adopting a peculiar register; by displaying feats of verbosity and memory that not everyone feels up to performing; by positioning themselves with confidence or trepidation in relation to worldly power; by manifesting a sensibility towards disagreement and its disagreeable consequences that can feel risky and even scary.

Political talk cuts to the core of identity. 'This is me speaking' is a not merely a claim to reveal identity, but an endeavour to enact a version of the self that will be recognized as possessing political agency. To imagine the voice as a bearer of direct and reliable messages from the subjective interior is ultimately naïve, for the notion that there is a pristine authenticity to disclose misses the performative nature of selfhood. The metaphor of the voice as a conduit to the soul fails to acknowledge the inherent ambivalence of any act of self-representation.

The grammar of political talk entails not only a responsibility to assert that 'This is me speaking', but to also do so within a context of address which is open to unrestricted interpretation. Expressive motivation minus receptive comprehension equals non-communication. So, speakers are bound to make themselves accountable to others. 'This is me speaking' counts for little if the people you are addressing do not know, accept or care who you are. Giving voice to the most urgent political intentions is pointless if one's goals are twisted, misconceived or nullified at the point of reception. Hence, most political expression is marked by nervous anticipation, revealed by tone and tilt – a reminder that much depends upon how precisely the grain of the voice is respected or devalorized by others.

Vocal value: Echoes of control and humiliation

Every time people begin to speak about politics they encounter genealogical traces of prohibition and derogation – bumps in the historical road upon which earlier expressive attempts faltered or were made to founder. Few would deny that speech, as a learned cultural code, renders people vulnerable to judgement, not only regarding the veracity of what they are saying, but also regarding their authority to speak. In the case of professional politicians, such considerations are commonplace and frequently tinged with resentment: Who is *he* to devise policies and make decisions that can affect *me*? How can someone whose life experience is so palpably different from mine claim to speak for my values? In the case of everyday political talk, evaluations of speakers' authority are rarely articulated. But they are there, the sedimentous remnants of centuries of dogma about entitlements to political voice and the acceptable forms that such restricted utterances should take. 'What does she know about the global economy?'; 'Why should I take any notice of him when he doesn't even have a degree/job/title in front of his name?'; 'Who gave her the right to argue with someone like me?'

When it is said of two people who have been exchanging views about political issues that they have been 'putting the world to rights', the observation serves a euphemistic purpose. What is really being said is that the exchange, while seeming to address grand geopolitical themes, can be expected to play no meaningful part in setting right what is wrong with the world. By ironically ascribing great efficacy to such casual talk, its inefficacy is highlighted. How much easier it is to say that Jack is 'on his soapbox' or 'giving another one of his lectures to his mates' or 'getting it off his chest' than that Jack has nothing whatsoever to say about politics that could be worthy of sustained attention. Metaphors and euphemisms, while appearing to report and illustrate situations, in fact gesture towards ways of evaluating them. When referring to mundane political talk, such tropes perform a boundary-setting function, dispelling any assumption that the words spoken possess discursive weight.

How do qualities of manifest authority come to assume such significance in contemporary political talk? Why do so many people experience a daunting sense that they are entering into an alien space when their expression broaches upon the subject of politics? The genealogy of this feeling can be found in a long history of explicit proscription, the trace memories of which seem to be woven into contemporary anxiety.

The Sins of the Tongue, elaborated by the Fourth Lateran Council of 1215, sought to criminalize forms of public talk that reflected critically upon established authority or contained the seeds of autonomous public opinion. The aim of this ruling and the subsequent sanctions against public political expression imposed by European courts in the late Middle Ages was 'to reinscribe traditional social hierarchies and discourage disruptive and inflammatory speech' (Bardsley, 2003: 146). A common response by lowly speakers to this injunction was to retreat into a language of semi-whispered truth-telling which James Scott (1990: 4) describes as 'hidden transcripts': 'discourse that takes place "offstage", beyond direct observation by powerholders'. A public political discourse comprising the speakable utterances of elites and their followers ran in parallel with an offstage repertoire of 'speeches, gestures and practices that confirm, contradict or inflect what appears in the public transcript' (1990: 4/5). Each transcript appeared to be indifferent to the other, while being unable to repress their mutual dependence. Voices of authority, however unaccountable, needed to be overheard by their subjects in order to carry weight. Hidden political transcripts, however surreptitiously subversive, aspired to enter and destabilize official scripts from which their presence had been effaced, diminished or distorted.

A sense that utterances by non-members of the elite about how they were or should be ruled constituted a form of moral trespass – an incursion by vulgar minds into domains of discourse that were beyond them in every sense – was disseminated without any attempt at subtlety. The people, explained Thomas Starkey, the author of *An Exhortation to the People instructing them to Unity and Obedience* (1536) are 'rude and ignorant, having themselves small light of judgment'; their 'weak and vulgar minds' are unfit for 'matters of weight and gravity' (Cressy, 1977: 10). In the same year the humanist scholar and diplomat Richard Morison asserted that 'It is not meet, every man to do that he thinketh best. . . . It is not part of the people's play to discuss acts made in the parliament' (Cressy, 1977: 11). Robert Dallington, the tutor to the future Charles I, declared that 'as sacred things should not be touched with unwashed hands, so state matters should admit no vulgar handling' (Cressy, 1977: 11). Queen Elizabeth's Lord Keeper Bacon warned against 'unbridled speech' which 'maketh men's minds to be at variance with one another' and would inevitably lead to sedition and then treason (Cressy, 1977: 6). Punitive sanctions against such vocal transgression were inscribed in the 1352 Treason Act and enforced by sophisticated practices of surveillance and suppression designed to silence impostors seeking to encroach upon the intellectual pastures of their masters.

Even those like John Locke, who challenged monarchical absolutism and argued for government by consent, made a point of casting doubt upon the intellectual fitness of labourers and servants for political reflection. It was the narrow experience of such humble folk, according to Locke, that limited their capacity for abstract thought or reasoning. Indeed, to go beyond the transmission of simple instructions and propositions would be to 'amaze the greatest part of Mankind; and [one] may as well talk Arabick to a poor day labourer'. This account of political talk as a foreign language, exposure to which would only confuse and frustrate the majority of people, was tested periodically in moments of popular transgression. Olivia Smith (1986: 30–4) has shown how a succession of late-eighteenth and early-nineteenth-century petitions to the British Parliament calling for extended male suffrage were dismissed without consideration because their language was deemed to be rough, indecent and disrespectful. Lord Canning's declaration that 'if such language were tolerated, there was an end to the House of Commons, and the present system of government' (1986: 32) was indicative of the agitated response of the elite not only to radical demands, but also to the cultural form in which they were stated. Given that nobody claimed that the petitions were either lewd or threatening, but simply that they fell short of an arbitrary (and hitherto unstated) semantic standard, Smith's view that 'Rejection of the petitions implied that the disenfranchised could not write in a language which merited attention' (1986: 34) seems justified. Indeed, such constitutional refusal to recognize the self-expression of the non-elite should be understood within the context of an ongoing cultural onslaught against so-called vulgar speech.

In the latter part of the eighteenth century, elitist anxieties about public political talk changed tone and emphasis. Rather than explicitly denying 'the vulgar masses' entry to the arena of political discussion, it was argued that the public sphere should be open to all, but only on terms of civility determined by the cultural elite. If the savage beast could not be encaged it must be tamed. This change of position and tone was a response – at least, in Britain – to the changing fortunes of democratic discourse. Until the seventeenth century it was easy to depict democratic aspirations as mere social pathology– the wild radicalism of deluded fanatics who were at odds with the laws of nature. The revolutionary turbulence of the seventeenth century; the new language of popular consent embraced by the Whig settlement; the outbursts of public protest against Lord Bute and in favour of John Wilkes; and the emergence of a radical democratic movement, supported by a new literature of uncompromising political egalitarianism, rendered the total disavowal of democratically inclusive politics unsustainable. Of course, some members of the political elite maintained their stance well into the nineteenth and even twentieth centuries, but by then their perspective had become something of an embarrassment. The commanding ethos was one of discursive inclusion, checked by rules of civility that welcomed all voices into the political sphere as long as they adhered to standards deemed to be congruent with 'reasonable' and 'agreeable' discourse.

It was this aspiration to refine the manners of the public sphere that prompted Addison and Steele to establish *The Tatler* – and later *The Spectator* and *The Guardian*. Theirs was a project to create an egalitarian conversational arena – a space of amicable communion that would transcend social distinctions. 'To render ourselves agreeable' was Addison's cultural aspiration, and this entailed encountering voices of all sorts, but always on terms of 'moderation, mutual tolerance and social comity' (Klein, 1997: 34). Readers of *The Spectator* were expected to behave as if they were friends among whom all differences could be ironed out without recourse to personal or partisan conflict. The model for such civic intercourse was the coffee house: a flourishing institution, despite unsuccessful attempts by the King to close them down in 1675 and 1676. As Markman Ellis (2004: 59) notes in his cultural history of coffee houses, once people entered these spaces of promiscuous association, 'unlike all other social institutions of the period, rank and birth had no place':

> Arriving in the coffee house, customers were expected to take the next available seat, placing themselves next to whoever else has come before them. No seat could be reserved, no man might refuse your company. This seating policy impresses on all customers that in the coffee-house all are equal . . . the coffee house allowed men who did not know each other to sit together amicably and expected them to converse.

This architecture of civic equality was intended to evoke a sense of classless amity. But these were merely surface feelings, for underlying them were permanent reminders of social positioning. Gendered and racist protocols of exclusion and discrimination were built into the basic architecture of coffee houses, condemning vast sections of society to civil exile. And even when debarment was not explicit, it was enforced by prejudices of cliquey attraction. 'Of course', Ellis goes on to say, 'this [egalitarian ethos] was always a fiction, as systems of respect were not abandoned totally. One of the attractions was meeting with *men* whose knowledge, interests, social position or trade might be of value to you, and to such *men* due deference was necessary' (Ellis, 2004: 59; emphasis added). Protocols of polite civility both masked and reflected such hierarchies of respect – and also disrespect, abandoning some coffee houses to the exclusive fellowship of the socially marginalized and politically insignificant.

The term 'bore' entered the popular vocabulary in the mid-eighteenth century and was commonly applied to coffee-house talkers whose verbosity appeared to exceed their rank and education. William Hazlitt wrote caustically of coffee-house politicians who 'do not seem to talk for the sake of expressing their opinions, but to maintain an opinion for the sake of talking':

> A dearth of general information is almost necessary to the thorough-paced coffee-house politician; in the absence of thought, imagination, sentiment, he is attracted immediately to the nearest commonplace, and floats through the chosen regions of noise and empty rumours without difficulty and without distraction. . . . There is certainly no principle of short-hand in his mode of elocution. He goes round for a meaning, and the sense waits for him. It is not conversation, but rehearsing a part.

In a rather vicious tirade against bores, the Anglo-Irish writer Maria Edgeworth noted: 'The bore is good for promoting sleep; but though he causeth sleep in others, it is uncertain whether he ever sleeps himself; as few can keep awake in his company long enough to see. It is supposed that when he sleeps it is with his mouth open.'

The bore became a euphemism for presumptuously intrusive people who took discursive equality too far; the rough mechanics who believed that open debate should include consideration of their grievances; autodidactic types, loquacious in response to new-found knowledge; and women who refused to adhere to the script of gendered quietude. The bore became a figure of ridicule who could be ignored within the terms of politeness. Never 'one of us', but always the impostor, adulterating the quality of accredited erudition, the bore became a conspicuous figure of admissible rebuff.

References to bores, who know too little and speak too much, were frequently combined with strictures against 'vulgar' language. The relatively recent standardization of spoken English had led to the enforcement of 'correct' forms of speaking and the stigmatization of verbal impropriety. Linkage between authorized pronunciation and authoritative speech gave the production of verbal distinction an ideological slant. Teaching children to speak 'properly' entailed more than maintenance of the standard; it was designed to warn against 'those offensive tones in reading and speaking' (cited in Mugglestone, 1995: 278) that characterized social inferiors. By the very form of their speech, the vulgar became justified targets of contempt.

The proliferation of published dictionaries and grammar books from the mid-eighteenth century coincided with attempts to demarcate the boundaries of civic discourse. As Janet Sorensen (2004: 435) notes, 'Defining a national standard meant devaluing certain linguistic practices and their speakers as outside of newly set linguistic norms, beyond the pale of polite, rational conversation.' The rationale for this position is explained by Olivia Smith (1984: 2):

> The political and social effectiveness of ideas about language derived from the presupposition that language revealed the mind. To speak the vulgar language demonstrated that one belonged to the vulgar class; that is, one was morally and intellectually unfit to participate in the culture. Only the refined language was capable of expressing intellectual ideas and worthy sentiments, while the vulgar language was limited to the expression of sensations or passions.

This position, according to Nicholas McDowell (2004: 40) was 'intimately connected to debates surrounding the extension of the franchise, for ideas about both suffrage and literacy revolved around the issue of who was considered capable of taking part in public life'. Indeed, the tradition of regarding the prospect of democracy in terms of pathological threat persisted even up to the point late in the nineteenth-century when it was reluctantly accepted by elites that working-class people had to be given the vote. As Walter Bagehot, the most prominent defender of the uncodified, but nonetheless ideologically encrypted English constitution put it, 'notwithstanding their numbers' the working class 'must always be subject, always at least be comparatively uninfluential. Whatever their capacity may be, it must be less than that of the higher classes, whose occupations are more instructive and whose education is more prolonged'. The result was the adoption of a liberal democratic model that values all voices equally for one brief plebiscitary moment every few years, while the rest of the time accommodating itself to structural economic inequalities and culturally self-replicating hierarchies that are incompatible with the inclusive norms of democracy. No longer disenfranchised, the bores, the vulgar and the dispossessed are less likely to be silenced than ignored, ridiculed or classified as 'chavs', 'white trash', 'the angry left-behind' or mere 'noise'.

Democratic theorists point to the various ways in which social groups are excluded not only from getting what they need but also from getting to interpret what they need. Discursive exclusion intensifies the injuries of distributive inequality, perpetuating the latter not only by sidelining its victims from discussions about justice but also by stripping the excluded from a sense of being worthy of notice. The iniquitous denial of full recognition to social groups ranging from women and children to ethnic minorities and 'the white working class' has led proponents of social justice to expand their sense of what it means to be a victim of inequality. For example, the philosopher Charles Taylor (1997: 25) states that

> our identity is partly shaped by recognition or its absence, often by the misrecognition of others, and so a person or group of people can suffer real damage, real distortion, if the people or society around them mirror back to them a confining or demeaning or contemptible picture of themselves. Nonrecognition or misrecognition can inflict harm, can be a form of oppression, imprisoning someone in a false, distorted, and reduced mode of being.

This thesis has been powerfully advanced by Axel Honneth, whose primary empirical concerns lie with people's experience and perception of being treated as diminished social agents. He observes that

> in the self-descriptions of those who see themselves as having been wrongly treated by others, the moral categories that play a dominant role are those – such as 'insult' or 'humiliation' – that refer to forms of disrespect, that is, to the denial of recognition. Negative concepts of this kind are used to designate behaviour that represents an injustice not simply because it harms subjects or restricts their freedom to act, but because it injures them with regard to the positive understanding of themselves that they have acquired intersubjectively.

According to Honneth (2007: 134), moral injuries of misrecognition occur in three ways: first, through the most basic denial of a person's right to enjoy well-being; second, through disregard of a person's moral accountability, whereby they are considered incapable of speaking or answering for their own actions; and third, through 'those cases in which it is made known to one or more persons through humiliation and disrespect that their capabilities do not enjoy any recognition'. In such cases people are stripped of any sense of being significant social beings. They can at best aspire to be onlookers, grumblers or subordinates.

Habits of political misrecognition emanate from an over-determined notion of cultural roles in which stereotypical classifications prevail. The work of countering misrecognition entails energetic commitment to demonstrating that one is not what one is taken to be. In this way women are required to demonstrate that they are not over-emotional; disabled people are expected to prove that they are unflaggingly resilient; working-class people are urged to distance themselves from Hogarthian mob images that strike fear into the politically respectable; black people are expected to show that they don't have a chip on their shoulder. In short, faced with prejudices of misrecognition, people are called upon to adopt strategies of appeasement, correcting those aspects of their political speech that might define them as being unworthy of serious attention.

It is hardly surprising, then, that a pervasive nervousness surrounds public political discourse. Seeming rather like 'a cramped and unimaginative space of committed replication', (Berlant, 2011: 259), the political is commonly experienced as a domain in which certain groups and individuals are over-recognized. The jarring and alienating linguistic tics and commanding gestures of political elites constitute an oppressive, hegemonic patois, imitated by some, but leaving most people to stumble along practising a form of enervated citizenship in which there seems to be a radical split between what they say and what circulates as consequential political discourse.

In a constitutional system that claims legitimacy on the basis that all people are included in democratic decision-making, failure to acknowledge social groups or persons by ascribing to them an inferior status amounts to unjust and indefensible disenfranchisement. As Nancy Fraser (interviewed by Dahl et al., 2004: 377) points out, the demand for recognition involves a reframing of democratic practice whereby 'parity-impeding cultural norms' are deinstitutionalized and replaced by 'parity-fostering alternatives'. The normative aim of democratic recognition is to reach a position where 'people's standing as full partners in social interaction, able to participate as peers with others in social life' (Dahl et al., 2004) is fully acknowledged.

Perhaps this is all best stated best by Jacques Rancière in the eighth of his *Ten Theses on Politics* (2001) when he reminds his readers that

> If there is someone you do not wish to recognize as a political being, you begin by not seeing them as the bearers of politicalness, by not understanding what they say, by not hearing that it is an utterance coming out of their mouths.

Feeling agency

Agency entails a capacity to exercise control over one's life by acting upon the environment in a goal-directed manner. Commonly experienced as a private history of small and large attempts to overcome what seems overwhelming, call out what appears to be unjust and counter random acts of disrespect, it is through feelings of agency that people come to register personal dignity. To deny that some people are capable of acting for themselves – are too fragile, vulnerable, reckless or stupid to be unworthy of making their own mark – is to insult their status as autonomous human beings. Political talk often entails a subtle battle for the right to be treated with dignity.

Even when its outcomes turn out to be more reproductive than transformative, there is something about the notion of agency that suggests a generative relationship between action and effect. Socio-culturally mediated though such action always is, its origin in some sort of creative impulse makes it politically appealing, reflecting a hope that someone doing something, however small or unnoticed, might just have an impact upon their own or others' history.

The voice as an instrument of agency intervenes through the breath of the body, the contingency of the moment and the barriers of social structure. It serves as a call to attention. Might what is being said here disturb the inertia of an over-determined scene? How might this voice alert us to something within the scene that has not been acknowledged, or something that is absent and will now be missed or desired? Could this voice remind us of 'the fact that everybody sees and hears from a different position' (Arendt, 1959: 198) and thereby expose us to perspectives that prod us to reorient ourselves? Such capacity for interruption gives voice a fertile quality, its animating potential a constant threat to the fixity of social relations.

Political agency is always tinged with fluctuating feelings of efficacy and inadequacy. The evidence of the previous chapters suggests that people's experience of agency is intimately associated with memories of being recognized, heard, understood, respected, liked, wanted – as well as the antonyms to these terms. When Moira (Chapter 2) described herself as having a permanent feeling of rage towards what she perceived as social injustice, she was not simply providing a rationale for her committed activism but also explaining how she sustains herself as a social actor. It is not that Moira, a person with a certain identity, possesses agency, but that Moira's agency embodies her identity. When Colin (Chapter 2) spoke of having made a conscious decision to remove himself from political conflict because 'life's too short' to endure the anxiety of agonistic discord, he was pointing to a set of deep and complex feelings that overwhelmed his instrumental desire to change the world. For Colin, giving up being a radical activist was not an act of political surrender, but a recovery of personal agency: 'The first real step is to try to disengage yourself from all these pressures to join something and buy into something that you don't want to be a part of'. Can refusal of 'cruel optimism' amount to an affirmation of self-confidence? When Sue (Chapter 3) expressed deep reluctance to engage in political debate because she felt estranged from what seemed like a remote and intimidating discourse that would take her far too long to catch up with, she was not only identifying barriers that stood between her and the exercise of political agency, but also expressing a certain freedom in removing herself from the emotional encumbrances of onerous political commitment. When Steve (Chapter 3), a committed and articulate political actor, offered the candid admission that there was something in his political tone that felt compromised and disingenuous, he was not confessing to a lack of integrity, but expressing frustration at being locked into a linguistic code that so often enhances political agency by resorting to guileful opacity. Like Steve, Gabby and Roland (Chapter 3) spoke eloquently about their wish to strike a balance between the contrasting communicative requirements of political solidarity and relatable sociability. This entailed making affective adjustments which were themselves subtle performances of agency. It soon became clear that the Brexit disagreements discussed in Chapter 4 were rarely only – or even mainly – about macro-politics. Interviewees recalled powerful feelings of constrained, injured and suppressed agency, not only as triggers for their stances towards Brexit, but also as framing backdrops to scenes of argumentative encounter in which power disparities were rehearsed in real time. As a site of affective investment, people apprehend their experiences of political agency as gauges of their standing in the world. They feel their agency.

The challenge of capturing the experience of political agency as a phenomenally conscious state is formidable because few people explicitly think or speak of themselves as 'doing agency' or being agentic (an adjective that is rarely used in ordinary speech). Complex sensate activities such as being in love (Swidler, 2013), losing one's mind (Hornstein, 2017) or 'doing being ordinary' (Sacks, 1984; Tolson, 2001) are surrounded by well-established expressive resources as well as emotional routines and repertoires. People's practical sense of how to perform and evaluate these activities make them discursively familiar. Being a political agent is not like that. Our culture lacks a popular vocabulary for describing or reflecting upon the work of making a social or political difference. People who are paid to bring about political change are called politicians – a label that rarely attracts positive connotations. But acts of everyday agency tend to be spoken of as 'just getting on with life' or, more positively, 'trying to make things work' or, more negatively, 'being a busybody'. It says something about our democratic culture that political agency is such an uncommon and enigmatic concept.

When one tries to explore how people feel about their political agency there is a danger of this quickly becoming a theoretical discussion about macro-political power: structural barriers to collective action, the skewed priorities of the economic system, group inequalities, the mendacity of politicians and so on. This fails to get at the ways in which the exercise of agency impinges qualitatively upon phenomenal consciousness. It is much easier to speak about agency as an abstract resource than as a dimension of felt subjectivity, vulnerable to injuries, insults and unease. Translating agency into the terms of lived experience entails thinking of it less as a strategic operation than an emergent event in which social actors contextualize 'the contingencies of the moment' in relation to historically shaped background feelings as well as the projective possibilities of the future. Political agency is in this sense 'a temporally embedded process of social engagement' (Emirbayer and Mische, 1998: 963): an event that is experienced over time, however brief or long.

It is within the unfolding vicissitudes of present moments that agency is lived out as a drama of possibility and frustration. As Lauren Berlant (2011: 4) brilliantly puts it, 'the present is what makes itself present before it becomes anything else, such as an orchestrated collective event or an epoch on which we can look back.' Present situations are invitations to agency:

> A situation is a state of things in which *something* that will perhaps matter is unfolding amid the usual activities of life. It is a state of animated and animating suspension that forces itself on consciousness, that produces a sense of the emergence of something in the present that may become an event (2011: 5).

Daniel Stern (2004: 4) makes a similar observation, but from a psychoanalytical perspective:

> The present moment does not whiz by and become observable only after it is gone. Rather, it crosses the mental stage more slowly, taking several seconds to unfold. And during this crossing, the present moment plays out a lived emotional drama.

It is as agents, capable of initiating or bringing about change in their environment, that people become protagonists in these dramas of throbbing immediacy. Becoming a political agent entails a capacity to regard the present moment as an opportunity for action within an extensive unfolding of dynamic time. Political talk is perhaps one of the most promising settings in which people exhibit such temporal sensibility. As they argue about how the world is and was and should be, people shift promiscuously from tense to tense, relating the present moment to background causes and future possibilities.

How does this temporal motility work? As agents, people make sense of situations by referring to personal memories and collective histories. Mustafa Emirbayer and Anne Mische (1998: 975) point out in their seminal conceptualization of agency that 'Although . . . all experience takes place in the present, this present is permeated by the conditioning quality of the past'. Agents rarely (and only rashly) respond to immediate contingencies by inventing a wholly novel way of acting. Instead, they selectively reactivate past patterns of thought and action that seem to fit the situation they are in (1998: 971). In chapter 1 we considered the ways in which people draw upon past interactions, beliefs and strategies as frames for present action. In this way, much everyday behaviour, including political talk, takes the form of tacitly absorbed social practice. Not only agents but also the scenes in which agency takes place have a past. When one walks into a political party meeting one encounters not only these people in that room on this evening, but a historical scent of all the party meetings that have ever taken place and contributed to a practical image of what it means to 'do politics'. This is what the philosopher Charles Taylor means by 'engaged agency', a term that refers to the ways in which agents are embedded in histories and forms of life that shape the way that the world makes sense to them. Taylor (1993: 328) argues that 'Engaged agents are creatures with a background sense of things'. This background sense is key to understanding the agency of political talk, for when people begin to communicate about politics they bring to their utterances, conversations and debates a *background feel* for what is really going on and how it came about. Taylor (1993: 325) very helpfully describes what this 'background sense of things' means:

> It is that of which I am not simply unaware (as I am unaware of what is now happening on the other side of the moon), because it makes intelligible what I am uncontestably aware of; but at the same time I cannot be said to be explicitly or focally aware of it, because that status is already occupied by what it is making intelligible.

This delicate dance between an awareness that is only implicit and an intelligibility that is informed by oblique context is routinely performed within the course of political talk, as interlocutors try to work out whether they are able to communicate within a common set of references. If they cannot agree about where they stand now in relation to the past years, weeks or seconds, they will need to move back a stage to explore how and why their senses of background are so different. Much political communication is focused on precisely such questions of background framing, which can often be more affectively charged than the topics that people think they are arguing about. This haunting presence of the background was particularly discernible in the Brexit disagreements considered in Chapter 4; when Kath recalled her argument with a work colleague, her grandparents, who were not physically present during the argument, were invoked as ghostly emblems of neglected working-class honour. Ultimately,

Kath believed that her argument about the forthcoming national referendum could only be understood in the context of this background reference. To cite Taylor (1993: 325) once more,

> The context stands as the unexplicited horizon within which . . . experience can be understood. To use Michael Polanyi's language, it is subsidiary to the focal object of awareness, it is what we are 'attending from' as we attend to the experience.

Studies of political talk tend to focus exclusively on its explicit object: the topic that speakers claim to be talking about. And that is, indeed, an obvious and sensible place to start. But how people speak about a political topic is likely to vary greatly depending upon the 'background sense of things' that frames their perspective. The sedimented ways in which the past is woven into people's experience play a crucial role in determining how it is registered.

But political talk is also about a relationship to the future. Indeed, agency is most commonly spoken about in this future-oriented sense: in terms of the effects of present action upon subsequent outcomes. As Emirbayer and Mische (1998: 971) put it, projective agency

> encompasses the imaginative generation by actors of possible future trajectories of action, in which received structures of thought and action may be creatively reconfigured in relation to actors' hopes, fears, and desires for the future.

Political talk, in this context, is not a precursor to agency, but a crucial devising stage of agentic action. The vitalizing force of future-oriented agency depends upon 'hypothesization of experience, as actors attempt to reconfigure received schemas by generating alternative possible responses to the problematic situations they confront in their lives' (1998: 984). As people weigh up the range of actions that they might be able to take, they operate as exploratory agents, devising and then reflecting upon hypothetical exercises of change-making. Talking about politics opens a space for the rehearsal of conceivable responses to situations. Few people move directly from recognizing that something is a social problem to articulating a clear-cut solution. They find themselves reflecting aloud about what could or should be done to address the problem. They might emphasize one possible response in one conversation and another in a subsequent discussion. In the course of these exploratory rehearsals they begin to frame explanations, justifications and mitigations for future action.

The rehearsal space of political talk is commonly constrained by what seem to be objective limits to expedient improvisation. Contemplation of imaginative trajectories all too often collide with the adamantine constraints of social structure. These systemically entrenched barriers to making a difference to the world are cruelly stubborn. Capacities for agentic action are unequally distributed. The horizons of vast social groups such as the poor, educationally unqualified, women, non-whites, non-heterosexuals, disabled and pre-adults are circumscribed by rules, institutions and practices that ascribe devalorizing roles and powers to them. Added to these are deeply rooted, internalized dispositional accommodations to social structure through which people customize their behaviour to conform to and perpetuate their status. Both the durability of structural impasse and the dragging weight of habitus stand as major obstacles to the realization of democratic agency.

The primary challenge facing creative political agents is to devise inventive ways of overcoming seemingly intractable impediments to change. This calls for imaginative effort, often involving encounters with hypothetical and counterfactual realities. It is through talking about politics that spaces for performative agency open up, allowing people to safely inhabit theoretical trajectories of future action without being tied to their consequences. When political talk turns to phrases such as 'if I had my way' or 'what needs to happen is' or 'if only', people are not simply indulging in utopian counter-narratives. They are inviting other imaginations to converge with their own in preparation for joint action. This kind of rehearsal of options entails experimental reframing of issues, experiences and values, transforming what might at first seem like wishful thinking into a plausible candidate for strategic action.

Efficacy as a political agent depends upon making confident connections between background feelings, creative future projection and a capacity to feel connected to and make sense of the emergent and unfolding present. Such efficacy is far from universal. Despite William Sewell's 1992: 20) claim that 'a capacity for agency – for desiring, for forming intentions, and for acting creatively – is inherent in all humans', many people remain convinced that their voices count for very little when it comes to major decisions and policies that will affect their lives. In the United Kingdom, eight out of ten people feel that they have little (42 per cent) or no (40 per cent) influence on national decision-making (Hansard Audit, 2017). In the United States almost half the population believe that there is 'not much that ordinary citizens can do' to influence the federal government. Asked to explain why they feel so politically powerless, people often speak of how 'people like us' are misunderstood, looked down upon and insultingly ignored by elite decision-makers. These are subjective perceptions that tell a story about agency not simply as an instrumental capacity, measurable in terms of empirical accomplishments but also as a state of feeling.

Why are so many people so routinely disappointed about their experience as democratic agents? According to Lauren Berlant (2011: 97–8), they are right to feel this way:

> Sovereignty, after all, is a fantasy misrecognized as an objective state – an aspirational position of personal and institutional self-legitimating performativity and an affective sense of control in relation to the fantasy of that position's offer of security and efficacy. But it is inadequate for talking about agency outside of the King's decree or other acts in proximity to certain performances of law, like executions and pardons. It is also a distorting description of the political, affective, and psychological conditions in which the ordinary subjects of democratic/capitalist power take up positions as agents.

Berlant's dismissal of the claim that citizens are sovereign agents is hardly contentious. As Jürgen Habermas (1997: 39) pointed out over two decades ago, the Enlightenment notion of the public as a confident, self-determining entity that will only submit to the authority of rational discourse 'has become so far removed from its intellectual and cultural origins that the revolutionary consciousness has ceased to be relevant at all'. But when Berlant (2011: 116) goes on to argue that 'Most of what we do . . . involves not being purposive, but inhabiting agency differently in small vacations from the will itself, which is so often spent from the pressures of coordinating one's pacing with the working day', she appears to be conflating agency with the very forms of bodily inertia that it resists. It is certainly true that getting on with life under the pressures of neoliberal capitalism frequently involves falling back upon internalized habits of acquiescence, but that surely constitutes an abandonment of agency, not a more modest or mundane form of it. Only when people find themselves engaging with social structure in ways that are neither automatic nor paralysing can they hope to sustain positive feelings of agency.

The formidable impediments that stand between most people and a positive sense of democratic agency have been widely catalogued: the enervation of civic solidarity; an absence of easy access to balanced information or opportunities for deliberation about complex issues; polarized public discourse, dominated by echo chambers and routine incivility; political knowledge gaps dividing the poorest from the richest; the prevalence of deep social inequalities and economic insecurities; the diffuse sway of a global, neoliberal ideology that refuses to register voices liable to challenge or interfere with the latitude of the market. Given these intractable obstacles to contemporary agency, it is little wonder that the term has become so commonly synonymous with circumscriptive aspiration at best and utopian fantasy at worst. Berlant's (2011: 262) urgent call 'to reinvent, from the scene of survival, new idioms of the political, and of belonging itself' is provocative, perhaps stirring, but what exactly might this mean from the perspective of the people whose accounts in previous chapters suggested that they felt locked into devitalized and frustrating practices of political discourse?

The creative project of inventing new idioms of the political depends upon a radical revitalization of agency. Too often 'the political' is regarded as a passing show – a spectatorial event in which some are engaged onlookers, assimilating the drama as an object of voyeuristic consumption, while others 'feel rather like a deaf spectator in the back row, who ought to keep his mind on the mystery off there, but cannot quite manage to keep awake' (Lippmann, 1927). The 'mystery off there' stems from an unclear affinity between the narrative preoccupations of grand politics and the insistent contingencies of personal experience. Any compelling new idiom of political agency would need to re-orientate meaningful subjective action, including everyday political talk, towards the realm of personally significant experience.

In any democracy worthy of the name there must be political openness to people's perception of what it feels like to be a social actor, both cumulatively, through the emerging amassment of impressions, interactions, observations and frustrations that enlarge their sense of being in the world, and immediately, through their visceral response to the dynamics of the present moment. It is only when people feel capable of intervening as experientially embedded actors in the unfolding dramas of social reality, rather than enduring them as abeyant spectators, however interested or indifferent, that they can claim to be political agents.

If political discourse in democracies is to reconnect with personal experience, this must include *all* experience and not only that which conforms to authorized narratives, a legitimized range of ideologies or forms of generically recognized expression. Routine exclusions, dismissals or mockeries of 'irrelevant' experience are examples of what Nancy Fraser refers to as 'parity-impeding cultural norms'. Several of the people whose accounts of political talk appear in this book expressed uncertainties and frustrations about what is allowed to count as political argument or evidence. Several of them expressed a desire to stretch the terms of political expressiveness to take account of experiences that might not at first seem to fit in within the language of political disputation. They wanted to connect themes, feelings and events that were not obviously connected or even connectable. They wanted to engage with politics in the language of direct experience rather than ossified ideology. People told stories in which the immediacy of – usually asymmetrical – felt relationships were just as politically relevant as the apparently substantive points at issue. These agentic endeavours to bring experience into the political domain might be classified as 'parity-fostering alternatives' (Fraser, interviewed by Dahl et al., 2004: 377). They serve to expand political space in order to accommodate a range of experiential evidence, thereby exposing the public sphere to a more generous spectrum of humanity.

Reconnecting agency to the broadest range and forms of experience is crucial, but, as Joan Scott (1991: 779) has compellingly argued, agents do not simply act on experience: 'It is not individuals who have experience, but subjects who are constituted through experience'. It follows, then, that a reinvented political idiom would need to entail an awareness that the subjects and categories of experience are not ontologically settled, but emanate from discursive processes which are themselves contestable. In short, agents do not simply respond to experiential realities, but engage with the ways in which social reality is authorized, sensed, embodied and contested. This does not mean that all political agents must be discourse analysts, deconstructing semiotic and semantic symbols as they argue with one another about politics. It does imply, however, that agency begins before the point at which people decide what they could or should do about a situation. Agency begins with attempts to apprehend and define situations: What is going on here? How does it relate to other situations that are or have been going on? Who or what is responsible for this happening? What is my responsibility for and in this situation? What can I – or we – do about it? What makes this kind of definitional agency political is its ontologically critical stance; its refusal to accept discursive claims that close down scope for critical interpretation by insisting that a situation can possibly be described only in one way or that it can conceivably turn out only one way; by compelling participants to adopt roles and duties that are the only ones available; are historically circumscribed because 'they are what they are'. Political agency must be intimately related to experience, but must be capable of de-essentializing the terms of such experience so that they are not caught up in an empiricist impasse.

When people talk about politics they often feel that they have been thrown into the midst of a polemical battle in which the trenches were dug long before they ever arrived. Moral positions have not only been adopted, but labelled, scrutinized, demarcated and tarnished by empirical association. Structures of power and modes of discourse have been internalized by political insiders, leaving new arrivals with little choice but to catch up and fall in line. To talk about politics in such circumstances involves adopting a language that purports to represent experience in some sort of holistic, indexical fashion. A more discursively conscious and creative approach to expressive agency would regard political talk as an interpretive experience in its own right. William James (1976) captured this well when he wrote of how speech and language are constitutive of the ways in which people come to feel their active presence in the world:

> Only new-born babes, or men in semi-coma from sleep, drugs, illnesses, or blows, may be assumed to have an experience pure in the literal sense of a that which is not yet any definite what . . . Pure experience in this state is but another name for feeling or sensation. But the flux of it no sooner comes than it tends to fill itself with emphases, and these salient parts become identified and fixed and abstracted; so that experience now flows as if shot through with adjectives and nouns and prepositions and conjunctions. Its purity is only a relative term, meaning the proportional amount of unverbalized sensation which it still embodies.

It is precisely this capacity to not merely *have* experiences, but to go to work on them expressively and imaginatively, that turns an actor into an agent. For the latter, political subjectivity becomes a fertile enterprise, characterized by an openness to the experience of others and willingness to envisage alluring historical possibilities. At stake here is a capacity for political reflection that transcends the experiential partiality of blinkered subjectivity. For Arendt (1968: 241), democratic agency is rooted in an intersubjective receptivity to the perspectives of others who do not inhabit our skin or social environment:

> I form an opinion by considering a given issue from different viewpoints, by making present to my mind the standpoints of those who are absent; that is, I represent them. . . . The more people's standpoints I have present in my mind while I am pondering a given issue, and the better I can imagine how I would feel and think if I were in their place, the stronger will be my capacity for representative thinking and the more valid my final conclusions, my opinion.

Must one be a utopian to imagine a political democracy in which the search for mutual intelligibility trumps the monological urge to have the first and last word? Is it beyond the scope of realistic expectation to envisage a culture in which the capacity to assert without ambiguity that 'This is me speaking' will not be rendered impenetrable by codes of intelligibility designed to put people in their place? Might the imaginary of voice as a call to intersubjective connection offer a normative basis for the reinvention of exhausted idioms of the political, and of belonging itself? These are questions that will be addressed in the final chapter.

6

We need to talk – but how?

Political talk, once regarded as a defining expression of popular sovereignty, has come to be thought of as a feel-bad activity – a nervous, cacophonous, resentful flow of public grumpiness. It is as if people have lost confidence in their ability to talk about politics. They expect it to go wrong. They sense that it is tainted by a debasement of language and coarseness of tone that sets it apart from more congenial social interaction.

The depth of this unease is illustrated by the frequency with which people claim that political discourse is poisonous. In 2018, the Oxford English Dictionary chose the word 'toxic' as its 'word of the year': the word or expression that they 'judged to reflect the ethos, mood, or preoccupations of the passing year, and have lasting potential as a term of cultural significance'. Equating political talk with poison has become commonplace:

> Whether political violence is rising or simply getting more attention, there is no doubt that we face an extraordinarily toxic political climate. (*The Hill*, 22 June 2017)
>
> Yes, we disagree constantly. But what makes our disagreements so toxic is that we refuse to make eye contact with our opponents, or try to see things as they might, or find some middle ground. Instead, we fight each other from the safe distance of our separate islands of ideology and identity and listen intently to echoes of ourselves. We take exaggerated and histrionic offense to whatever is said about us. (*New York Times*, 24 September 2017)
>
> How did the language of politics get so toxic? (*The Guardian*, 21 July 2016)
>
> Is it possible to resurrect civility amid a tsunami of toxicity? (*Washington Post*, 11 January 2019)
>
> So how do we make our political conversation less toxic? How do we stop bad faith preventing us from discussing politics with people on the other side? (*New Statesman*, 29 August 2018)

Are Toxic Political Conversations Changing How We Feel about Objective Truth? (*Scientific American*, February 2018)

Caught up doubly in this pathological plight, both as vulnerable victims of noxious discourse and as the apparent source of the contagion, there seems to be no way out for everyday citizens. Unless they express themselves, they are doomed to political irrelevance, but when they do so they cannot stop producing infectious toxins that pollute the public sphere. Faced with such an impasse, some wonder whether democracy is sustainable. Former BBC Director General Mark Thompson (2016: 19) states that 'For me, the critical risk is not in the realm of culture but that of politics and, in particular, democracy – its legitimacy, the competitive advantage it has historically conferred over other systems of government, and ultimately its sustainability'. The popular sociologist William Davies (2018: 118) suggests that 'As the language of politics grows more violent, and attacks on the "elites" becomes more vociferous, democracy starts to inch closer to violence, with more instruments and institutions being "weaponised"'. In her final speech as the British prime minister, Theresa May 2019 asserted that 'Today an inability to combine principles with pragmatism and make a compromise when required seems to have driven our whole political discourse down the wrong path. . . . It has led to what is in effect a form of "absolutism" – one which believes that if you simply assert your view loud enough and long enough you will get your way in the end. . . . This descent of our debate into rancour and tribal bitterness – and in some cases even vile abuse at a criminal level – is corrosive for the democratic values which we should all be seeking to uphold. It risks closing down the space for reasoned debate and subverting the principle of freedom of speech.'

Similarly, in the interviews about experiences of political talk discussed in previous chapters, distaste for what many regarded as a tone of generically sanctioned incivility seemed to trouble people, often more than the subjects about which they found themselves disagreeing.

The most common response to these anxieties has been to call for more 'political civility', a normative demand that is complicated by the fact that 'providing a settled definition of civility is all but impossible' (Jamieson et al., 2017: 208). Toni Miassaro and Robin Stryker (2012: 383) define civility as 'an inherently interactive and relational concept that implies that participants observe rules of engagement that are mutually respectful, that avoid ad hominem vitriol, and that otherwise preserve others' dignity'. While attempts to identify the forms of behaviour that constitute uncivil discourse have pointed to a broad range of communicative offences (Stryker et al., 2016), it has proved to be rather more difficult to formulate generalized norms of civility that can be applied to specific contexts of interpersonal disagreement. For example, 60 per cent of respondents to Stryker et al.'s (2016: 543) survey stated that 'making disrespectful statements in a political discussion' is clearly uncivil. But what exactly does that mean? That political interlocutors should engage with one another only after they have established mutual respect? That speakers should not refer disrespectfully to people, policies or ideologies that treat them disrespectfully? That one should offer complete respect to one's opponent's integrity, even if one suspects him or her of arguing deceptively?

Calls for more political civility are typically raised in response to the pugnacious tone of macro-political discourse: the polarizing aggression of political leaders; the vituperative *ad hominem* of campaign ads; and the scathing language of opinionated journalists. In response to these temporizing injunctions, Lance Bennett (2011: 2) argues that, when faced with political opponents who are determined to win the political game at any moral cost, 'civility becomes a losing strategy' and 'incivility may be a more honest response to some challenges than remaining polite in the face of assaults upon one's values'. Bennett may be right to observe that the frenetic nature of star-turn demagogic performances at raucously partisan election rallies, character attacks unleashed in over-heated television studios or eruptive psychodramas played out promiscuously within the non-place of Twitter cannot be tempered by naïve appeals to communicative courtesy. But the overwhelming majority of political talk in contemporary democracies does not take place in these contexts. It is local, casual and interpersonal. It arises from real people's attempts to make sense of, and address, socially generated problems that affect them. Given that social problems are not like mechanical malfunctions, but appear to people as experiential challenges evoking intense personal feelings, it is hardly surprising that people spend a great deal of time and energy thinking about what to do with their emotions when talking about them.

From early childhood human beings learn to act upon their unreflective emotional experience with a view to assessing and managing their expressive performances. Emotional assessment entails reflecting upon whether the kind of feelings one has are appropriate to the situation one finds oneself in. Emotional management involves determining how best to express or suppress feelings, bearing in mind the existence of cultural codes which value some feelings and modes of display more than others. As we have seen in previous chapters, managing and evaluating affect within political talk is a common source of anxiety. When Sebastian (Chapter 2) reported an encounter with a constituent who was trembling with fear when she came to see him because she had never met a Member of Parliament before, he expressed concern that this reflected something that was fundamentally wrong with representative politics. The implication of his comment was that there are better ways of feeling and speaking that democracy should encourage. When Kieran (Chapter 3) complained about political insiders constantly interrupting each other and that the quality of democratic discourse was degraded by routine displays of disrespect, he no doubt had in mind an idea of what showing respect should look like. He was suggesting that the currently accepted feeling rules governing political talk needed to be replaced by more respectful ones. When Gabby (Chapter 3) observed that some political activists fail to 'feel the concept', she was highlighting what she regarded as over-intellectualized habits of political articulation. She wanted the rules of political discourse to be more open to affective expression. When Sian's stepfather (Chapter 4) imposed his racist views upon the guests at her birthday gathering, Sian's perception that he had violated a basic feeling rule hardly required elaborate justification. Most people hearing Sian's story would feel uncomfortable on her behalf. When some of her friends felt so angry that they walked away from the situation, refusing to engage any further with Sian's stepfather, they were collectively affirming their commitment to a feeling rule. At stake in all of these cases was a search for appropriate norms of subjective performance.

Styling the speaking subject

> In an oration, as in life, nothing is harder to determine than what is appropriate.
>
> —(Cicero, *De Oratore*, 21:70)

How do people determine what constitutes appropriate behaviour when they find themselves in the midst of stark political disagreement? This was a question that came up repeatedly as interviewees told me their stories of political talk not working out well for them. For many of them it seemed as if there was no language available for addressing the sensitivities raised when two or more people encounter one another as inhabitants of a world viewed from inimical perspectives. Lurking in the background of so many of the frustrated accounts of political talk I heard were fundamental questions about who is entitled to speak first and most and loudest; what needs to be acknowledged before differences can be aired and attended to; appropriate proxemics and gestural dynamics of conversational space; how to manage feelings of being judged and cravings for appreciation; and the silent choreography of interpersonal decency and dignity. These are questions about apt social practice and answering them is an inevitably political matter.

As with other everyday practices like walking through the city streets, being part of a cinema audience, attending a job interview or going on a date, when people talk politics they draw upon (though are not fully bound by) norms of appropriate behaviour. Such rules of conduct tend to be tacit, informing social practice through what Judith Butler (1993: 95) refers to as 'a regularized and constrained repetition of norms'. Sometimes these rules are culturally embedded and widely shared; sometimes they become problematically unsettled and a source of cultural anxiety.

What being a political subject entails is no longer a matter of cultural consensus. Over the course of the past 250 years, modernist, industrial societies came to privilege norms of social action rooted in a preference for rationality over feeling; the subordination of the everyday lifeworld to the impersonal dynamics of the administrative system; the celebration of strategic and regulatory control over people and the rest of nature; attempts to separate tameable cognition from somatic impulsiveness; and a preference for linguistic parsimony, plain-spokenness and expressive indexicality to the real. Modernist feeling rules surrounding the practice of political talk reflect these sanctioned dispositional qualities. When people talk about politics they are expected to refer authoritatively to facts, chronologies and other archives of objective knowledge; justify their conclusions with claims of incontrovertible logic; display a commanding confidence by adopting a balanced, dispassionate ('scientific') perspective towards evidence and counter-arguments; and resist being drawn into exercises of psychological introspection or revelations of personal fragility or vulnerability. Generic political performances that are tonally insensitive to biographical and experiential differences between people are admired for exhibiting objectivity. These norms appeared to work well when a small minority of the population, all of the same gender, colour and educational background, were the principal acknowledged speakers about politics. They felt *appropriate*.

But what it means to be a political subject is no longer a matter of cosy cultural accord. As societies have come to value unbridled performances of self over normative conformity, knowing how to perform political talk, gesture, comportment, argumentation, protest and acquiescence is no longer clear-cut. And, as Ann Swidler (2001: 94) reminds us, 'In unsettled lives . . . people use culture to organize new strategies of action and to model new ways of thinking and feeling.' Current anxieties surrounding political discourse should therefore be understood less as a symptom of democracy succumbing to the toxicity of an over-excited public than as an emerging sense that modernist norms are inadequate for the expressive tonalities and rhythms of the early twenty-first century. While the old regulative strictures continue to dominate the administrative state (albeit increasingly creakily), the ethos of everyday relationships is veering away from them and towards a more reflexive sense of how people might communicate on their own terms.

In the absence of agreed norms of political expression, feeling rules are routinely transgressed, not because they are rejected, but because they are no longer a matter of shared acceptance or even comprehension. In its extreme form, such discursive confusion degrades much that passes for political debate online, where quaint notions of respect, sensitivity and politesse are discounted by mutual neglect. But even in mundane face-to-face political exchanges, the path from animated disagreement to awkward disagreeableness is commonly short and slippery. In post-Brexit-referendum Britain and Trump's America there are reports of families that can no longer sit down together in the same room (*The Independent*, 8.12.16; *The Guardian*, 27.6.16; *New York Times*, 9.3.19; *The Atlantic*, 26.11.18; *Scientific American*, 1.6.18).

It is here that the notion of civility is regarded by some as a potential panacea for the belligerent *tone* that has come to characterize mundane political discourse. Even if civility cannot be imposed as a prescriptive ideology, repudiating specific speech acts and insisting upon certain standards of interpersonal courtesy, might it serve as a form of affective orientation, evoking a kinder, more munificent tone of political discourse? When Massaro and Stryker (2012: 227) sought to train their textual coders to spot campaign ads that offended the norms of civility they urged them to look out for content that relied 'on a more uncivil tone (e.g., overly strident, rude, discourteous)'. In characterizing the prevailing style of rhetorical incivility, Bennett (2011: 2) refers to an 'often harsh and hyperbolic tone'. In her study of *Rude Democracy*, Susan Herbst (2010: 3) locates civility within the 'fundamental tone and practice of democracy'.

Rarely defined or even discussed in political studies, the concept of tone raises important questions about the nuanced ways in which social relations are played out within an affective register. Unlike the denotative content of speech, which can be described, transcribed, deconstructed and challenged, tone is elusive, hinting at pre-spoken intentions and post-spoken resonances which operate at the level of feeling. As Mladen Dolar (2006: 21) puts it, 'the particular tone of the voice, its particular melody and modulation, its cadence and inflection, can decide the meaning . . . can turn the meaning of a sentence upside down;

it can transform it into its opposite'. And George Steiner (1975: 10) sees tone as operating 'behind and beneath the surface of language, indicating a complex field of semantic and ethical values'. When one person says to another that 'I don't like the tone in which you said that' or 'I sensed what you really meant by the tone of your voice' or 'You should try to adopt a civil tone', they are referring to an intersubjective quality that cannot be evaluated simply in terms of what has been said, but in terms of the relational affects generated by the act of speaking as well.

Deborah Tannen (2005) offers a striking illustration of the significance of tone in her ethnographic study of a Thanksgiving dinner party in Berkeley, California. Her initial plan was to write about the conversational style of each of the six dinner guests, but as she proceeded it became clear that the conversation as a whole was dominated by two somewhat mutually incomprehensible tones: one adopted by participants who came from New York Jewish families and the other adopted by those who did not. It turned out that 'the non-New York participants had perceived the conversation to be "New York" in character and they had felt out of their element' (2005: 5). Tannen (1984: 182) identifies the loudness, pitch, pauses and tone of the New York speakers' voices as causes of this conversational failure. Everybody present had a reasonable sense of what everyone else was saying, but the relational affects produced by tone and style meant that some participants (the non-New Yorkers) 'were often puzzled about what would be an appropriate comment, or what was appropriate about others' comments' (1984: 5). In a strictly functional gathering, such as a board meeting or a university seminar, terms of conversational engagement – or even rules of order – might have been outlined at the outset in a bid to *set the tone*. In most informal contexts, however, this would be regarded as a highly officious intervention. It is, after all, spontaneity and unconstraint of tone that gives speech flavour and diversity. But if, as is increasingly being said of contemporary public discourse, the predominant tone is aggressive, boorish, uninformed and monological, the temptation to regulate it intensifies.

As a pedagogical project to manage public tone, the promotion of civility entails an attempt to cultivate a collective affective demeanour. It arises historically from an impulse that citizenship is a complex embodied practice that needs to be primed and rehearsed. To be a citizen in this context is not simply to possess rights or potential agency, but to bear oneself in a fashion that exhibits expressive self-mastery or confidence as well. The civil-toned subject becomes recognizable by a readiness to engage in matters of shared public interest – an orientation towards mutual communication that reflects a fundamental investment in community.

Classical Athenian democracy and Roman republicanism were laboratories for the pedagogical promotion of a certain form of civil tone. Rhetoricians sought to cultivate speaking subjects capable of entering the public domain and participating in an ongoing civic conversation. Rhetorically instructed citizens were expected to make a commitment to a form of public presence in which they would show themselves to be willingly vulnerable to the judgement of others. Defined by their right – and duty – to speak candidly within the assembly, citizens of Athenian democracy were taught to exhibit courage in the face of the possibility of being 'shouted down, informally harassed for their views or, perhaps worst of all, haled before a court on the charge of making an illegal proposal' (Balot, 2005: 234). The task of civic education was to instil in citizens a commitment to a form of public performance that subordinated self-expressiveness to a recognized template of displayed character virtues. Such an accommodation to public tone entailed not simply knowing what to say but also displaying sensibility towards the communication environment.

Classical rhetorical pedagogues contrasted their interests to the wordy abstractions of the philosophers by focusing on the somatic, visceral and aesthetic dimensions of citizenship. The production of a civil tone, they insisted, called for intensive work on every aspect of corporeal expression, from posture, gesticulation and facial expression to the pitch, pace and mellifluousness of vocal sound. The classical scholar Joy Connolly (2007: 139) shows how Roman rhetoricians like Cicero and Quintilian sought to nurture 'the corporeal citizen' whose 'body proffers an almost inexhaustible series of significations that operate on both rational and emotional grounds'. It was through techniques of bodily self-control that the well-trained classical citizen learned the display rules of politics. Imbued with an almost Goffmanesque sensitivity to the effects of positive self-presentation, rhetorical performers realized that their reception depended on well-rehearsed, finely toned displays. Aristotle's advice to a speaker entering the public domain was to 'make his own character look right and put his hearers . . . into the right frame of mind'. Cicero urged the vocal citizen to 'attain such success as to seem to be what he would wish to seem' (Cicero, 2.176). Training in *hupokrisis*, which originally meant acting, but came to mean oral delivery, focused upon the animation, suppleness, mobility and energy of the human voice. Political talk came to be regarded as an aesthetic performance, governed by explicit feeling rules of public expression.

This aestheticization was to have enduring consequences for post-classical political discourse by creating a marked separation between form and content. Rhetoric came to focus upon stylistic presentation more than political substance.

By late antiquity and the early Middle Ages, rhetoricians had cultivated a highly technical approach to their subject, emphasizing formulaic rules of argumentative arrangement above anything else (Copeland and Sluiter, 2009: 8). Rhetorical speech ceased to focus upon the expression of individual identity within civic engagement. Instead, it was dominated by phonetic proprieties derived from elocution manuals and syllogistic argumentation promoted by logicians. As political speech evolved into an impersonal, technicized performance genre, its generic obsession with tonality overwhelmed other more intellectually or somatically idiosyncratic aspects of political communication. The objective was to sound like someone engaged in political speech rather than saying anything original – or in an original fashion.

Many of the anxieties surrounding contemporary political discourse stem from this sense that there is a separation between rhetorical form and content. There is a pervasive public sense that political talk is 'all just clever words' and wily performance. The political genre is overshadowed by an intuition that form and style untethered from content and conviction ought not to be trusted and that the political speech genre is designed to realize effects rather than clarify meaning. To speak plainly and meaningfully about politics entails a willingness to engage with the dilemmas of worldly context rather than obsession with the arrangement of wordy text. The popular criticism that political slickness is about perpetuating an authoritative tone rather than creatively exploring disagreement turns the adjective 'political' into a euphemism for 'fake'.

The history of debate training within schools and universities has contributed to this fetishized image of political argumentation as mere form. Rather than being taught to display the courage of their convictions, students within these institutions have commonly been encouraged to see debate as an end in itself – a game in which one might take either side of any argument as long as one has the wit to win. 'Switch-side debating', as it became known in the United States from the 1920s onwards, entailed student-speakers debating both sides of a single proposition, regardless of their personal convictions, with a view to demonstrating their technical capabilities as disinterested exponents. In their summary of the ensuing debate about the ethics of college debating, Ronald Greene and Darrin Hicks (2005: 112) show how, in forcing students to debate both sides, 'training was no longer simply a mechanism for developing critical thinking or advocacy skills, but . . . a performance technique that made possible the self-fashioning of a new form of liberal citizen'.

This emphasis upon speaking as a mode of technique, detached from agonistic commitment or affective attachment, is now a central part of training people for employability. Acquiring a set of functional communication skills has become a requirement for young people wishing to enter the job market, often at the lowest service level. They are expected to acquire a capacity to 'communicate' (even though they already know how to speak) and to exhibit 'the right tone' (even though they might prefer the way they emoted before being trained). In a report for the Organisation for Economic Co-operation and Development (OECD), Frank Levy (2010: 10) argues that technology-rich workplaces require employees capable of practising what he calls 'complex communication', defined as follows:

> Interacting with humans to acquire information, to explain it, or to persuade others of its implications for action. Examples include a manager motivating the people whose work she supervises, a sales person gauging a customer's reaction to a piece of clothing, a biology teacher explaining how cells divide, an engineer describing why a new design for a DVD player is an advance over previous designs.

According to Levy (2010: 8), 'the skill of Complex Communication cannot be learned by simply reading the right book. It requires extensive practice and teacher-student interaction.' In short, training complex communicators involves habituating them to a set of practices through repetition and ongoing surveillance.

As the act of speaking has been turned into a technical competence, inculcated via compulsory school and workplace instruction, it has come to be perceived by some as a political project to constrain the content of speech by sanctioning its form. Recall Rita's lament in Chapter 4: 'We're like kids when we have to go on those courses . . . we've got to learn, this e-learning and stuff like that . . . and how people can take offence to certain stuff.' In her critique of contemporary efforts to fashion talk as a saleable commodity, Deborah Cameron (2000: 180) argues that

> communication training does not empower people on the grounds that people are never empowered by being denied the opportunity to exercise choice and judgement. That is in effect what many regimes of communication training do, even as they claim to be developing 'communication skills' – a paradox that arises because the prevailing notion of 'skill' is mechanical and decontextualized.

In criticizing the idea of communication as a set of skills to be imparted through disciplinary training, Cameron is challenging the fundamentally undemocratic assumption that most people are not the best judges of how they should speak. The notion that there are right and wrong ways of speaking, comparable to right or wrong ways of changing a tyre on a car or performing an appendectomy raises form and style to an ontological status, to be validated as proper or discredited as defective. By trying to impose political and aesthetic standards upon people who are in a weak position to resist them, liberal authorities reinforce a popular suspicion that, despite claiming that how people speak is a private matter, they are determined to meddle in the tone, style and content of self-expression.

The pedagogical strategies that we have been considering all focus on communication skills as an individual accomplishment. Students of the classical rhetorical masters were trained to embody and exhibit a set of individually incarnated virtues. College debaters were taught to demonstrate a capacity to speak about any subject thrown at them by displaying personal skills of verbal dexterity and stylistic wit. Well-trained employees are expected not only to recite required scripts but also to possess a degree of expressive versatility that will enable them to respond independently to unplanned contingencies. In all of these cases, the individual appears to be standing at the centre of a communication force field, emitting expressive energy in the form of messages and responding in appropriate ways to actual or anticipated feedback. Normative behaviour refers here to a domain of appropriate personal conduct.

Persuading people to feel confident about expressing themselves as democratic citizens is commonly spoken about as if it were a similarly personal challenge. The promotion of personal confidence is at the centre of current pedagogical schemes designed to encourage people to work on their emotional experience and self-expression. A wide range of contemporary projects to promote 'confidence' and 'resilience', to cultivate 'emotional intelligence' and boost and measure 'happiness', are integral to neoliberal technologies of self. Upon critical scrutiny, many of these programmes are revealed as attempts to revise feeling rules for a post-industrial economy in which the commoditization of emotional experience requires people to be in a permanent state of high sensory alert. In an astute critique of what they call 'confidence (cult)ure', Rosalind Gill and Shani Orgad (2016: 6) reflect on both the gendered targeting implicit in confidence pedagogies and their ideological sub-text of blaming women for being somehow deficient as social agents:

> Academics and think tanks, politicians and newspaper columnists, call on women to recognise that they are being held back not by patriarchal capitalism or institutionalised sexism, but by their own lack of confidence – a lack that . . . is presented as being entirely an individual and personal matter, unconnected to structural inequalities or cultural forces.

In urging people (especially women) to take responsibility for their negative self-images, promoters of personal confidence ideologies stand accused of devaluing political feelings:

> In favouring positive affect and outlawing 'negative' feelings, the confidence culture disavows affect that is considered 'political', specifically anger, indignation and complaint, systematically repudiating such feelings or refiguring them in terms of injunctions to work on the self. (Gill and Orgad, 2016: 17/18)

In the context of political expression, advice couched in simple terms of finding the strength to speak up reduces discursive inequality to matters of individual psychological fitness and technical competence. People are left out of political conversations for many more reasons than having low self-esteem or failing to sound like a strong leader. Like communication training, confidence-enhancing pedagogies address personal challenges in ways that ignore the structural roots of individual powerlessness. If confidence is defined as the reasonable expectation that things will go well, there has to be an objective basis for such optimism. Encouraging people to believe that they are capable of achieving things that they are not able to accomplish on their own is not confidence-building, but cynicism.

Despite these strong reservations, I want to suggest that building confidence must be at the core of any attempt to engender what I would call a *courageous democracy*. I have in mind here Hannah Arendt's (1959: 186) observation that

> The connotation of courage, which we now feel to be an indispensable quality of the hero, is in fact already present in a willingness to act and speak at all, to insert one's self into the world and begin a story of one's own . . . courage and even boldness are already present in leaving one's private hiding place and showing who one is, in disclosing and exposing one's self.

Arendt is surely right in saying that it takes courage to begin a story that is one's own – to have the strength to flourish as a vocal agent rather than a docile dupe. Reference to democratic courage is timely at a historical moment when traditional forms of political communication are being abandoned, while the direction and limits of adaptation remain unclear. In the face of historical indeterminacy, strategies of confidence-building amount to acts of political resistance by the routinely unheard. When the radical educationalist Paulo Freire (1970: 76) declared that 'Those who have been denied their primordial right to speak their word must first reclaim and prevent the continuation of this dehumanizing aggression' he was making a direct connection between confident self-expression and political agency.

So, while acknowledging the fuzzy superficiality and suspect didactic ambition of much of the rhetoric from the confidence-boosting industry, I persist in the claim that confidence remains a vital democratic resource – and one that is unequally distributed. The most fundamental claim of democracies is that everyone has a voice and each voice counts. For that claim to become more than platitudinous, democratic confidence needs to be conceptualized as a pervasive political quality rather than a psychic form of body-building, focused entirely on the personality traits of discrete individuals.

The challenge is to think of democratic confidence as an intersubjective phenomenon. This entails moving beyond a conception of politics as a clash between atomized subjectivities. When people are asked about their memories and experiences of political talk they tend to speak of the political as if it were a personal trait: 'I'm not really a political person'; 'Politics is part of who I am and what I do'; 'I sometimes talk about political things when I'm with friends, but it's not really me'. (Each of these statements was taken from interview transcripts.) In this sense, politics is conceived as an object of interest that is encountered by pre-formed political subjects. Whether people feel attached to this external object, and with what degree of firmness or looseness, is regarded as a matter of personal predilection. From this individualistic perspective, the work of fashioning confident political subjects seems to be vitally important, for it is only by equipping individuals with specific capacities to recognize, comprehend, engage with, speak about and act upon the political that they can be expected to exercise their political agency.

In contrast to this conception of pre-formed individual actors taking to the political stage and declaring themselves is the idea that subjective identities are produced and reproduced through political transaction. Political subjects are relational beings who 'are inseparable from the transactional contexts in which they are embedded' (Emirbayer, 1997: 297; see also Somers and Gibson, 1994; Somers, 1995; Crossley, 2010; Donati, 2010). To the extent that people acknowledge and act upon their relatedness to others they cannot ignore the extent to which their identities as individual actors depend upon how they are regarded, treated, spoken about, rewarded or discriminated against by those others. They could try to exist as subjectively autonomous, solipsistic units, striving painfully to ignore or work around their social interdependence, but in doing so they would become trapped in a monological bubble, like loud speakers that can only ever hope to drown out other loud speakers.

Writing of intersubjectivity as a primary adaptation to sociality, Alfred Schutz (1970: 164) suggested that 'the sphere of the we' is the natural outcome of nonpathological communication: 'This means that the world is not only mine but my fellow men and women's environment; moreover, these fellow men and women are elements of my own situation, as I am of theirs.' Becoming political involves a process of attunement to intersubjective possibilities – to the imaginative opportunities and precarious tensions inherent to daily adjustment between 'mine' and 'we'. Politics as a relational concept can be thought of not so much as a substance or territory that individuals enter into, but as a way of forming and disclosing oneself as an actor within a world in which substance and territory are never fully settled or determinate.

The most pressing argument that I wish to advance in this book is that democratic political talk depends upon forms of confidence that are engendered through intersubjective recognition. This is consistent with Hannah Arendt's (1959: 198) conception of politics as a space in which people appear before one another:

> The reality of the public realm relies on the simultaneous presence of innumerable perspectives and aspects in which the common world presents itself and for which no common measurement or denominator can ever be devised. For though the common world is the common meeting ground for all, those who are present have different locations in it, and the location of one can no more coincide with the location of another than the location of two objects. Being seen and being heard by others derive their significance from the fact that everybody sees and hears from a different position.

The political in Arendt's sense comprises a complex process of mutual disclosure through which subjects become meaningfully present to one another as neither friends nor strangers, but as interdependent beings. Disclosure through speaking amounts to more than simply making known one's formed perspectives and opinions to others. In the midst of the 'sheer inexhaustible flow of arguments' that characterize 'the common world' it is incumbent upon people to develop an 'enlarged mentality', whereby they learn to look 'upon the same world from one another's standpoint'. In one of the most evocative phrases in the history of democratic theory, Arendt refers to this normative obligation to attend to the plurality of surrounding experiences and perspectives as 'training one's imagination to go visiting'. Only by cultivating such a political sensibility does it become possible to 'take our bearings in the world' (1994: 323).

The extent to which these Arendtian norms have been lost, repressed, fragmented or undiscovered in Western political discourse frames much of the apocalyptic talk about the fateful toxicity of the contemporary political mood. Overwhelmed by an impasse in which, far from 'going visiting', political imaginations seem to be locked into repertoires of well-rehearsed bellicosity and exhausted ideological posturing, it seems to many people that taking their bearings in the world is a task to be conducted against rather than within the language of the political. Nervous and irritable public talk makes the kind of self-disclosure proposed by Arendt feel risky and unavailing. When dogmatic claims are insisted upon by 'silent minorities', often hiding behind bullying demagogues and propagandistic media slogans, political expression becomes tonally insensate and the task of translating meanings across experience is abandoned as a lost cause or an unnecessary chore.

Without the efforts to translate meanings across experiential contexts, as outlined in Chapter 1, there can be no possibility of finding a common political language within which intersubjective recognition can be embedded, because there is no democratic option but to embrace the reality that 'everybody sees and hears from a different position' and accept the challenges involved in establishing interpretive arteries through which experiences and values can become more comprehensible and sharable. For, as George Steiner (1975: 205) puts it:

> The tensions between private and public meaning are an essential feature of all discourse. . . . Vital acts of speech are those which seek to make a fresh and 'private' content more publicly available without weakening the uniqueness, the felt edge of individual intent.

The most obvious part of political translation involves the transfer of cognitive meaning between people, but the much more difficult challenge is to communicate affective intention. The most significant inflections within political talk are those that neither fully reveal nor conceal meaning but convey intentional ambivalence and offer scope for polysemic interpretation. To quote Steiner (1975: 220/1) one last time:

> We communicate motivated images, local frameworks of feeling. All descriptions are partial. We speak less than the truth, we fragment in order to reconstruct desired alternatives, we select and elide. It is not 'things which are' that we say, but those which might be, which we would bring about, which the eye and remembrance compose. The directly informative content of natural speech is small. Information does not come naked except in the schemata of computer language or the lexicon. It comes attenuated, flexed, coloured, alloyed by intent and the milieu in which the utterance occurs.

Translation works towards an attunement to communicative feeling and tone no less than to semantic meaning. Anything that people say in the course of political talk is but a first version of what is heard and mediated by interpretation. For politics is never only about what is said but also about the manner of its saying and reception, including those pregnant pauses between words within which affective currents flow and intentions lurk. Political translation depends upon practices of sensibility that exceed the formulaic demands of syllogistic logic.

For the political to emerge as a register of experience there needs to be a sensitivity to the reasons that people have for caring and disagreeing about things that matter to them. These include not only obviously political questions about who gets what; who is deserving of what; how best to compensate unfair losses or restrain excessive privilege; and how to create and maintain just social rules and structures, but also which voices get to be heard and taken seriously; resentments resulting from being wrongly labelled, classified or valued; and who is free to feel and express what. Whether political disagreements appear to be primarily about distribution or recognition, beliefs or affects, the object of contention might turn out to be quite different once it has been subjected to argumentative scrutiny. At the same time, disagreeing subjects might turn out to occupy different positions – or the same positions, but for different reasons – once they have disclosed themselves to one another.

It is this translatory exposure to intersubjective judgement that makes political talk such a risky activity, for both the object of contention and the contending subjects may not be the same after it has taken place as when it begins. As we have seen, some people feel more confident and competent about expressing themselves politically than others, although this often depends upon the circumstances in which they are invited to do so. A person who might be very eloquent and persuasive when talking about an issue with his or her neighbours might freeze and stammer when asked to present verbal testimony at a council meeting. A group of school friends capable of arguing vociferously among themselves about instances of everyday sexism might find themselves retreating into murmuring timidity when asked to give a presentation about the subject before a school assembly. The social space and context in which political talk occurs matters.

Political talk never takes place in a vacuum. In his discussion of the relational dynamics of participatory democracy, Maarten Hajer (2005: 626) raises the important question of how settings for political discussions 'influence what is said, what can be said and what can be said with influence'. By shifting the burden of expressive efficacy from the lone individual – orator, debater, scripted employee, 'skilled' communicator – to the social conditions in which political talk takes place, Hajer and other relational theorists move the argument from being one about the nurture and regulation of individual communicative competence to a much more productive inquiry into the best ways of enabling people to flourish as members of a democratic polity. In short, responsibility is transferred from the individual speaker to the norms governing the speaking situation.

The setting, arrangements and protocols of spaces of democratic interaction are addressed by Iris Marion Young (2002) in her groundbreaking book *Inclusion and Democracy*. Young lays bare a range of ways in which democratic societies exclude citizens from participating in decision-making, even when the latter is supposed to be public and participatory. She outlines a number of *external exclusionary* factors, such as the frequent inaccessibility of venues, timings and jargon when people are formally invited to engage in participatory exercises; the ways in which politicians and bureaucrats often broker deals within political back-channels, thereby nullifying the value of public input; and, of course, the strategies through which some people with vast amounts of money and other resources exercise domination by shaping political agendas or economically vetoing popular decisions. Such external exclusions are largely structural and can only be addressed by tackling deep-rooted, systemic enablers of inequality and injustice. Young (2002: 65) then goes on to outline what she calls *internal exclusion* whereby

> Having obtained a presence in the public, citizens sometimes find that those still more powerful in the process exercise, often unconsciously, a new form of exclusion: others ignore or dismiss or patronize their statements and expressions. Though formally included in a forum or process, people may find that their claims are not taken seriously and may believe that they are not treated with equal respect. The dominant mood may find their ideas or modes of expression silly or simple, and not worthy of consideration. (Young, 2002: 55)

Indeed, Young suggests that these forms of internal exclusion often occur even within progressive democratic exercises, such as when a cross-section of the public are invited to deliberate as members of a citizens' jury or deliberative poll. Because such participatory exercises privilege a certain kind of rational, dispassionate argumentation, they inadvertently silence certain forms of experiential testimony. In seeking to promote an atmosphere of civility, organizers of such 'democratic' exercises can fall into the trap of expecting all participants to possess a shared notion of what constitutes reason, decorum and the common good. Like in the New England town meetings studied by Jane Mansbridge (1983) in which culturally non-conforming 'outsiders' tended to be classified as disruptive and best excluded from proceedings, the price of normative consensus can too often be cultural homogeneity.

Faced with the risk of democracy being undermined by exclusionary practices, Young sets out three ways in which the invitation to participate in democratic politics could be made more attractive and meaningful to the widest range of people. The first entails gestures of acknowledgement. Shorthand summaries of Young's proposal tend to focus upon the importance of greeting people when they arrive at political meetings, but her suggestion is rather broader than that. She is advocating the development of a psychological ethos of recognition through which the substantive communication of ideas is rooted in a commitment to interpersonal attunement. In short, it is when people feel able to go beyond speaking *at* one another and take the time to speak *with* one another, as if their presence really matters, that they stand the best chance of communicating as equals. Acknowledgement entails not just noticing or hearing the other but also looking and listening out for them. It is a gesture of proactive recognition.

Second, Young makes a case for the value of rhetorical expression that is rooted in the particularities of situated experience. Rather than advocating rhetoric as a form of pedagogical regulation, her purpose here is to countenance a pluralistic range of expressive vocabularies, tones and gestures. She is particularly concerned to legitimize styles of speech which are overtly emotional. As discussed in Chapter 1, these have tended to be disparaged by the guardians of the hyper-rationalist public sphere. When people begin to speak with feeling about how it is to experience life from positions that are not white, male or middle-class, they are vulnerable to being labelled as rhetorically over-heated or theatrical. Young (2002: 64) retorts that

> The only remedy for the dismissiveness with which some political expressions are treated on grounds that they are too emotional, dramatic or figurative is to notice that any discursive argument and content is embodied in situated style and rhetoric. Rhetoric, then, becomes a feature of expression to which we ought to attend in our engagement with one another, rather than an aspect of expression we try to bracket in order to be truly rational.

Third, Young (2002: 71) argues for the value of narrative 'as a means of giving voice to kinds of experience which often go unheard'. Storytelling enables people who face common problems to recognize their affinity and people who have never faced, or even imagined, such problems to empathize with those facing them. Narratives perform the important performative function of connecting sequences of real events with a view to expressing their meaning. As Hayden White (1980: 14) puts it, narrativity is 'a function of the impulse to moralize reality'. Unlike the rational-world paradigm, which infers that only through rigorous scrutiny of factual evidence and procedurally appropriate argumentation can 'truth' be found, narrativity takes a pragmatic and pluralistic approach to the establishment of meaning. As Lance Bennett and Murray Edelman (1985: 160) put it,

> The creation of a social world through narrative is . . . compelling because there are always conflicting stories – sometimes two, sometimes more – competing for acceptance in politics. The awareness that every acceptance of a narrative involves the rejection of others makes the issues politically and personally vital. In a critical sense, the differences among competing narratives gives all of them their meaning.

All three of Young's proposals for democratizing political engagement are directly relevant to the theme of this book. But whereas Young's primary concern is to outline a 'normative ideal of democracy as a process of communication among citizens and public officials, where they make proposals and criticize one another, and aim to persuade one another of the best solution to collective problems' (1985: 52), the focus of this book is on everyday exchanges that people have with one another when they are not making collective decisions, participating in policy consultations or even maintaining a sustained discussion. This calls for a different way of thinking about communication, focusing more on habitual social practice than sanctioned institutional protocol. It is one thing to try to incorporate innovative features of inclusiveness and equality into formal processes of public participation and deliberation, but quite another to reshape practices of everyday political talk that can take place anywhere, typically surfacing and fading with casual ephemerality. While such embryonic agonistic moments cannot be fashioned by procedural reform, they can be exposed to critical political reflection.

One of the most important contributions to social understanding and practice that has been made by feminist theorists like Iris Young has been to acknowledge the significance of seemingly casual and personal micro-exchanges in relation to the exercise of social power (see also Elshtain, 1993; Gilligan, 1993; Pateman, 2018). Thanks to these theorists it is now widely recognized that the locally personal is intrinsically political and that macro-politics cannot be fair or just without respecting micro-feelings. By insisting that people can be oppressed by the ways that they are spoken to, gestured towards and casually misrepresented at the most local level, feminists have discredited the disingenuous claim that power and its abuses can only ever be substantial at the macro-structural level. The pernicious forms that micro-exchanges take can be aggressive, diminishing and enduringly harmful. While everyday political talk cannot be reshaped by design, in the ways that Iris Young proposes for more formal democratic activities, it would be a mistake to ignore what happens to people when they give expression to their political thoughts and feelings within informal interpersonal contexts. For, it is in precisely such mundane contexts that people make their way, often stumblingly, from being lone actors to intersubjectively attuned political agents. If we are to make sense of what has gone wrong with political discourse, it is to practices of everyday talk that we must turn and in particular to those moments of communicative interaction in which intersubjectivity is realized or stymied.

Becoming intersubjective

Almost everyone agrees that the health of our democracy depends upon vibrant, reflective, inclusive and consequential political talk. Hardly anyone agrees on precisely what we mean by 'our democracy'. As a constitutional arrangement, democracy comprises procedures for pursuing public interests, securing rights and making and enforcing decisions, but these in themselves are insufficient to stimulate or sustain the kind of subjective engagement that is necessary if 'the demos' is to rule itself in any meaningful sense. For that to happen people must possess the confidence and capacity to exercise democratic voice, both at the macro-level of determining decisions that affect them and at the micro-level of everyday reflexivity. Unless democracy is grounded in practical experience it is in danger of being seen as a tokenistic symbol – as it has rightly been regarded in regimes such as the 'people's democracies' where there was not only a failure to encourage the right to speak freely about politics but also a brutal effort to stamp it out.

Defenders of proceduralist versions of liberal democracy have tended to regard political talk as a functional opportunity for citizens to search the marketplace of ideas with a view to discovering what is in their best interest and then promote that self-interest as effectively as possible (McClurg, 2006; Kim and Kim, 2008; Mansbridge et al., 2010; Weeden and Kurzban, 2016; Conover and Miller, 2018). Conceived in this way as an individualist endeavour to maximize social advantage, political talk is reduced to a strategic act of information-seeking or network-influence enhancement. But as social animals, humans are motivated by more than the rational pursuit of self-interest. Quite often people talk about politics because they feel a need to be understood or because they find it hard to contain their feelings or because they value the person or people with whom they are speaking or because they believe that they can articulate ideas in a way that deserves to be heard or because they cannot bear the thought of others dominating a discussion or because they have experiences to talk about that they believe might alter people's perspectives. People speak out politically because they like their own voice and despite the fact that they are embarrassed by their own voice. They speak because they feel entitled to and because they feel a need to challenge others who doubt whether they are entitled to. They speak to affirm that 'This is me speaking', but also to surprise people by refusing to conform to their known identity. Political talk can be instrumental, but it can also be much more than that. Just as talk between people is a fundamental feature of the networks that bind society, so does it provide the expressive tone and reciprocal ties that embed politics within the domain of communal experience. It is a practice of attunement between disjointed, but correlative, states of feeling.

Considered as a social activity through which people learn, rehearse and enact political agency, political talk can be understood as a precondition for the emergence of relations of intersubjective recognition. Axel Honneth, following John Dewey, defines a democratic public as a group of people who are faced with a social challenge that can only be addressed by their establishing an intersubjective relationship:

> Social action unfolds in forms of interaction whose consequences in the simple case affect only those immediately involved; but as soon as those not involved see themselves affected by the consequences of such interaction, there emerges from their perspective the need for joint control of the corresponding actions either by their cessation or by their promotion. . . . The term 'public' is attributed to that sphere of social action that a social group can successfully prove to be in need of general regulation because encroaching consequences are being generated; and, accordingly, a 'public' consists of the circle of citizens who, on the basis of a jointly experienced concern, share the conviction that they have to turn to the rest of society for the purposes of administratively controlling the relevant interaction (Honneth, 1998: 774)

Talking performs several roles in this process of constituting democratic publics. First, it is a means by which those who are 'immediately involved' in a problem acknowledge one another and begin to coordinate their concerns.

Second, through wider social talk, people who originally think of themselves as 'not involved' begin to see that they might be affected by the problem as it unfolds. Third, political talk becomes a practice through which 'a jointly experienced concern' is rhetorically constructed as an issue that can be more widely recognized as political. Finally, talk might turn strategic, focusing on ways of responding to, resisting or 'controlling' what has become established as a shared public problem. This sequence of intersubjective public-building might occur discretely over a protracted period or through messily overlapping stages; styles of communicative interaction might vary as talk moves through different environments and is mediated by technologies of circulation; shared problems might be categorized as being manifestly political in some cases and seemingly interpersonal or pre-political in others. In short, the realization of democratic intersubjectivity is a dialectical process through which political subjectivities are both formed and exercised.

Failure to develop practices and habits of democratic intersubjectivity can be fateful. Let us return briefly to our discussion at the beginning of Chapter 1 about the 'national conversation' that was supposed to take place in the run-up to the UK's Brexit referendum. Finding themselves involved as key participants in this 'national conversation', people had to think hard about what it might mean to organize and sustain an energetic and rewarding political debate comprising millions of separate but interconnected interpersonal conversations. Most people already had a strong sense of what a futile, uninformed, cacophonous political conversation would sound like, but the formula for a productive one seemed rather elusive. No manual existed. There were few obvious precedents to draw upon. It was hardly surprising, then, that after the referendum was over few people felt that their reasons for voting had been properly understood and almost everyone felt that they had not been listened to by the other side. Indeed, they were right: when pollsters asked both pro-Brexit and pro-Leave supporters whether they would be prepared to enter into a conversation with one another 'respondents readily expressed prejudice toward the out-group and favouritism toward the in-group' (Hobolt et al., 2018). It seemed as if Britain had proved itself to be a political echo chamber filled with the kind of shouty, brash reverberations that one might have expected to witness at a bad-tempered 1970s football match. The absence during the referendum process of any well-conceived attempt to urge political opponents to listen to one another, let alone modify their viewpoints, resulted in acute polarization, with most voters only speaking and listening to others who thought as they did. It was as if, once people had reached a position in relation to the referendum question, listening to the other side was regarded as a wholly irrelevant gesture.

Scholars and commentators have expressed deep concerns about the quality of the national debate that preceded the Brexit vote. In its analysis of national discourse in the run-up to the referendum, the Electoral Reform Society (Brett, 2016: 8) observed that 'There was a marked lack of 'real conversations' between the campaigns and the voters – genuine two-way discussions that offered proper deliberation' and concluded that 'most of the information people received was largely one-directional, with no sense of dynamic two-way debate involved' (2016: 21). The Constitution Unit's (Renwick and Palese, 2018: 171) study of lessons to be learned from the referendum noted that 'Having said he wanted a referendum, Cameron . . . made no suggestion that there should be any inclusive discussion of what kind of relationship with the EU voters in the UK wanted'. Consequently, 'debate during the referendum campaign was of often miserable quality'. We are not focusing here on an obscure or trivial political judgement. Many believe that no peacetime electorate has ever before been invited to arrive at such a momentous decision about its national future. To have done so on the basis of a 'miserable quality' of public discussion is very worrying.

Much has been written about what the Brexit decision was really about (Shipman, 2017; O'Toole, 2018; Dorling and Tomlinson, 2019); the failure of the mass media to hold political leaders to account and provide adequate information to voters during the referendum campaign (Deacon et al., 2016; Cadwalladr, 2017; Gavin, 2018; Zelizer, 2018); the dire quality of online debate about Brexit (Howard and Kollanyi, 2016; Lilleker and Bonacci, 2017; Del Vicario et al., 2017; Bastos and Mercea, 2019) and the pervasive atmosphere of 'post-truth' that surrounded the referendum (Coleman, 2018; Bennett and Livingston, 2018; Waisbord, 2018). In contrast to this wealth of critical analysis, hardly any studies have been published exploring how people discussed Brexit with one another face to face in domestic, workplace and leisure settings. And yet that is where the vast majority of discussions and arguments about Brexit took place. The precise relationship between these micro-interactions and the larger public and media spheres is a matter for empirical and theoretical investigation. But it cannot be disputed that most of the discursive action in the months leading up to and following the Brexit decision did not take place through the mass media or online. Why is this important?

The health of democracy depends upon the quality and inclusiveness of political talk. That does not mean that most people need to engage regularly in political discussion. As a social practice, political talk is something that everyone needs to be able to do, even if people are rarely inclined to do it. Rather like knowing how to help someone in a medical emergency or what to do when facing a red traffic light, having the basic capacity to speak up, listen to others and arrive at shared understandings when a critical political decision is being made that is likely to fundamentally affect your long-term future should be regarded as basic civic capabilities. If enough people lack these capabilities society is vulnerable. If there is a critical mass of people who feel too unconfident to engage in a democratic debate – or, just as bad, so over-confident that they prefer to arrive at democratically binding decisions without needing to participate in democratic discussion with anyone else – the outcome could be catastrophic, resulting in bad public judgements or unjust ones that exclude the reflective input of groups likely to be affected by them.

While there is general agreement that possessing a political voice and having the confidence to use it is a precondition of any kind of meaningful democratic citizenship, there is a scarcity of detail about what this actually entails. What follows is an attempt to develop an evaluative language for thinking about interpersonal political talk. Three basic communicative actions are considered:

- *expressing* what one thinks and feels in ways that are meaningful
- being heard by, and *listening* to, others with a view to sharing meaning;
- *working through* the ramifications of contested meanings with an openness to arriving at revised perspectives.

The first two of these actions are often referred to atheoretically, as if expressing and listening were hard-wired, natural human activities. The third, 'working through', tends to be confined to psychoanalytical explorations of deep angst rather than accounts of political disagreement. My aim in the following three sections is to problematize these basic communicative actions by asking how we might explain their significance and relatedness to an imaginary being who has no awareness of what these practices involve; how we might become more confident in appraising their normative character; and how the recurrent anxieties that emerged in my interviews might be allayed by establishing a more reflexive account of what is going on when political talk occurs.

(i) Expressing

There are two silences. One when no word is spoken. The other when perhaps a torrent of language is being employed. This speech is speaking of a language locked beneath it. That is its continual reference. The speech we hear is an indication of that which we don't hear. It is a necessary avoidance, a violent, sly, anguished or mocking smoke screen which keeps the other in its place. When true silence falls, we are still left with echo, but are nearer nakedness. One way of looking at speech is to say that it is a constant stratagem to cover nakedness. (Pinter, 2013: 14)

When people give voice to their political thoughts and feelings they invariably say less or more than they had intended. In saying less, the unsaid simmers beneath articulation, often comprising what Christopher Bollas (1987: 263) calls 'the unthought known': those latent sensations that shape disposition without being able to express it as commutable sense. The unsaid reverberates not only through pregnant silences, hesitant pauses and random stuttering but also through the employment of euphemistic and metaphorical strategies which protect raw and unformed feeling from the riskiness of public disclosure and scrutiny. Often, when people seem to be speaking about the micro-biographies of their everyday lives, they are shooting at the shadows of apparently impermeable social structures and codes of political exclusion. And often, when people seem to be engaging with the well-rehearsed scripts of macro-politics, they are really reflecting upon their own position in the global topography of social power. When people say more about politics than they had intended to, voice becomes a channel for leakage, whereby apparently innocent words, phrases, tones and gestures 'give off' (Goffman, 1959) clues to subliminal, but unveiled resentments, disappointments, anxieties, fears and fantasies.

People do not simply exchange political views in the unscrupulous manner in which operators on the money market trade currencies. They invest emotionally in positions, placing their feelings where their mouths are. Self-expression is not simply a matter of finding the right words. It is a matter of finding the right feelings. One of the greatest misunderstandings in relation to political talk is that people know what they want to express before they start to speak. Were that so, speaking would be a technical act of simple transmission through which pre-existing thoughts and affects were loaded and fired off into public space. The psychoanalyst Donald Stern (2009: 326) describes how 'unscripted speech' emerges when 'there is something in mind that wants expressing':

This process, which usually takes split-seconds or seconds, is unpredictable, messy, widely distributed in the body and mind and usually involves conscious and unconscious bodily happenings. This non-linear process is perhaps what makes us most human. It would include how the word search gets performed, with what deliberation or rising excitement, with what burst of enthusiasm or calm when it 'catches' a word. It is a process that can rush forward, hesitate, stop, restart gently, etc. It can express itself in various dynamic forms of vitality. It is quintessentially a process of soft assembly – a continual improvisation to fit found reality.

This sense of fraught tension between nuanced feeling and available language was evocatively captured by T. S. Eliot:

> So here I am...
> Trying to use words, and every attempt
> Is a wholly new start, and a different kind of failure
> Because one has only learnt to get the better of words
> For the thing one no longer has to say, or the way in which
> One is no longer disposed to say it. And so each venture
> Is a new beginning, a raid on the inarticulate
> With shabby equipment always deteriorating
> In the general mess of imprecision of feeling,
> Undisciplined squads of emotion

Pursuing a similar point, the philosopher Sue Campbell (1997) argues that most people are unable to name many of the feelings that they experience. Feelings exist as powerful, but ineffable, frames, shaping perception and belief in ways that are typically beyond unambiguous classification. Campbell argues that articulation, defined as 'performing the appropriate acts ... to give something the form by which it may be recognized' (105) is not simply a matter of translating thoughts and feelings into words. The shape of experience is mediated through the expressive possibilities that are available. In a complex and groundbreaking analysis, Campbell makes two claims that have an important bearing on the sense in which articulation is politically shaped. The first is that

> When people express a feeling, they are trying to make clear the meaning or significance of something in the context of how they view their lives. When we identify, recognize or respond to behavior as experience of feeling, we are attempting to understand or interpret how something is significant for a particular person. (126)

Indeed, the political significance that is attached to any experience is to a great extent determined by the expressive resources that are available to describe it. Forms of oppression, for example, are less likely to be recognized as injustices when words and phrases that adequately characterize them do not exist. Feeling abused by sexist language is almost impossible to communicate if there is no socially understood notion of 'sexist language'. Words and other resources of articulation frame experience. This leads to Campbell's second important claim: that the extent to which feelings 'can be either successfully communicated to others or can be subject to suppression, distortion and manipulation' (4) is a matter of political contestation. Specifically, she argues that 'people have considerable power over our feelings through their acts of interpretation' and 'those who already occupy positions of social power will interpret our feelings through emotion categories that serve *their* needs and interests' (147; Campbell's emphasis). It follows from this that 'Once we do recognize these facts we may then be forced into a position where our best political option is to gain control of the categories through which we are interpreted and to change the meaning of certain emotion concepts through our revisionary participation in practices associated with these categories' (147/8). When, for example, the #MeToo movement emerged, its first task was to translate forms of experience and feeling that had hitherto been labelled as 'exceptional incidents' or 'just part of the casting-couch culture' or 'over-friendly flirting' into unequivocal accounts of harassment and assault. Behaviour that had up until then been institutionally prevalent and covered up had to be named in ways that would counter claims that women were merely being 'over-sensitive' or 'naïve' for feeling violated. Because politics is not simply a matter of arid dialectic disputation but is rooted in the affectively laden dramas of experience, finding modes of articulation through which people are able to reclaim and report their experiences is crucial.

It is not enough, however, simply to express what one thinks or how one feels, without considering its effects on listeners. O'Keefe and McCornack's (1987) distinction between expressive and rhetorical talk, discussed in Chapter 1 is relevant here. In their theoretical model, expressive speakers simply '"dump" their current mental state' on listeners without systematically altering it 'in the service of achieving effects'. They assume that if what they are saying is valid it will be accepted by right-thinking people. For rhetorical speakers, on the other hand, 'all meaning is treated as a matter of social negotiation'. They express themselves with a view to framing the political reception of what they want to say. Realizing that their addressees may well have a political interest in adopting positions of cognitive or emotional dissonance, disingenuity or ridicule, rhetorical speakers set out to interrupt such responses by gaining control of the categories through which their expression is interpreted. This entails not simply dumping their opinions on listeners but making claims about how things should be named; what things really mean; what is true and what is false; and which experiences matter.

When people are repeatedly unable to find words, phrases and gestures that will make their experiences interpretable to others they are likely to suffer loss of epistemic confidence. Acknowledging the hermeneutic barriers that routinely thwart the uptake of certain messages, they begin to tell their own stories, outline their own opinions and relate their own feelings with the assumption that they will probably be misunderstood. When conventional acts of interpretation are recalcitrantly insensitive and undermining, the challenge of translating private feelings into public terms seems too overwhelming to pursue. The right to name their own feelings is taken away from them. A woman who has been patronized might feel anger but find it difficult to sustain that description in the face of interpreters who insist that she is really acting haughtily or bitterly or too intensely. Becoming politically articulate entails a refusal to come to terms with this kind of hermeneutic injustice, defined by Miranda Fricker (2006: 100) as 'the injustice of having some significant area of one's social experience obscured from collective understanding owing to a structural prejudice in the collective hermeneutic resource'. In the face of such injustice some people feel discouraged from speaking about what matters to them for fear of hitting walls of cultural amnesia, incomprehension or scepticism. Having the courage to defend one's feelings and identity in the face of an interpretive community that claims authority over them is therefore a precondition of articulacy.

Contrary to the romantic notion of self-expression as an authentic baring of the unique self, what one says can never fully reflect who one is and what one means. As Judith Butler (2005: 26) puts it, 'the account of myself that I give in discourse never fully expresses or carries this living self', for when

> I give an account *to* someone . . . I am compelled to give the account away, to send it off, to be dispossessed of it at the very moment that I establish it as *my* account. No account takes place outside the structure of address, even if the addressee remains implicit and unnamed, anonymous and unspecified.

It is in the medial space of incipient intersubjectivity that the dynamics of political talk are played out. Speakers can never fully control what they say or how it is interpreted, for, as Pocock (1973: 37) reminds us, language is 'a medium which cannot be wholly controlled by any single or isolable agency'. Effective political expression depends upon a metacommunicative search for ways of controlling the terms of reception. Its starting assumption is the probability of misinterpretation. Its strategic fixation is to determine the terms on which meanings and intentions are understood. When people say that political talk is rhetorically loaded, they are right, not in the sense that all politics is about underhand manipulation, but because the adjective 'political' implies a heightened sense of attention to communicative effects. Political articulation arises precisely because individuals and groups have diverse experiences, values and affective moods which distract them from acknowledging a shared reality.

At its best, politics translates across divergent realities. The most effective political communicators are pragmatic cultural brokers who are adept at fostering dispositional alliances that transcend narrowly subjective perspectives. As Ronald Burt (2005: 11) notes, 'The value of a relationship is not defined inside the relationship; it is defined by the social context around the relationship.' Political self-expression is most effectively intersubjective when speakers apply a dextrous sensibility towards and between contexts.

The contemporary political domain has become radically unsettled by disagreement about appropriate ways of expressing disagreement. At the elite level this has tended to manifest itself in an agitated conflict between proponents of the old rules of democratic decorum and brash new leaders who are more than happy to abandon the protocols of civility in order to perform their 'authentic selves' through narcissistic displays of method-acting. Ugly and dangerous to observe though this clash of communicative styles often is, it reveals a deep normative uncertainty about how best to perform political subjectivity. Generic performative practices of dutiful political citizenship have fallen by the wayside in recent decades (Bennett et al., 2011). Popular political discourse has come to be increasingly framed by personal, experiential narratives rather than partisan or ideological attachments; affective expressiveness rather than the privileging of cognitive reason; and the availability of a much broader, more pluralistic range of communicative styles than were hitherto admissible within the political domain. This is not to suggest that partisanship, ideological commitment, rationalism or political genre have disappeared, but that they are no longer unconditionally hegemonic. In a world of phone-ins, online forums, 'reality' formats, TV debates dominated by questioning from 'ordinary people' and popular valorization of the qualities of sincerity and authenticity, forms of political articulation are no longer amenable to the strictures once associated with civic duty and legitimate eloquence. This movement towards a pragmatics of 'situated style' (Young, 2002: 64) and cross-cutting discourse (Mutz, 2002) has rendered the political domain more porous than it once was, and less aesthetically rigid.

As we have seen, this moment of cultural flux has accentuated performative uncertainties. More inclusive – some might say democratized – attitudes towards political talk are in tension with embedded prejudices about speakers' social positions and their attendant cognitive, emotional and moral capacities.

Popular tolerance for more localized, vernacular styles of political expression has extended the range of ways in which people talk about politics, but when some of these ways are frowned upon or even suppressed there are suspicions that 'political correctness' is serving as a form of soft censorship. The open expression of political emotion is less likely to be immediately dismissed as hysteria than it once was, but there are still well-rehearsed concerns about the value and validity of non-propositional political pronouncements. In short, practices are in transition and cultural instability prompts loud contestation. Political talk about how to do political talk is now at the very centre of the political agenda.

(ii) Listening

> When someone with the authority of a teacher, say, describes the world and you are not in it, there is a moment of psychic disequilibrium, as if you looked into a mirror and saw nothing. Yet you know you exist and others like you, that this is a game done with mirrors. It takes some strength of soul – and not just individual strength, but collective understanding – to resist this void . . . and to stand up, demanding to be seen and heard. (Rich, 1986: 199)

Listening is a social practice that is learned, no less than speaking. People are taught how to pay attention, sometimes in quite coercive ways, within the confines of educational institutions. Introduced at an early age to an economy of attention in which certain voices (elders, educators and employers) have to be listened to, while other voices (advertisers, spiritual leaders, elected representatives) compete to be heard and most voices (the majority of people in the world) are unlikely ever to be heard, people learn that the attention economy is profoundly unequal. Codes of recognition depend upon the regular misrecognition of voices that are deemed to be insignificant or, in Rancière's terminology, mere noise.

Nobody has ever rioted in the street because they were being listened to too much. Nobody ever takes offence because an interlocutor is too eager to make sense of what they are trying to say. It is *not* being listened to that is bruising. When one is not recognized because one's interpretation is sure not to matter, political conflict shifts from the validity of arguments to the recognition of subjects. The struggle for respectful attention becomes the paramount consideration.

Listening as a social practice entails an awareness that attention is necessarily selective. It is impossible to attend to everything. As Jonathan Crary (2001: 24/5) states, 'Attention as a process of selection necessarily meant that perception was an activity of *exclusion*, of rendering parts of a perceptual field unperceived'. He quotes William James's (2001: 62; James, 1890: 19) observation that 'Each of us literally chooses, by way of attending to things, what sort of universe he shall appear to himself to inhabit'. Political expression is a call for attention within a crowded field of communication, inviting listeners to choose to attend to one thing rather than another. These selective choices are inescapably political.

Learning to listen entails coming to terms with not being listened to, even when one thinks one has something to say that ought to be heard. Just as speaking up in public takes courage, it demands a certain bravery to call out cursory inattention. Refusing to be routinely ignored as if one does not exist is a political response to the embedded disparities of the attention economy. But it is rare. More commonly, the experience of being overlooked and unheard generates resentment rather than resistance. Resentment spurs convictions that those doing the ignoring are not worth talking to anyway; that they could never understand one's experiences and are secretly contemptuous of them; that theirs is a language of mendacity and hypocrisy; and that only by remaining at a distance from their cultural power is it possible to avoid the worst risks of humiliation. Such resentment is intensified when it is surrounded by what often seem like disingenuous claims by elites to be highly committed to listening to what 'ordinary people' have to say. From community-wide policy consultations that are completely decoupled from decision-making to talking exercises geared towards catharsis rather than efficacy, when attention is staged as political performance it is more likely to exacerbate suspicion on the part of the routinely unheard than to assuage their umbrage. People recognize experientially that there is a crucial difference between being heard (often through forms of impersonal surveillance) and being truly listened to. And this sense of scepticism seeps through to the culture of interpersonal political talk, where haughty interlocutors are perceived as having been educated with a view to exercising selective inattention. Much political talk is overshadowed by this kind of mistrust, often dooming it to failure even before the first words have been uttered.

People become politically attuned to the pretence of pseudo-listening. Leonard Waks's (2010) distinction between cataphatic listening, which is motivated by a will to hear what is already known, and apophatic listening, motivated by a sensibility towards thoughts and sensations that cannot be readily named or categorized, is relevant here. Cataphatic listening tends to be confirmatory, as when people listen out for statements that reinforce what they already think or for flawed logic and weak evidence offered in support of arguments that might challenge their own. The cataphatic listeners attend defensively, so busily guarding their own truth from confutation that they are highly unlikely to appreciate the broad meaning or intention of what is being said to them. Apophatic listening entails an openness to being surprised or even contradicted.

When political talk moves beyond a functional speaker–listener relationship and becomes dialogical, participants transcend a solely denotative focus upon what is being said and begin asking metacommunicative questions about why and how things are being said and the ways in which their expressive forms forge relationships between communicators. Typical metacommunicative questions asked by people engaged in political dialogue are 'Why is this person saying this? Why say it to me? What sort of person do they think of themselves as being? What do they want me to know about them? What is different about me now that I have witnessed this act of telling? What is it about the teller that will be different now that I have listened to her?' In short, dialogue depends upon ongoing reflection upon the dynamics of intersubjective orientation. This necessitates a particular kind of listening which goes beyond simply appraising the 'validity' of propositions and attends to the experiences and intentions that shape political positions and utterances. If, as I am suggesting, the quality of listening is a crucial determinant of the vitality of political discourse, much depends upon how well political talkers are willing to reflect upon the ways in which their relationships are politically framed.

The discursive failings of the Brexit referendum – and of many other 'democratic events' across the world in which echo-effects trumped reflective dialogue – reflect a normalization of pathological listening, with many, claiming to think and speak in the name of 'the people', hearing what they want to hear, while others, cast as non-people, are deemed undeserving of a hearing. This has led some political and communication theorists to suggest that democracies are now facing a crisis of listening (Bickford, 1996; Dreher, 2017; Bassel, 2017; Morrell, 2018; Macnamara, 2018; Hendriks et al., 2019). For too long, they argue, political communication has been regarded as a message-oriented genre (Brown, 1981), revolving around the efficient establishment of linear pathways between proactive speakers and reactive listeners. Such a conception reduces attentiveness to a passive and unreflective exercise of message consumption, leaving speech as the central, generative act of communication. Andrew Dobson (2014: 2) captures the essence of this perspective:

> Although much prized in daily conversation, good listening has been almost
> completely ignored in political conversation, and particularly the form we know
> as democracy. Speaking has gathered the lion's share of attention, both in terms

of the skills to be developed and the ways in which we should understand what improving it might entail.

Dobson and the new wave of 'democratic listening' theorists and practitioners are right to recognize this lacuna in political communication theory and practice. To think of listening as a subsidiary element of communication, functionally distinct from speaking, is to foster an illusion that discussion is primarily a matter of message dissemination. In contrast to this conception of political talk stands the dialogical perspective, most famously elaborated by Bakhtin for whom communication is an event that can never be reduced to the controlling intentions of a speaker. For Bakhtin (1986: 68), the work of listening is active and interpretive from the outset:

> The fact is that when the listener perceives and understands the meaning . . . of speech, he simultaneously takes an active, responsive attitude towards it. He either agrees or disagrees with it (completely or partially), augments it, applies it, prepares for its execution and so on. And the listener adopts this responsive attitude for the entire duration of the process of listening and understanding, from the very beginning – sometimes literally from the speaker's first word.

In dialogical talk there are no fixed speaking or listening roles, but ceaseless interplay between intentions, meanings and interpretations. In contrast to the idea of 'political conversation' as strategic interaction, dialogue envisages attentive transaction.

Genuine dialogue starts with the primary impulse to seek the attention of another person. As Martin Buber put it, 'the fundamental fact of human existence is . . . rooted in one being turning to another as another, as this particular other being, in order to communicate with it in a sphere which is common to them but which reaches out beyond the special sphere of each'. Turning towards another person constitutes an invitation to enter into a form of communication through which interlocutors are able to become meaningfully present to one another. Buber (1947: 19) states that

> There is genuine dialogue . . . where each of the participants really has in mind the other or others in their present and particular being and turns to them with the intention of establishing a living mutual relation between himself [or herself] and them. There is technical dialogue, which is prompted solely by the need of objective understanding. And there is monologue which is disguised as dialogue, in which two or more [people] meeting in space speak with [themselves] in strangely tortuous and circuitous ways.

Missing from monological and merely technical dialogical communication is any inclination to reach out towards others in their biographical particularity. In such circumstances, antagonists talk past one another, standing their ground, but failing to inhabit a common ground. Before people can meaningfully disagree, they have to truly meet. Buber referred to this meeting ground as the 'between', a relational space that, paradoxically, would be less likely to emerge (or matter) 'between two friends or intimate partners' than 'between two persons who profoundly disagree with each other and yet struggle to make each other present even as they stand their own ground' (Czubaroff, 2000: 181). It is within this transitional space that communicative reciprocity can be rehearsed, even in the midst of the fiercest disagreement. Buber's 'between' bears a close conceptual resemblance to psychoanalytic notions of 'potential space' as 'a resting-place for the individual engaged in the perpetual human task of keeping inner and outer reality separate yet inter-related' (Winnicott, 1953: 90) and the 'third' as 'a field of intersection between two subjectivities' (Benjamin, 2017: 34). Whatever we may choose to call this intermediary, dialogical space, without it there is little hope for the kind of moments of meeting in which interactants do not merely encounter one another as inimical subjectivities, but find themselves in an intersubjective relationship, however unresolved.

As they spoke about their experiences of political talk, several of my interviewees recalled experiences of political disagreement as feeling like a standoff between parallel monologues. In such situations they felt not only unheard but also unrecognized. It was as if their experiences did not exist. For Axel Honneth (2007: 71), to be unrecognized as an agent in one's own right is to be excluded from meaningful communication, for 'the normative presupposition of all communicative action is to be seen in the acquisition of social recognition: subjects encounter each other within the parameters of the reciprocal expectation that they be given recognition as moral persons and for their social achievements'. Becoming politically visible, argues Judith Butler (2001: 23–4), depends upon 'a set of norms concerning what will and will not constitute recognizability'. In short, practices of listening are never neutral, but constitute a normative filter to democratic inclusion.

The task of democratic subjects, then, is to recognize one another. The psychoanalyst Donnel Stern (2010: 111) – not to be confused with Daniel Stern – goes to the crux of what it means to recognize and be recognized when he states that 'We need to feel that we exist in the other's mind, and that our existence has a kind of continuity in that mind; and we need to feel that the other in whose mind we exist is emotionally responsive to us, that he or she cares about what we experience and how we feel about it'. In such moments of focused acknowledgement people accept that it is precisely because of their differences – of experiences, interests, feelings and values – that the effort to understand one another is worth undertaking. They then commit to the hard work of translating their views into a language that can be comprehended by the other, while at the same time trying to make sense not only of what the other person says but also of what they mean by what they say. This entails generously interpretive listening – a willingness to work through what is being said with a view to engaging with it beyond the calculus of exchange.

(iii) Working through

Democracy needs a new way to talk.

(Lasswell, 1941)

There are moments in history when conventional ways of talking about things that matter seem inadequate. In the midst of a world that seemed vulnerable to the abominable rhetoric of Hitler, Stalin and their followers, many democrats, including the political scientist Harold Lasswell, felt that only by discovering a new way of talking to one another could people hope to protect the norms that stood between them and barbarism. Lasswell (1941: 89) came to the conclusion that

> Existing methods of debate . . . do not deal successfully with the flow of words. They allow words to contribute to public confusion, not clarification. . . . We need methods of introducing discipline into the handling of language in public discussion.

His solution was ingenuously simplistic:

> Someone should be charged with the responsibility for clarifying what is said. The job of the clarifier would be to make words make sense. . . . The clarifier will not take sides. He will not express personal preferences. He will perform a strictly technical function. (90)

In providing a purely impartial interpretation of publicly significant meaning, the 'clarifier' would put an end to the confusion of language by offering imperious certainty in place of messy contestation. Although Lasswell's main aim was for the 'clarifier' to provide authoritative elucidation of the terms of *public* debate within settings such as policy hearings or community forums, he seemed also to imagine that the role could be applied to the arbitration of private disagreements:

> The idea of the clarifier can be extended to all occasions where there is collective discussion, public or not. (92)

Lasswell believed that a key function of 'the clarifier' would be to protect political talk 'from the interference of non-rational tendencies' (93). This would involve 'patient study' of the ways in which people think and speak with a view to introducing 'many ingenious ideas for improving the strength of the rational elements' (95). The notion that epistemological neutrality could counter the intensifying mid-twentieth-century climate of totalitarian mendacity was naïve. But faced with increasingly normalized forms of insidious political talk in which, as George Orwell put it, lies were made to sound truthful, murder respectable and pure wind given an appearance of solidity, the imaginary of a disinterested public interpreter reflected an edifying impulse to redeem the public sphere.

In seeking to render political talk invulnerable to interpretive unsettlement by applying a universal standard of semantic meaning, Lasswell was pursuing a favourite objective of the seventeenth-century natural philosophers. Francis Bacon (2011: 518) had warned against 'the juggleries and charms of words' that 'seduce and forcibly disturb . . . judgement'. The remedy was to be found in the eradication of semantic ambiguity through the emancipation of expression from rhetorical framing. The natural philosophers' ideal was to establish an impersonal, decontextualized political language, abstracted from the particularities of contingency. As John Locke put it, 'Words become general by being made the signs of general ideas; and ideas become general by separating them from the circumstances of time and place.' This ambition to estrange political talk from the rhythms of everyday sociality provoked one of the recurrent anxieties expressed by my interviewees: that the political genre appears to privilege homogenizing abstraction over the idiosyncrasies of private experience and unique feeling.

All of these attempts to proscribe polysemous incertitude by insisting upon a universally standardized lexicon fail to acknowledge the crucial point that meanings do not reside within the dictionary definitions of words and phrases, but emerge out of intentions, habits and interpretations that are rarely fully settled at the moment of utterance. Because what they really mean is not always clear or fully resolved to the individuals and groups involved in political talk, one of the most valuable democratic endeavours they can undertake is to talk about what it is that they are really trying to talk about; work at getting to the core of what actually matters to them; and be candid about their competencies and incapacities to articulate thoughts, feelings, intentions, positions, propositions and questions. This entails engaging in a process of ongoing 'working through'.

As the term is being used here, 'working through' refers to the practice of thinking and talking about a matter over time with a view to developing insight into what it is really about and why it matters. It entails a commitment to recognizing the meaning of conflicting truth claims and minimizing misconceptions arising from resistance to available evidence. Such working through can take place over micro-seconds or over years. It is rarely a planned event or process – 'Let's work through!' – but a reflective urge, resisting the simplicity of instant judgement. As suggested by the theoretical account of agency set out in the previous chapter, people act on experiences through a combination of attention to background sense, the unfolding of present moments and the projection of hypothesized futures. It is in the passage of integration of these temporal modalities that people become attuned to experience and prompted to act upon it. This can sometimes be an introspective enterprise, conducted over a long period of time, as when someone tries to make sense of a biographically shaping experience that has to be worked through again and again before it can be interpreted in fresh ways. Or it can occur during single, scattered moments of barely registered self-reflection. From a democratic perspective, 'working through' is most significant when it is not a solitary exercise, but a joint heuristic activity providing a vital foundation to intersubjectivity by giving new meaning to notions of 'we' and 'us':

> When two people cocreate an intersubjective experience . . . the phenomenal consciousness of one overlaps and partly includes the phenomenal consciousness of the other. You have your own experience plus the other's experience of your experience as reflected in their eyes, body, tone of voice and so on. Your experience and the experience of the other need not be exactly the same. They originate from different loci and orientations. They might have slightly different colouration, form and feel. But they are similar enough that when the two experiences are mutually validated a 'consciousness' of sharing the same mental landscape arises. (D .N. Stern, 2004: 125)

Working through is not simply a quest for psychological awareness, but a crucial enabler of democratic coordination. When women who have survived domestic violence, people of colour who have experienced racism, soldiers who have experienced the trauma of war or people exposed to long-term economic deprivation begin to work through their unjust experiences together, not simply recounting them, but seeking joint clarification as to what they mean and how they should be responded to, the realization of an intersubjective relationship is not simply inspiriting, but empowering.

Democracy, if it is to be more than a constitutional formula that only touches people's lives tangentially, needs to develop a stronger sensibility towards these moments of affective grappling, stuttering word-searching, attempts to label seemingly inchoate moods and consciousness of what is really at stake in an argument. This entails turning to everyday political talk, even in its most fragmented and incoherent forms, as a site of dynamic contention – the crucial stage in political consciousness in which meaning is still open to revision through forms of working through that contrast sharply with the resoluteness of position-taking.

In a seminal article, Michael Schudson (1997) has argued that 'conversation is not the soul of democracy'. Criticizing theorists who argue that democratic legitimacy depends upon 'public conversation' (Benhabib, 1996: 74) or that managing challenging public controversies calls for a 'rhetoric of conversation' (Campbell, 2003), Schudson makes a forceful case for distinguishing between informal, spontaneous conversation and seriously democratic talk. Because 'democracy is a contrivance', he argues, 'democratic talk is not essentially spontaneous but essentially rule-governed, essentially *civil*, and unlike the kinds of conversation often held in highest esteem for their freedom and their wit, it is essentially oriented to *problem-solving*' (Schudson, 1999: 298; his italics). Unlike well-managed political discourse, which cannot be abandoned to the risks of erratic spontaneity, Schudson argues that 'conversation has no end outside itself' (1999: 299). It merely comprises comfortable encounters between social intimates who are unwilling to be troubled by the embarrassment of conflict or the burden of reaching a conclusion. Empirically, this is simply not so. As we have seen in previous chapters and know from other studies of political talk (Gamson and Gamson, 1992; Walsh, 2004: Perrin, 2009; Hochschild, 2016), people engage in political conversations with friends and with strangers, in unfocused, fragmented chats as well as intensely focused arguments. More importantly, these encounters are part of an intellectual and affective continuum which might start with a glance or a grunt and end in meticulous forensic disputation. Schudson's distaste for the lack of rules or controlled tone that characterize informal political talk is a perfectly reasonable personal choice but makes for bad normative democratic theory. In suggesting that the messy flow of extemporaneous interaction is so lacking in obvious, or even potential, clarity as to make it ineligible as real politics, Schudson sometimes seems to be yearning for the arrival of Lasswell's 'clarifier' who can explain what people mean without their needing to work through it themselves. I want to argue for the opposite position: that politics is defined by an absence of shared intelligibility and therefore disagreements have to be worked through with a view to understanding what they are about and what might be done about them.

To return to the anxieties about the contemporary quality of political talk with which this chapter began, I want now to suggest that the pathologies of public discourse that have aroused such alarm recently are most likely to be addressed by paying attention to what people are trying to achieve (and avoid) through political talk, and in particular by encouraging at every level of our democracy practices of working through. The most promising moves in this direction thus far have been made by theorists and practitioners of democratic deliberation (Dryzek, 2002; Fishkin, 2011; Parkinson and Mansbridge, 2012; Steiner, 2012; Elstub, 2014; Bachtinger et al., 2018, Bächtiger and Parkinson, 2019). What has been called the 'deliberative turn' is motivated by a desire to move beyond a head-counting democracy, based on the disembodied aggregation of secret preferences, with a view to creating spaces in which people can talk openly about where they stand in relation to issues likely to affect them, while remaining open to the possibility of changing their stances in the light of dialogue. Proponents of deliberation value talk and are not only interested in what elite actors have to say. Indeed, after the Brexit referendum in the United Kingdom sustained and rigorous attention was addressed to the possibility of arriving at future momentous national decisions (and, for that matter, working out the meaning of the last one) via some sort of deliberative citizens' assembly (Renwick et al., 2018; Gastil et al., 2018; Farrell et al., 2019; Hansard, Committee on Exiting the European Union, 24 July 2019).

While deliberation, as it has been practised in various contexts (Fishkin and Mansbridge, 2017; Suiter, 2018; Pow and Garry, 2019), is certainly a move in a more effectively democratic direction, it is open to three kinds of criticism. First, that the kind of talk valued by its advocates is overly prescriptive. With their emphasis upon expressions of sober reasoning, most deliberative events are more like the proceedings of a university seminar than everyday political talk in the home, workplace or pub. With rare exceptions (Neblo, 2003), the characterization of deliberation as a dispassionate activity leaves little space for participants to work out what to do with their feelings, even though these are often critical shapers of their beliefs (Redlawsk, 2006; Thrift, 2008; Marcus, 2010; Cvetkovich, 2012; Highmore, 2017). Working through feelings such as anger, disappointment and fear, as well as hope, desire and excitement, is an aspect of political talk that cannot be wished away.

A related second criticism of deliberative exercises is that, while conducted on the assumption that all participants are equal, the reality is that participants bring their pre-existing inequalities with them into the process and differences of status affect the ways in which people feel able to express themselves and react to input from others. In a highly astute exploration of the unequal terms of entry to the deliberative domain, Kevin Olson (2011: 530) argues that the question of who gets to determine what constitutes legitimate deliberative speech is crucial to any claim to be a democratic project. When people who are not part of hegemonic speech communities attempt to be taken seriously as deliberators they are obliged to

> make a public case that the accepted, 'legitimate' standards of political speech should be broadened to include idioms normally termed signs of failure and incompetence. They must overcome the stigma and delegitimation of their own idiom to argue for its legitimation. And they must make this argument within or in contrast to hegemonic idioms themselves. This task is difficult because of the dilemma it poses: to legitimate oneself either by using a dominant idiom poorly as a non-native speaker, or a stigmatized idiom well as a native speaker. Either choice can be considered a sign of incompetence. (2011: 539)

The need to work through the consequences of unequal status cannot be dismissed on the grounds that that would take much longer than the few hours or days set aside for a selected deliberative mini-public to meet. Working through the positions that people assume for themselves, ascribe to others and resist or resent is a constitutive part of being political. To leave it aside is to encourage a form of unequal politics in which sensitivities to the effects of inequality are suppressed.

A third criticism of deliberative practice focuses on the 'cultural vocabularies' in which the terms of discussion are embedded. This is not so much about the unequal expressive resources that participants bring to deliberation as the background assumptions and customary political language that frame what political talk is supposed to be about. Such frames often mask hegemonic values and interests that are not on the table for discussion. This has led Scott Welsh (2002: 697) to argue that a core part of deliberation should involve opportunities for rhetorical contestation with a view to determining the categories defining what is at stake. Traditional antipathy towards rhetorical interventions in processes of deliberation, argues Welsh, amounts to a means of preventing culturally marginalized groups from formulating problems and potential solutions in their own terms. Welsh suggests that, rather than allowing the language of problem-framing to be determined by institutional initiators of deliberative exercises, the legitimacy of the terms of discussion should be regarded as a rhetorical accomplishment, arrived at through thorough political contestation. This again is a form of working through, probably incompatible with the institutional design of most current deliberative exercises.

A promising response by some deliberative theorists to these – and other – criticisms has been to move away from the idea of organizing one-off deliberative events in which 'everything' about a particular issue is talked through. They acknowledge that while singular mini-publics might generate interesting conclusions as a counterfactual microcosm of the mass population, they cannot possibly replicate the complex cultural dynamics that shape political judgement in the real world. This has led theorists to think beyond the role that deliberation can play within individual public engagement exercises and explore how a *deliberative system,* operating at every level of macro-democracy (government and legislative institutions, the mass media, digital platforms and social media, schools and universities, workplaces and communities, as well as specialized deliberative forums) might generate a more vibrant talk-based democracy.

A recent year-long research project led by the global civil society alliance, CIVICUS, went to 80 countries to conduct informal, citizen-led discussions with a view to finding out what people want from democracy. In their report entitled *Democracy for All: Beyond a Crisis of Imagination* (2019), they reported that in places where functioning representative democracy does not yet exist people want it. In places that have representative democracy, people want a more deliberative version of it in which their voices are taken seriously. For that to happen, there will have to be a cultural shift towards valuing the vernacular expression of experience. Attitudes of paternalistic condescension towards grass-roots voices need to be challenged. Dogmatic assumptions that public voices are only worth registering when they conform to the logic of market priorities need to be abandoned. The intimate connection between expression and agency needs to be acknowledged. If democracy is to come anywhere close to its professed ideals, the 'how' in the title of this chapter needs to be addressed. This entails moving beyond the cultivation of instrumental communication skills; the aesthetic obsession with 'proper' forms of speech; and the notion that self-confidence can be generated through pep-talks. It entails a direct challenge to the presumption that political speech is only significant if it takes place in a TV studio or emanates from a demagogue working a crowd. It entails an appreciation of what happens when people begin to think of themselves as democratic agents, capable of making a difference to their world.

This needs to begin with the education of our children, for whom the confidence and courage to speak up for themselves in their own voices should not be left to chance or unequal structures of educational opportunity. In recent years there have been energetic efforts to teach school students to speak and listen in ways that might enhance their capacity to enter into public acts of intersubjective discourse, clear meaning-making and personal efficacy. Much of this work has been inspired by Andrew Wilkinson's (1970) pioneering work on oracy developed in the late 1960s and early 1970s. Mercer et al's Cambridge Oracy Skills Framework, which focuses on the physical, linguistic, cognitive and social and emotional aspects of confident self-expression has been particularly useful. There are encouraging trends in current educational work pursued by Voice 21, the Brilliant Club and the All-Party Parliamentary Group on Oracy around the teaching of critical thinking and dialogical problem-solving. Vitally important though teaching children to become the next generation of articulate citizens is, its success depends upon not simply reinforcing generic scripts of appropriate civic performance. Young people's capacity for creative expressive improvisation is an invaluable source for the reinvigoration of political talk as social practice. If we focus our attention on the well-rehearsed cleverness of Oxbridge debaters, we are likely to miss the electrifying energy of the poets, rappers, street campaigners, school-student activists, playwrights and countless others who are contriving imaginative ways to quicken the pulse of the public conversation.

Encouraging people to leave their private hiding place and show who they are will surely involve unlearning debilitating rituals of citizenship that have played on the vulnerability of atomised actors caught up in a performance that is not of their own making. We should avoid being prescriptive about the text or tone of new variants of civic expression. This might be what John Dewey (1927 [1954]) had in mind when he wrote that to 'form itself the public has to break existing political forms'. Dewey's argument was that the public would only ever be able to exercise its agency robustly by resisting formal functions ascribed to it by others and creating its own practices of acting politically. This applies equally to the micro-enactments of self-expression through which people enter into politics and the macro-coordination of collective action through which political outcomes are realised. The more our conversations about what matters go off-script, off-cliché and off-form the better it will be for politics. Lasswell was right: Democracy needs a new way to talk.

Political talk about political talk:
A methodological appendix

In conducting the interviews reported in this book, I was interested in hearing from people what it felt like to be in the thick of raw political discourse; to be animated by an urge to be acknowledged as a vocal political actor; or to regard political contention as an aggravating background noise, best avoided. Talking about talking is an inherently metacommunicative enterprise (Ruesch and Bateson, 1951; Watzlawick et al., 1967). Not only does it focus people's minds on who said what to whom and to what effect, but it also involves finding the right words to describe the feeling of being in the midst of talk – of attempting to make oneself known through word and gesture.

There have been several excellent studies based on the observation of political talk (Gamson, 1992; Charlesworth, 2000; Cramer Walsh 2004, 2016; Hochschild, 2016), but it is only when people are invited to reflect on their own experiences of political talk that they are able to add captions to the emotional drama of agonistic interaction. It is in the second iteration of their political talk that people often realize what it was really all about.

Interpersonal talk involves translation across expressive orbits, and political talk focuses upon the contested terms of such translation. This is a book about the translatory sensibilities upon which reciprocal political communication depends. Its aim is not to urge people to learn to agree but to learn how to disagree well.

Methodologically, Erving Goffman's approach to the study of talk has been a crucial starting point. Goffman (1981: 3) has been strangely neglected by political communication scholars, but his observation that 'When a word is spoken, all those who happen to be in perceptual range of the event will have some sort of participation status relative to it' strikes me as a first principle of analysis if one wishes to understand how political ideas travel and political action emerges.

Goffman (1981: 4) was surely right to recognize as an 'insufficiently appreciated fact' the observation that

> words we speak are often not our own, at least our current 'own'. Who it is who can speak is restricted to the parties present (and often more restricted than that), and which one is now doing so is almost always perfectly clear. But although who speaks is situationally circumscribed, in whose name words are spoken is certainly not. Uttered words have utterers; utterances, however, have subjects (implied or explicit), and although these may designate the utterer, there is nothing in the syntax of utterances to require this coincidence. We can as handily quote another (directly or indirectly) as we can say something in our own name.

The work of talking about talk entails probing these tacit rites of entitlement, often discovering, as I have in the pages of this book, that what is being contested, more than anything else in political dispute, is the right to speak and be taken seriously. Astute as ethnographic observers may be, they can only hope to guess at what is going on in the minds of social actors. To find out about how words and tones made them feel, the phrases they almost uttered, the histories they sensed between the lines or the sensations that hit them as they walked away from a scene of political argument, there is only one mode of investigation: it is necessary to talk to people about their memories of being in situations that they would characterize as 'political talk'.

But how best to do this? It is one thing to invite a selection of people to talk about their talk and quite another to avoid this becoming an intrusive, emotionally detached exercise in academic smash and grab. There are some basic principles that can help us to avoid such a parasitic outcome. First, researchers must really care about the questions that they are asking. For me, that was not difficult. All of my questions to interviewees had been on my mind for years if not decades. I had never conceived of them as particularly academic questions. They mattered to me because I enjoy hearing people talking, really enjoy people disagreeing and tend to feel depressed when the scope for productive disagreement is marred by conditions of miscommunication that undermine the prospect of reciprocity. The best way to elicit answers that are meaningful is to ask questions that matter to you.

Second, the interview must be given time and space to breathe. Participants in an interview need time to get to know one another and determine what is really going on between them. The interviewer who is like a mechanical mouthpiece for a list of prepared questions and the interviewee who is conceived as a mere data-generator will never communicate beyond a surface that was probably discoverable without either being present. At their best, interviews should constitute a recognition of presence. The people who leave the room at the end of the interview should never be quite the same as the ones who came in. There is never such a thing as a completed answer to a question, only ever a pause that might be filled if the interviewee feels trusting enough to do so.

Third, interviews are not about revealed truth but about exercised memory. We are dealing here with 'I said, they said' accounts of politics in which the terms of reported speech are just as real and open to contestation as their object. Memory is always political, not simply in the post hoc sense of selective recall, but insofar as it pervades real-time interaction by importing culled aspects of the past into the present. In focusing upon narratives of political talk, we are acknowledging that life is 'made social through constant work of reassembling' (Frank, 2012: 15). Memory is not only unreliable but also creative, and subjectivity inflects both what is told and the manner of its telling. As Merleau-Ponty (1964: 44) states,

> To speak is not to put a word under each thought; if it were, nothing would ever be said. We would not have the feeling of living in the language. . . . Language signifies when instead of copying thought it lets itself be taken apart and put together again by thought. . . . The empirical use of already established language should be distinguished from its creative use.

Fourth, there is, of course, the unavoidable matter of the researcher's presence within the interview. The most important acknowledgement that needs to be made at the outset is that there are always (at least) two people in the room during an interview and only one of them is called upon to offer their voice and its political history as an object of critical scrutiny. Mishler (1991: 82) is surely right to note that 'the interviewer's presence and form of involvement – how she or he listens, attends, encourages, interrupts, digresses, initiates topics and terminates responses – is integral to a respondent's account'. Indeed, Mishler refers to interviewees' stories as 'a joint production' (1991) and this leads him to ask, 'How can the presence and influence of an interviewer be taken into account in the analysis and interpretation of a respondent's story?' (p. 96). To be sure, research interviews are rhetorically constructed situations in which people meet artificially and verbal exchange is dominated by the premeditated intentions of the interviewer. Interviewees will have their own ideas about what the interviewer expects from them. In this sense, communicative exchange is haunted by apprehensions about status and positioning. Committed as I was to avoid judgemental responses to what they told me, the very act of inviting my interviewees to speak out loud about their experience of public disagreement may well have evoked the very elemental anxieties about self-value, recognition and agency that inflected the reported conflict.

Interview sample

Eighty interviews were conducted as part of the research reported in this book. Fifty of them took place before the Brexit referendum of 2016. Interviewees were recruited to fit into one of four categories. The first group (of sixteen) comprised people who claimed that they rarely or never talked about politics. I wanted to understand why these people were averse to political talk or, as it transpired in some interviews, why they had been made to feel like outsiders whose political voices were unlikely to be acknowledged. The second group (of sixteen) comprised people who thought of themselves as political talkers. This ranged from people who spent a lot of time talking about politics to family and friends to activists who talked to much wider social networks. The third group (nine people) were politicians, ranging from Members of Parliament to local councillors. The fourth group (nine people aged eleven to twenty) were young people who were at school or college. I was interested in how they might have been influenced by institutional notions of appropriate political form (Mertz, 2007). Thirty more interviews were conducted after the Brexit referendum, with an equal split between leavers and remainers.

I make no claim that the distribution of views or perceptions about political talk in the interviews I conducted reflect the British population. Although my sample was designed to avoid unrepresentativeness of gender, age, socio-economic status, ethnicity or ideological strata within the UK population, and seemed to me to provide an unbiased account of a complex cultural phenomenon, it is not the purpose of qualitative research to engender generalizable conclusions. Indeed, interviewees were often keen to emphasize that they could only talk about how a situation felt to them, sometimes acknowledging that another person might have read it differently. I wanted to encourage people to speak in such personal terms – to recall political talk through the lens of autobiographical narrative (Habermas, 2007) rather than to conform to a socio-demographic type or generate median data.

The interviews themselves were conducted in rooms within the University of Leeds. On average they were an hour in length, but several were much longer. I began most of the interviews by asking people to talk about themselves. Did they think of themselves as talkative – as being persuasive; as having strong values; as sociable; as interested in politics; as leaders; as followers? I asked them a number of questions about whether, how often and with whom they talked about politics. I showed interviewees pictures of people arguing about politics and asked them to describe what was going on – and how it made them feel. Did it throw up any memories of having been in situations like that? I asked each interviewee whether they had ever disagreed with something someone had said to them about politics and/or felt it necessary to justify their own political viewpoint. I asked whether they had ever felt uncomfortable in the presence of political argument; whether they had ever felt under pressure not to say what they thought; or whether there were situations in which talking about politics seemed inappropriate or unacceptable. I then asked a lot of questions about growing up. I usually began by asking people whether they came from noisy or quiet families. Most interviewees knew what I was getting at here and talk about the soundscape of early family life gave rise to a lot of recollections about family dynamics. I asked whether they recalled any extended family members being vocal about politics and in a surprising number of cases, aunts, uncles, cousins, in-laws and neighbours were recalled as key figures in their earliest awareness of politics. I asked interviewees if they could recall an occasion when they argued with someone else about politics. I made it clear that I was interested in interactions that were memorable to them, for whatever reason. It might have been because they felt that they had really argued their case well, or let themselves down, or fallen out with a good friend, or resented the energy expended. Not a single interviewee failed to come up with an account of a political argument that was lodged in their memory. I asked them to try to tell me about this interaction in the form of a story. I asked for as many details as they could remember, not only about the substance of the disagreement but also about its tone and temper and topography. I pressed for the kind of detail that would allow me to close my eyes and imagine being a witness to the situation they were telling me about. My sense was that people liked this opportunity to reflect on their experiences, habits and feelings and particularly enjoyed telling stories about moments in which they had been unsure how the story would end.

Several interviewees made a point of telling me that they appreciated having the time to talk about an aspect of their life that they had not previously thought much about. Much of what went on in the interview had less to do with cognitive accounting than affective sharing. Indeed, exploring the phenomenology of political talk entails paying close attention to feelings as well as motives; contexts as well as norms; polysemic readings as well as definitive meanings. In the words of the great chronicler of lived experience Svetlana Alexievich (2017: xix), 'I turn more and more into a big ear, listening all the time to another person. I "read" voices.' She goes on (2017: xxvi), 'I listen when they speak. . . . I listen when they are silent. . . . Both words and silence are the text for me.'

As I listened to people recalling their experiences of finding, using, losing and neglecting their political voices, I was struck by the reflective ways in which they monitored and appraised their performances. They listened to their own voices and contemplated the echoes of their utterances long after the words had been spoken. They were aware that certain phrases, tones and stances were legitimate and effective and others best left unexpressed. They wanted to understand how their political talk related to the unarchived political lexicon of everything that anyone has ever said before them. They were curious about the ways in which they spoke themselves into existence, performing identities that positioned them in relation to indeterminate flows and levers of political power.

Making sense of it all

My aim was to discover memories, impressions and interpretations rather than truths. As Mishler (1991: 110) rightly notes, the assumption that 'there is one "true" interpretation of an array of data and . . . that this interpretation may be determined by standard, universally applicable technical procedures' is not well founded. The discussion of interviews in this book would certainly not pass any kind of positivist test for analytical 'reliability'. In seeking to learn about the discursive resources that people bring to accounts of political talk, a sharp focus has been cast upon the strengths and vulnerabilities of subjectively experienced political agency. The inherent ambiguity and provisionality of subjective consciousness are insusceptible to quantifiable measurement and best observed through an impressionistic lens.

Such a mode of analysis entails coming to terms with the indeterminacy of everyday political talk. Just as the interpretation of impressionist painting is unlikely to be accomplished by searching for fixed, indexical meanings, so non-positivist readings of political talk should proceed on the assumption that significance typically lies beneath the semantic surface of articulation. By 'privileging blur' (Prendergast, 2000: 26), one acknowledges that ambiguity, contradiction, pregnant pauses and half-formed points are not enemies of meaning, but common features of politics as a work in progress.

McCormack (2000) recommends that the interpretation of transcripts should entail two stages:

1. Viewing the interview transcript through multiple lenses, which involves the following:
   - immersing oneself in the transcript through a process of active listening;
   - identifying the narrative processes used by the storyteller;
   - paying attention to the language of the text;
   - acknowledging the context in which the text was produced; and
   - identifying moments in the text where something unexpected is happening.
2. Developing interpretive stories using the views highlighted through the multiple lenses

There is much to be said for adopting an interpretive approach that draws upon narrative theory (Labov and Waletzky, 1997; Hymes, 2003; Frank, 2010; Gibbs, 2018). Interpreting the interviews discussed in this book involved a sensitivity not only to the stories that people told but also to the emotional energy that inflected their telling. When people talk about talk, they not only recall its substance and effects but also inflections, rhythms and tonalities. In listening to these one becomes attuned to what Allison Pugh (2013: 43) refers to as the interviewee's 'emotional landscape that brings a broader, social dimension to individual motivation'. She goes on to say that

> Informants tell us not just what they think and feel, but how it feels to feel that way – for example the emotional environment that they inhabit and the particular pressures that this cultural world puts on them. (p.49)

In her critically important article on 'What good are interviews for thinking about culture?', Allison Pugh (2013: 50–1) introduces a way of reading interview material through four distinct but overlapping frames. There are 'honourable' responses to questions in which interviewees seek to 'present themselves in the most admirable light, actively conducting a form of display work as they put forward a sense of what counts as honourable behavior'. When my interviewees spoke about how they 'ought to' follow political discussions or sought to be 'in the know' when they spoke, they were performing a form of citizenship that they might have assumed I was looking for from them. Pugh's second frame is 'schematic'. Here interviewees present a view of the world – 'politicians are permanently evasive' or 'well-educated people are best placed to make political pronouncements' or 'they're trying to stop us saying what we really think'. Schematic frames of political talk edit narratives to emphasize a dominant view of the world. Third, Pugh refers to visceral responses which emerge from 'an emotional landscape of desire, morality and expectations that shapes their actions and reactions, a landscape that researchers must somehow be able to divine and portray'. Much of my own interpretive energy in writing this book was devoted to precisely that task. The success of the book depends to a great extent on how well that was realized. But this must be considered in relation to Pugh's fourth frame of interpretation which she calls 'meta-feelings'. These reflect upon 'how we feel about how we feel':

> These kind of data offer a powerful account of the individual embedded in culture, for it is often a measure of the distance between how someone feels and how they feel they ought to feel (Hochschild, 1983). . . . Meta-feelings, then, are the emotional expression of our relative ease with the prevalent worldviews that surround us; they are like the expansion joints that show whether bridges are expanding or contracting with the prevailing weather. (2013: 51)

Allison Pugh's notion of 'meta-feelings' is discussed explicitly in Chapter 2, but it served as a constant methodological lens as I listened again and again to the interview transcripts, picking up the modulations in storytelling form that corresponded to distinct or imbricated frames of feeling. The performative potential of such affective excavation is explored by Lauren Berlant (2011: 247) in her discussion of the 'sonic activist' group, Ultra-Red. It is their practice to interview people whose voices are usually silenced or subjugated:

> But Ultra-Red's method is more selective than reproducing testimony. . . . Members of Ultra-Red came to notice that, along with telling their stories about injustice, their interviewees talked a lot about their feelings. . . . So Ultra-Red embarked on a project of sifting out political feeling statements from the statements generally. As the interviewees spoke their speech into the record a technician would remix it and play back the voices in a new feedback loop made up of sentences reflecting on political feeling, until the room was thick with the hangover of everyone's feelings and the noise of newly connected atmosphere.

This methodological innovation points to the sense in which interpreting interviews is an art, seeking to represent meaning in forms that might at first seem antithetical to cognitive translation. There is room for many approaches to the art of hearing voices, ranging from classical strategies such as Ronald Grele's (1975) *Envelopes of Sound*, Eliot Mishler's (1991) *Research Interviewing*,

Robert Weiss's (1995) *Learning from Strangers*, Pierre Bourdieu et al.'s (1999) *The Weight of the World*, Arthur Frank's (2010) *Letting Stories Breathe* and Svetlana Alexievich's (2017) *The Unwomanly Face of War*, to more innovative experiments that focus on the sound of interviewees' voices (Hall et al., 2008; Bray, 2014) or the unvoiced moods and gestures of their accounts (Sklar, 2000; Csordas, 2009; Coleman and Brogden, 2020). Perhaps we should think more carefully about interviews as performances of self and qualitative interpretations as representations of selves. And, like all translations between performance and representation, veracity depends to a considerable extent upon the quality of commitment driving the translatory impulse.

Hartmut Rosa's (2019: 163) complex and inspiring notion of 'resonance' is relevant here. One definition of resonance that he offers is as follows:

> . . . a specifically cognitive, affective and bodily relationship to the world in which subjects are touched and occasionally even 'shaken' down to the neural level by certain segments of the world, but at the same time are also themselves 'responsively', actively and influentially related to the world and experience themselves as effective in it – this is the nature of the responsive relation or 'vibrating wire' between subject and world. When a person's *eyes light up*, we can read this as visible and perhaps measurable evidence their 'wire' is resonating in both directions. The subject develops an intrinsic, generally action-oriented interest that opens *outward* to the world while at the same time being affected or set in motion *from without* (his emphases).

How might we observe and register these phenomena of being 'touched', 'shaken down to the neural level', 'eyes lighting up' and synergistic relation between interior thought and feeling and external forces and affects? There are no simple methodological answers to that question but searching for them may well move the study of political communication from its current cognitive preoccupations to a vantage point from which experiential politics can be sighted.

Bibliography

Addington, D. W. (1968). The relationship of selected vocal characteristics to personality perception. *Speech Monographs, 35*(4), 492–503.

Alexander, J. C. (2010). *The Performance of Politics: Obama's Victory and the Democratic Struggle for Power*. Oxford: Oxford University Press.

Alexander, J. C. (2011). *Performance and Power*. Cambridge: Polity.

Alexievich, S. (2017). *The Unwomanly Face of War* (R. Pevear & L. Volokhonsky, Trans.). London: Penguin Books Limited.

Allen, J. (2011). *Lost Geographies of Power* (Vol. 79). Hoboken, New Jersey, NJ: John Wiley & Sons.

Altieri, C. (2003). *The Particulars of Rapture: An Aesthetics of the Affects*. Ithaca: Cornell University Press.

Archer, M. S., & Archer, M. S. (2000). *Being Human: The Problem of Agency*. Cambridge: Cambridge University Press.

Arendt, H. (1959). *The Human Condition*. London: University of Chicago Press.

Arendt, H. (1968). *The Concept of History: Between Past and Future*. New York: Penguin.

Arendt, H. (1994). *Hannah Arendt: Critical Essays* (L. P. Hinchman & S. Hinchman, Eds). NYC: State University of New York Press.

Asen, R. (2002). Imagining in the public sphere. *Philosophy & Rhetoric, 35*(4), 345–67.

Asen, R. (2010). Reflections on the role of rhetoric in public policy. *Rhetoric & Public Affairs, 13*(1), 121–43.

Ashforth, B. E., & Humphrey, R. H. (1993). Emotional labor in service roles: The influence of identity. *Academy of Management Review, 18*(1), 88–115.

Astington, J. W. (2014). Intention in the child's theory of mind. In *Children's Theories of Mind* (pp. 165–80). Hove, East Sussex: Psychology Press.

Atkinson, P., & Silverman, D. (1997). Kundera's immortality: The interview society and the invention of the self. *Qualitative Inquiry, 3*(3), 304–25.

Austin, J. L. (1962). *How to Do Things with Words* (J. O. Urmson, Ed.). Oxford: Clarendon Press.

Bächtiger, A., Dryzek, J. S., Mansbridge, J., & Warren, M. E. (2018). *The Oxford Handbook of Deliberative Democracy*. Oxford: Oxford University Press.

Bächtiger, A., & Parkinson, J. (2019). *Mapping and Measuring Deliberation: Towards a New Deliberative Quality*. Oxford: Oxford University Press.

Bacon, F. (2011). *The Works of Francis Bacon* (J. Spedding, R. L. Ellis, & D. D. Heath, Eds). Cambridge: Cambridge University Press.

Bagehot, W. (1883). *Essays on Parliamentary Reform*. London: K. Paul, Trench & Company.

Bakhtin, M. M. (1986). *Speech Genres and Other Late Essays*. Austin: University of Texas Press.

Balot, R. (2005). Greek freedom. *The Classical Review, 55*(1), 207.

Bamberg, M. (2011). Who am I? Narration and its contribution to self and identity. *Theory & Psychology, 21*(1), 3–24.

Bardsley, S. (2003). Sin, speech, and scolding in Late Medieval England. In T. Fenster & D. L. Smail (Eds), *Fama: The Politics of Talk and Reputation in Medieval Europe* (pp. 145–64). Ithaca: Cornell University Press.

Barnett, C. (2008). Political affects in public space: Normative blind spots in non-representational ontologies. *Transactions of the Institute of British Geographers, 33*(2), 186–200.

Barnidge, M. (2017). Exposure to political disagreement in social media versus face-to-face and anonymous online settings. *Political Communication, 34*(2), 302–21.

Barthes, R., & Howard, R. (1975). *The Pleasure of the Text*. London: Macmillan.

Bassel, L. (2017). Why a politics of listening? *The Politics of Listening* (pp. 1–15). New York: Springer.

Bastos, M. T., & Mercea, D. (2019). The Brexit botnet and user-generated hyperpartisan news. *Social Science Computer Review, 37*(1), 38–54.

Bauman, R., Briggs, C. L., & Briggs, C. S. (2003). *Voices of Modernity: Language Ideologies and the Politics of Inequality*. Cambridge: Cambridge University Press.

Bauman, Z. (1999). *In Search of Politics*. Palo Alto, CA: Stanford University Press.

Bayard, D. (2000). The cultural cringe revisited: Changes through time in Kiwi attitudes toward accents. *New Zealand English*, 297–324.

Beattie, G. (2003). *Visible Thought: The New Psychology of Body Language*. Hove: Psychology Press.

Benhabib, S. (1996). *Democracy and Difference: Contesting the Boundaries of the Political*. Princeton, NJ: Princeton University Press.

Benjamin, J. (2017). *Beyond Doer and Done To: Recognition Theory, Intersubjectivity and the Third*. Abingdon: Taylor & Francis.

Benjamin, M. (1990). *Splitting the Difference: Compromise and Integrity in Ethics and Politics*. Lawrence: University Press of Kansas.

Bennett, S. E., Flickinger, R. S., & Rhine, S. L. (2000). Political talk over here, over there, over time. *British Journal of Political Science, 30*(1), 99–119.

Bennett, W. L. (1980). The paradox of public discourse: A framework for the analysis of political accounts. *The Journal of Politics, 42*(3), 792–817.

Bennett, W. L. (2011). *What's Wrong with Incivility? Civility as the New Censorship in American Politics*. Center for Communication and Civic Engagement, University of Washington.

Bennett, W. L., & Edelman, M. (1985). Toward a new political narrative. *Journal of Communication, 35*(4), 156–71.

Bennett, W. L., & Livingston, S. (2018). The disinformation order: Disruptive communication and the decline of democratic institutions. *European Journal of Communication, 33*(2), 122–39.

Bennett, W. L., Wells, C., & Freelon, D. (2011). Communicating civic engagement: Contrasting models of citizenship in the youth web sphere. *Journal of Communication*, *61*(5), 835–56.

Berlant, L. (2010). Thinking about feeling historical. In *Political Emotions*. London: Routledge.

Berlant, L. G. (2011). *Cruel Optimism*. Durham, NC: Duke University Press.

Bickford, S. (1996). *The Dissonance of Democracy: Listening, Conflict, and Citizenship*. Ithaca: Cornell University Press.

Bitzer, L. (1968). The rhetorical situation. *Philosophy and Rhetoric*, *1*(3), 1–14.

Blackman, L. (2012). *Immaterial Bodies: Affect, Embodiment, Mediation*. New York: Sage.

Bland, A. (2016, 31 July). How did the language of politics get so toxic? *The Guardian*. Retrieved from https://www.theguardian.com/politics/2016/jul/31/how-did-the-lang uage-of-politics-get-so-toxic

Blendon, R. J., Benson, J. M., Brodie, M., Morin, R., Altman, D. E., Gitterman, D., . . . James, M. (1997). Bridging the gap between the public's and economists' views of the economy. *Journal of Economic Perspectives*, *11*(3), 105–18.

Blum-Kulka, S. (1997). Discourse pragmatics. *Discourse as Social Interaction*, *2*, 38–63.

Bollas, C. (1987). *The Shadow of the Object: Psychoanalysis of the Unthought Known*. New York: Columbia University Press.

Boltanski, L., & Thévenot, L. (2006). *On Justification: Economies of Worth* (Vol. 27). Princeton, NJ: Princeton University Press.

Bourdieu, P. (1979). *Distinction: A Social Critique of the Judgement of Taste* (R. Nice, Trans.). Cambridge, MA: Harvard University Press.

Bourdieu, P. (1991). *Language and Symbolic Power*. Cambridge, MA: Harvard University Press.

Bourdieu, P. (1992). *An Invitation to Reflexive Sociology*. Chicago, IL: University of Chicago Press.

Bourdieu, P., Accardo, A., Waryn, S. T., Ferguson, P. P., Emanuel, S., & Johnson, J. (1999). *The Weight of the World: Social Suffering in Contemporary Society*. Stanford, CA: Stanford University Press.

Bray, M., Adamson, B., & Mason, M. (2014). *Comparative Education Research: Approaches and Methods*. New York: Springer.

Brennan, T. (2004). *The Transmission of Affect* (Vol. 15). Ithaca: Cornell University Press.

Brett, W. (2016). *It's Good to Talk: Doing Referendums Differently After the EU Vote*. Retrieved from https://www.electoral-reform.org.uk/latest-news-and-research/publ ications/its-good-to-talk/

Brewer, M. B., & Sedikides, C. (2001). *Individual Self, Relational Self, and Collective Self: Partners, Opponents or Strangers?* Hove: Psychology Press.

Brockriede, W. (1975). Where is argument? *The Journal of the American Forensic Association*, *11*(4), 179–82.

Brown, G. (1981). Teaching the spoken language. *Studia Linguistica*, *35*(1–2), 166–82.

Brown, G., & Yule, G. (1983). *Teaching the Spoken Language* (Vol. 2). Cambridge: Cambridge University Press.

Brundidge, J. (2010). Toward a theory of citizen interface with political discussion and news in the contemporary public sphere. *International Journal of Communication, 4,* 1056–78.

Bruner, J. S. (1983). *Child's Talk: Learning to Use Language.* London: W.W. Norton & Co.

Bruner, J. S. (1990). *Acts of Meaning* (Vol. 3). Cambridge, MA: Harvard University Press.

Buber, M. (1947). *Between Man and Man* (R. G. Smith, Trans.). London: Kegan Paul.

Buber, M. (2003). *Between Man and Man* (2nd edn). London: Routledge & Kegan Paul.

Burke, E. (1872). *Reflections on the Revolution in France, and on the Proceedings in Certain Societies in London Relative to that Event.* Seeley, London: Jackson and Halliday.

Burt, R. S. (2005). *Brokerage and Closure: An Introduction to Social Capital.* Oxford: Oxford University Press.

Butler, J. (1993). *Bodies that Matter: On the Discursive Limits of "Sex."* New York and London: Routledge.

Butler, J. (2001). Giving an account of oneself. *Diacritics, 31*(4), 22–40.

Butler, J. (2005). Gender trouble: Feminism and the subversion of identity GT. *Political Theory, 4,* 4–24.

Cadwalladr, C. (2017). The Great British Brexit robbery: How our democracy was hijacked. *The Guardian.*

Cameron, D. (2000). *Good to Talk?: Living and Working in a Communication Culture.* New York: Sage.

Cameron, D. (2012). *Verbal Hygiene: The Politics of Language.* London: Routledge.

Campbell, N. D. (2003). Reading the rhetoric of 'compassionate conservatism'. In Cynthia Burach, and Jyl J. Josephson (eds), *Fundamental Differences: Feminists Talk Back to Social Conservatives* (pp. 113–26). Lanham, MD: Rowman and Littlefield.

Campbell, S. (1997). *Interpreting the Personal: Expression and the Formation of Feelings.* Ithaca: Cornell University Press.

Campbell-Kibler, K. (2007). Accent, (ING), and the social logic of listener perceptions. *American Speech, 82*(1), 32–64.

Cavarero, A. (2005). *For More than One Voice: Toward a Philosophy of Vocal Expression.* Stanford, CA: Stanford University Press.

Chan, M. (2018). Reluctance to talk about politics in face-to-face and Facebook settings: Examining the impact of fear of isolation, willingness to self-censor, and peer network characteristics. *Mass Communication and Society, 21*(1), 1–23.

Charlesworth, S. J. (2000). *A Phenomenology of Working-Class Experience.* Cambridge: Cambridge University Press.

Chen, H., Rattanasone, X., Cox, F., & Demuth, K. (2017). Effect of early dialectal exposure on adult perception of phonemic vowel length. *The Journal of the Acoustical Society of America, 142*(3), 1707–16.

Cicero. (1948) [58 BC]. *De Oratore* (H. Rackham & E. W. Sutton, Eds). Cambridge, MA: Harvard University Press.

CIVICUS. (2019). *Democracy for All: Beyond a Crisis of Imagination*. Retrieved from http://www.waccglobal.org/articles/democracy-for-all-beyond-a-crisis-of-imagination

Cockerell, M. (1989). *Live from Number Ten: Inside Story of Prime Ministers and Television*. London: Faber & Faber.

Coleman, S. (2005). New mediation and direct representation: Reconceptualizing representation in the digital age. *New Media & Society*, 7(2), 177–98.

Coleman, S. (2013). *How Voters Feel*. Cambridge: Cambridge University Press.

Coleman, S. (2018). The elusiveness of political truth: From the conceit of objectivity to intersubjective judgement. *European Journal of Communication*, 33(2), 157–71.

Coleman, S. (2020). Taking a position: Contemporary dance and the communication of deep political feeling. In S. Rai, M. Gluhovic, S. Jestrovic, & M. Saward (Eds), *Oxford Handbook of Politics and Performance*. Oxford: Oxford University Press.

Coleman, S., Blumler, J., Moss, G., & Homer, M. (2015). *The 2015 Televised Election Debates; Democracy on Demand?* Retrieved from https://pvac-sites.leeds.ac.uk/demo cracyondemand/files/2015/12/Coleman-et-al-Democracy-on-Demand.pdf

Coleman, S., & J. Brogden (2020). *Capturing the Mood of Democracy; The British General Election 2019*. London: Palgrave.

Colleoni, E., Rozza, A., & Arvidsson, A. (2014). Echo chamber or public sphere? Predicting political orientation and measuring political homophily in Twitter using big data. *Journal of Communication*, 64(2), 317–32.

Committee on the Future Relationship with the European Union (2019). *Committee Consider Citizens' Assemblies and a Further Referendum Ahead of New Prime Minister's Arrival*. Retrieved from https://committees.parliament.uk/committee/36 6/committee-on-the-future-relationship-with-the-european-union/news/142246/ committee-consider-citizens-assemblies-and-a-further-referendum-ahead-of-new -prime-ministers-arrival/

Connolly, J. (2007). The new world order: Greek rhetoric in Rome. *A Companion to Greek Rhetoric*, 139–65.

Connolly, W. E. (2002). *Neuropolitics: Thinking, Culture, Speed* (Vol. 23). Minneapolis, University of Minnesota Press.

Connor, S. (2000). *Dumbstruck: A Cultural History of Ventriloquism*. Oxford: Oxford University Press on Demand.

Conover, P. J., & Miller, P. R. (2018). Taking everyday political talk seriously. In *The Oxford Handbook of Deliberative Democracy* (p. 378). Oxford: Oxford University Press.

Copeland, R., & Sluiter, I. (2009). *Medieval Grammar and Rhetoric: Language Arts and Literary Theory, AD 300–1475*. Oxford: Oxford University Press.

Cosslett, R. l. (2016). Family rifts over Brexit: 'I can barely look at my parents'. *The Guardian*. Retrieved from https://www.theguardian.com/lifeandstyle/2016/jun/27/br exit-family-rifts-parents-referendum-conflict-betrayal

Couldry, N. (2004). Theorising media as practice. *Social Semiotics, 14*(2), 115–32.

Couldry, N. (2010). *Why Voice Matters: Culture and Politics After Neoliberalism*. NY: Sage Publications.

Cowan, S. K., & Baldassarri, D. (2018). "It could turn ugly": Selective disclosure of attitudes in political discussion networks. *Social Networks, 52*, 1–17.

Craib, I. (1990). *Psychoanalysis and Social Theory*. Amherst, MA: University of Massachusetts Press.

Cramer, K. J. (2016). *The Politics of Resentment: Rural Consciousness in Wisconsin and the Rise of Scott Walker*. Chicago: University of Chicago Press.

Cramer Walsh, K. (2004). *Talking About Politics: Informal Groups and Social Identity in American Life*. Chicago: University of Chicago Press.

Crary, J. (2001). *Suspensions of Perception: Attention, Spectacle, and Modern Culture*. Cambridge, MA: MIT Press.

Cressy, D. (1977). Levels of illiteracy in England, 1530–1730. *The Historical Journal, 20*(1), 1–23.

Crossley, N. (2010). *Towards Relational Sociology*. London: Routledge.

Crowley, T. (2003). *Standard English and the Politics of Language*. NY; Springer.

Csordas, T. J. (1999). Embodiment and cultural phenomenology. In G. Weiss & H. Fern Haber (Eds), *Perspectives on Embodiment: The Intersections of Nature and Culture* (p. 143). Abington: Taylor & Francis.

Csordas, T. J. ed. (2009). *Transnational Transcendence: Essays on Religion and Globalization*. Berkeley: University of California Press.

Cvetkovich, A. (2012). *Depression: A Public Feeling*. Durham, NC: Duke University Press.

Czubaroff, J. (2000). Dialogical rhetoric: An application of Martin Buber's philosophy of dialogue.

Dahl, H. M., Stoltz, P., & Willig, R. (2004). Recognition, redistribution and representation in capitalist global society: An interview with Nancy Fraser. *Acta Sociologica, 47*(4), 374–82.

Dahl, R. (1998). *On Democracy*. New Haven, Conn: Yale University Press.

Dahlgren, P. (2002). In search of the talkative public: Media, deliberative democracy and civic culture. *Javnost - The Public, 9*(3), 5–25.

Dahlgren, P. (2009). *Media and Political Engagement: Citizens, Communication, and Democracy*. Cambridge: Cambridge University Press.

Dalton, R. J., & Welzel, C. (2014). *The Civic Culture Transformed: From Allegiant to Assertive Citizens*. Cambridge: Cambridge University Press.

Davidson, R. J. (2003). Seven sins in the study of emotion: Correctives from affective neuroscience. *Brain and Cognition, 52*(1), 129–32.

Davies, B., & Harré, R. (1990). Positioning: The discursive production of selves. *Journal for the Theory of Social Behaviour, 20*(1), 43–63.

Davies, W. (2018). *Nervous States: How Feeling Took over the World*. New York: Random House.

Davis, M. H. (2018). *Empathy: A Social Psychological Approach*. London: Routledge.

Deacon, D., Harmer, E., Downey, J., Stanyer, J., & Wring, D. (2016). *UK News Coverage of the 2016 EU Referendum*. Retrieved from Centre for Research into Communication & Culture.

Del Vicario, M., Zollo, F., Caldarelli, G., Scala, A., & Quattrociocchi, W. (2017). Mapping social dynamics on Facebook: The Brexit debate. *Social Networks, 50*, 6–16.

Denworth, L. (2018, 1 June). Thanksgiving dinner may end sooner if guests pass the gravy across a partisan divide. *Scientific American*.

Dobson, A. (2014). *Listening for Democracy: Recognition, Representation, Reconciliation*. Oxford: Oxford University Press.

Dolar, M. (2006). *A Voice and Nothing More*. Cambridge, MA: MIT Press.

Donati, P. (2010). *Relational Sociology: A New Paradigm for the Social Sciences*. London: Routledge.

Dorling, D., & Tomlinson, S. (2019). "Sneak Peek": Rule Britannia: From Brexit to the end of Empire.

Drager, K. (2010). Sociophonetic variation in speech perception. *Language and Linguistics Compass, 4*(7), 473–80.

Dreher, T. (2017). Social/participation/listening: Keywords for the social impact of community media. *Communication Research and Practice, 3*(1), 14–30.

Dryzek, J. (2000). *Deliberative Democracy and Beyond*. Oxford: Oxford University Press.

Dryzek, J. S. (2002). *Deliberative Democracy and Beyond: Liberals, Critics, Contestations*. Oxford: Oxford University Press

Dunn, J., Brown, J., Slomkowski, C., Tesla, C., & Youngblade, L. (1991). Young children's understanding of other people's feelings and beliefs: Individual differences and their antecedents. *Child Development, 62*(6), 1352–66.

Dunn, J., Brown, J. R., & Maguire, M. (1995). The development of children's moral sensibility: Individual differences and emotion understanding. *Developmental Psychology, 31*(4), 649.

Dvora, Y. (2015). *Constructing "Race" and "Ethnicity" in America: Category-making in Public Policy and Administration*. Taylor and Francis.

Easton, D. (1968). The theoretical relevance of political socialization. *Canadian Journal of Political Science / Revue canadienne de science politique, 1*(2), 125–46.

Elgie, R. (2015). Scientific realist accounts of political leadership: Political psychology. In *Studying Political Leadership* (pp. 108–37). New York: Springer.

Eliasoph, N. (1998). *Avoiding Politics: How Americans Produce Apathy in Everyday Life*. Cambridge: Cambridge University Press.

Eliot, T. S. (1971). East Coker (Four Quartets). In *The Complete Poems and Plays of T.S. Eliot*. London: Harcourt Brace & Company.

Ellis, M. (2011). *The Coffee-House: A Cultural History*. London, UK: Weidenfeld & Nicolson.

Elshtain, J. B. (1993). *Democracy on Trial*. Toronto: House of Anansi.

Elstub, S. (2014). *Deliberative Democracy: Issues and Cases*. Edinburgh: Edinburgh University Press.

Emde, R. N., Biringen, Z., Clyman, R. B., & Oppenheim, D. (1991). The moral self of infancy: Affective core and procedural knowledge. *Developmental Review, 11*(3), 251–70.

Emirbayer, M. (1997). Manifesto for a relational sociology. *American Journal of Sociology, 103*(2), 281–317.

Emirbayer, M., & Mische, A. (1998). What is agency? *American Journal of Sociology, 103*(4), 962–1023.

Erickson, F. (1982). Money tree, lasagna bush, salt and pepper: Social construction of topical cohesion in a conversation among Italian-Americans. *Analyzing Discourse: Text and Talk*, 43–70.

Eveland Jr., W. P., Morey, A. C., & Hutchens, M. J. (2011). Beyond deliberation: New directions for the study of informal political conversation from a communication perspective. *Journal of Communication, 61*(6), 1082–103.

Eveland, W. P., & Kleinman, S. B. (2013). Comparing general and political discussion networks within voluntary organizations using social network analysis. *Political Behavior, 35*(1), 65–87.

Farrell, D. M., Suiter, J., & Harris, C. (2019). 'Systematizing' constitutional deliberation: The 2016–18 citizens' assembly in Ireland. *Irish Political Studies, 34*(1), 113–23.

Felski, R., & Fraiman, S. (2012). Introduction: In the mood. *New Literary History, 43*(3).

Fernald, A., & O'Neill, D. K. (1993). Peekaboo across cultures: How mothers and infants play with voices, faces, and expectations. *Parent-Child Play: Descriptions and Implications*, 259–85.

Finlayson, A. (2007). From beliefs to arguments: Interpretive methodology and rhetorical political analysis. *The British Journal of Politics and International Relations, 9*(4), 545–63.

Fisher, M., Knobe, J., Strickland, B., & Keil, C. (2018, February). Are toxic political conversations changing how we feel about objective truth? *Scientific American*. Retrieved from https://www.scientificamerican.com/article/are-toxic-political-co nversations-changing-how-we-feel-about-objective-truth/

Fishkin, J. S. (1991). *Democracy and Deliberation: New Directions for Democratic Reform* (Vol. 217). New Haven: Yale University Press.

Fishkin, J. S. (2011). *When the People Speak: Deliberative Democracy and Public Consultation*. Oxford: Oxford University Press.

Fishkin, J. S., & Mansbridge, J. J. (2017). *The Prospects & Limits of Deliberative Democracy*. American Academy of Arts and Sciences.

Fitzgerald, J. (2013). What does "political" mean to you? (Report). *Political Behavior, 35*(3), 453.

Flatley, J. (2009). *Affective Mapping: Melancholia and the Politics of Modernism*. Cambridge, MA: Harvard University Press.

Flax, J. (1993). The play of justice: Justice as a transitional space. *Political Psychology, 14*(2), 331–46.

Fonagy, P. (2018). *Attachment Theory and Psychoanalysis*. London: Routledge.

Frank, A. W. (2010). *Letting Stories Breathe: A Socio-Narratology*. Chicago: University of Chicago Press.

Fraser, N. (1995). Politics, culture, and the public sphere: Toward a postmodern conception. *Social Postmodernism: Beyond Identity Politics, 291*, 295.

Fraser, N. (2000). Why overcoming prejudice is not enough: A rejoinder to Richard Rorty. *Critical Horizons, 1*(1), 21–8.

Freire, P. (1970 [2007]). *Pedagogy of the Oppressed* (MB Ramos, Trans.). New York: Continuum.

Freire, P. (2018). *Pedagogy of the Oppressed*: London: Bloomsbury Publishing.

Fricker, M. (2006). Powerlessness and social interpretation. *Episteme, 3*(1–2), 96–108.

Gallie, W. (1956). Essentially contested concepts. *Proceedings of the Aristotelian Society, 56*, 167.

Gamson, W. A. (1992). *Talking Politics*. Cambridge: Cambridge University Press.

Garfinkel, H. (1967). *Studies in Ethnomethodology*. Englewood Cliffs, NJ: Prentice-Hall.

Gastil, J., Knobloch, K. R., Reedy, J., Henkels, M., & Cramer, K. (2018). Assessing the electoral impact of the 2010 Oregon Citizens' Initiative Review. *American Politics Research, 46*(3), 534–63.

Gavin, N. T. (2018). Media definitely do matter: Brexit, immigration, climate change and beyond. *The British Journal of Politics and International Relations, 20*(4), 827–45.

George, L. K. (1998). Self and identity in later life: Protecting and enhancing the self. *Journal of Aging and Identity, 3*(3), 133–52.

Gergen, K. J. (1991). *The Saturated Self: Dilemmas of Identity in Contemporary Life* (Vol. 166). New York: Basic Books.

Gibbs, G. R. (2018). *Analyzing Qualitative Data*. New York: Sage Publications.

Gill, R., & Orgad, S. (2016). The confidence cult (ure). *Feminist Studies, 30*(86), 324–44.

Gilligan, C. (1993). *In a Different Voice: Psychological Theory and Women's Development*: Cambridge, MA: Harvard University Press.

Goffman, E. (1959). *The Presentation of Self in Everyday Life* (Vol. 259). New York: DoubleDay.

Goffman, E. (1981). *Forms of Talk*. Oxford: Blackwell.

Goldinger, S. D., Kleider, H. M., & Shelley, E. (1999). The marriage of perception and memory: Creating two-way illusions with words and voices. *Memory & Cognition, 27*(2), 328–38.

Goodwin, B., & Taylor, K. (1982). *The Politics of Utopia*. New York: Martin's Press.

Grandey, A. A. (2015). Smiling for a wage: What emotional labor teaches us about emotion regulation. *Psychological Inquiry, 26*(1), 54–60.

Gray, S. W. (2015). Mapping silent citizenship: How democratic theory hears citizens' silence and why it matters. *Citizenship Studies, 19*(5), 474–91.

Grele, R. J. (1975). *Envelopes of Sound: Six Practitioners Discuss the Method, Theory, and Practice of Oral History and Oral Testimony*. Chicago: Precedent Pub.

Greene, R. W., & Hicks, D. (2005). Lost convictions: Debating both sides and the ethical self-fashioning of liberal citizens. *Cultural Studies, 19*(1), 100–126.

Grele, R. J. (1991). *Envelopes of Sound: The Art of Oral History.* Praeger.

Grosz, E. (2004). *The Nick of Time: Politics, Evolution, and the Untimely.* Durham, NC: Duke University Press.

Gubrium, J. F., & Holstein, J. A. (1998). Narrative practice and the coherence of personal stories. *Sociological Quarterly, 39*(1), 163–87.

Gunn, J. (2010). On speech and public release. *Rhetoric & Public Affairs, 13*(2), 175–215.

Guru-Murthy, K., White, M., Cochrane, L., Price, L., & Schneider, D. (2014, 2 April). Rebranding Ed Miliband *The Guardian.* Retrieved from https://www.theguardian.com/politics/2014/apr/02/rebranding-ed-miliband-broadcast-guru

Habermas, J. (1984). *The Theory of Communicative Action* (T. McCarthy, Trans.). Portsmouth, NH: Heinemann.

Habermas, J. (1997). *Modernity: An Unfinished Project.* Cambridge, MA: MIT Press.

Habermas, T. (2007). How to tell a life: The development of the cultural concept of biography. *Journal of Cognition and Development, 8*, 1–31.

Habermas, T., & Bluck, S. (2000). Getting a life: The emergence of the life story in adolescence. *Psychological Bulletin, 126*(5), 748.

Habermas, T., & Köber, C. (2015). Autobiographical reasoning in life narratives buffers the effect of biographical disruptions on the sense of self-continuity. *Memory, 23*(5), 664–74.

Hajer, M. A. (2005). Setting the stage: A dramaturgy of policy deliberation. *Administration & Society, 36*(6), 624–47.

Hajer, M. A. (2009). *Authoritative Governance: Policy Making in the Age of Mediatization.* Oxford: Oxford University Press.

Hall, T., Lashua, B., & Coffey, A. (2008). Sound and the everyday in qualitative research. *Qualitative Inquiry, 14*(6), 1019–40.

Hample, D. (2007). The arguers. *Informal Logic, 27*(2), 163–78.

Hansard Society. (2017). *Audit of Political Engagement 14: The 2017 Report.* London: Hansard Society.

Hansard Society (2018). *Audit of Political Engagement.* Retrieved from https://www.hansardsociety.org.uk/publications/reports/audit-of-political-engagement-15-2018

Hansard Society cic (2019). *Audit of Political Engagement.* Retrieved from London: https://www.hansardsociety.org.uk/publications/reports/audit-of-political-engagement-16

Hardin, R. (2002). Street-level epistemology and democratic participation. *Journal of Political Philosophy, 10*(2), 212–29.

Harré, R. (1999). *Trust and Its Surrogates: Psychological Foundations of Political Process.* Cambridge: Cambridge University Press.

Harris, R. [@Robert_Harris]. (2016, 16 June). How foul this referendum is. [Twitter]. Retrieved 6 April 2020 from https://twitter.com/Robert___Harris/status/743440375981936640

Hart, R. P., Childers, J. P., & Lind, C. J. (2013). *Political Tone: How Leaders Talk and Why.* Chicago: University of Chicago Press.

Hendriks, C. M., Ercan, S. A. & Duus, S. (2019). Listening in polarised controversies: A study of listening practices in the public sphere. *Policy Sciences*, *52*(1), 137–51.

Herbst, S. (2010). *Rude Democracy: Civility and Incivility in American Politics*. Philadelphia, Penn: Temple University Press.

Highmore, B. (2013). Feeling our way: Mood and cultural studies. *Communication and Critical/Cultural Studies*, *10*(4), 427–38.

Highmore, B. (2017). *Cultural Feelings: Mood, Mediation and Cultural Politics*. London: Routledge.

Hitchens, P. (2010). Leave it aht, Samanfa . . . Mrs Cameron's Estuary English typifies a society that mistrusts aspiration and mocks excellence. *The Mail on Sunday*. Retrieved from https://www.dailymail.co.uk/debate/article-1259388/PETER-HIT CHENS-Leave-aht-Samanfa--Samantha-Camerons-Estuary-English-typifies-society -mistrusts-aspiration-mocks-excellence.html

Hitchens, P. (2012). What the papers didn't say – And what they did. *Mail Online*. Retrieved from https://hitchensblog.mailonsunday.co.uk/2012/07/index.html

Hobolt, S. B., Leeper, T., & Tilley, J. (2018). *Divided by the Vote: Affective Polarization in the Wake of Brexit*. American Political Science Association, Boston.

Hochschild, A. R. (1979). Emotion work, feeling rules, and social structure. *American Journal of Sociology*, *85*(3), 551–75.

Hochschild, A. R. (1983). *The Managed Heart: Commercialization of Human Feeling*. Berkeley: University of California Press.

Hochschild, A. R. (2016). *Strangers in Their Own Land: Anger and Mourning on the American Right*. NY: The New Press.

Honneth, A. (1996). *The Struggle for Recognition: The Moral Grammar of Social Conflicts*. Cambridge, MA: MIT Press.

Honneth, A. (1998). Democracy as reflexive cooperation: John Dewey and the theory of democracy today. *Political Theory*, *26*(6), 763–83.

Honneth, A. (2007). *Disrespect*. Cambridge: Polity.

Hornstein, G. A. (2017). *Agnes's Jacket: A Psychologist's Search for the Meanings of Madness*. (Revised and Updated ed.). London: Routledge.

Howard, D. (2008). Necessary fictions: The "swinish multitude" and the rights of man. *Studies in Romanticism*, *47*(2), 161–78.

Howard, P. N., & Kollanyi, B. (2016). *Bots, #StrongerIn, and #Brexit: Computational propaganda during the UK-EU referendum*. Available at SSRN 2798311.

Hunt, C., & Sampson, F. (2006). *Writing: Self and Reflexivity*. London: Palgrave Macmillan.

Hymes, D. (2003). *Foundations in Sociolinguistics: An Ethnographic Approach*. London: Routledge.

Inglehart, R. (1988). The renaissance of political culture. *The American Political Science Review*, *82*(4), 1203–30. Retrieved from www.jstor.org/stable/1961756. doi:10.2307/1961756

Iris, Y. (2000). *Inclusion and Democracy*. Oxford: Oxford University Press.

Isenbarger, L., & Zembylas, M. (2006). The emotional labour of caring in teaching. *Teaching and Teacher Education, 22*(1), 120–34.

James, W. (1890). *The Principles of Psychology* (Vol. 1). Cosimo, Inc.

James, W. (1905). The thing and its relations. *The Journal of Philosophy, Psychology and Scientific Methods, 2*(2), 29–41.

James, W. (1976). *Essays in Radical Empiricism* (Vol. 3). Cambridge, MA: Harvard University Press, p. 93

Jameson, F. (1976). Authentic ressentiment: The "experimental" novels of Gissing. *Nineteenth-Century Fiction, 31*(2), 127–49.

Jamieson, K. H., Volinsky, A., Weitz, I., & Kenski, K. (2017). The political uses and abuses of civility and incivility. In K. Kenski & K. H. Jamieson (Eds), *The Oxford Handbook of Political Communication*. Oxford: Oxford University Press.

Jasper, J. M. (1998). *The Emotions of Protest: Affective and Reactive Emotions in and Around Social Movements*. Paper presented at the Sociological Forum.

Jepperson, R. L., & Swidler, A. (1994). What properties of culture should we measure? *Poetics, 22*(4), 359–71.

Jones, J. P. (2005). *Entertaining Politics: New Political Television and Civic Culture*. Lanham, MD: Rowman & Littlefield.

Jones, O. (2015, 13 October). Labour must unify around the anti-austerity message. *The Guardian*. Retrieved from https://www.theguardian.com/commentisfree/2015/oct/13/labour-austerity-tax-credits-economic

Katriel, T., & Philipsen, G. (1981). "What we need is communication": "Communication" as a cultural category in some American speech. *Communication Monographs, 48*(4), 301–17. Retrieved from https://doi.org/10.1080/03637758109376064. doi:10.1080/03637758109376064

Kendon, A. (2004). *Gesture: Visible Action as Utterance*. Cambridge: Cambridge University Press.

Kiley Bense. (2018, 26 November). How politics in Trump's America divides families. *The Atlantic*.

Kim, J., & Kim, E. J. (2008). Theorizing dialogic deliberation: Everyday political talk as communicative action and dialogue. *Communication Theory, 18*(1), 51–70.

Kim, J., Wyatt, R. O., & Katz, E. (1999). News, talk, opinion, participation: The part played by conversation in deliberative democracy. *Political Communication, 16*(4), 361–85.

Klein, L. E. (1997). The figure of France: The politics of sociability in England, 1660–1715. *Yale French Studies* (92), 30–45.

Klinnert, M. D., Campos, J. J., Sorce, J. F., Emde, R. N. & Svejda, M. (1983). Emotions as behavior regulators: Social referencing in infancy. In *Emotions in Early Development* (pp. 57–86). Cambridge, MA: Academic Press.

Knoke, D. (1990). Networks of political action: Toward theory construction. *Social Forces, 68*(4), 1041–63.

Kostić, A., & Chadee, D. (2015). Emotional recognition, fear, and nonverbal behavior. In *The Social Psychology of Nonverbal Communication* (pp. 134–50). New York: Springer.

Kreiman, J., & Sidtis, D. (2011). *Foundations of Voice Studies: An Interdisciplinary Approach to Voice Production and Perception*. Hoboken, NJ: John Wiley & Sons.

Kristeva, J. (1991). *Strangers to Ourselves*: New York: Columbia University Press.

Kuklinski, J. H., Luskin, R. C., & Bolland, J. (1991). Where is the schema? Going beyond the "S" word in political psychology. *American Political Science Review*, 85(4), 1341–80.

LaBelle, B. (2014). *Lexicon of the Mouth: Poetics and Politics of Voice and the Oral Imaginary*. London: A&C Black.

Labov, W. (1972). *Sociolinguistic Patterns*. Philadelphia: University of Pennsylvania Press, Incorporated.

Labov, W., & Waletzky, J. (1997). Narrative analysis: Oral versions of personal experience. *Journal of Narrative & Life History*, 7(1–4), 3–38. doi:10.1075/jnlh.7.02nar

Lahire, B. (2011). *The Plural Actor*. Cambridge: Polity.

Lane, R. (1992). Political culture: Residual category or general theory? *Comparative Political Studies*, 25(3), 362–87. doi:10.1177/0010414092025003004

Lasswell, H. D. (1941). *Democracy Through Public Opinion*. Menasha, WI: George Banta Publishing Co.

Lawrence, J. (2009). *Electing Our Masters: The Hustings in British Politics from Hogarth to Blair*. Oxford: Oxford University Press.

Le Bon, G. (1895). *The Crowd: A Study of the Popular Mind* (pp. 5, 18). London: T. Fisher Unwin.

Le Bon, G. (2006). *The Crowd: A Study of the Popular Mind*. New York: Cosimo Classics.

Lev-On, A., & Lissitsa, S. (2015). Studying the coevolution of social distance, offline- and online contacts. *Computers in Human Behavior*, 48, 448–56.

Levy, D. A., Aslan, B. & Bironzo, D. (2016). *UK Press Coverage of the EU Referendum*. Oxford: Reuters Institute for the Study of Journalism.

Levy, F. (2010). *How Technology Changes Demands for Human Skills*. OECD Education Working Papers, No. 45. OECD Publishing *(NJ1)*.

Lewis, H. (2018, 29 August 2019). How Britain's Political Conversation Turned Toxic. *The New Statesman*. Retrieved from https://www.newstatesman.com/politics/uk /2018/08/how-britain-political-conversation-turned-toxic

Leys, R. (2011). The turn to affect: A critique. *Critical Inquiry*, 37(3), 434–72.

Liestøl, G., Morrison, A. and Rasmussen, T. eds (2004). *Digital Media Revisited: Theoretical and Conceptual Innovations in Digital Domains*. Cambridge: MIT Press.

Lilleker, D. G., & Bonacci, D. (2017). The structure of political e-expression: What the Brexit campaign can teach us about political talk on Facebook. *International Journal of Digital Television*, 8(3), 335–50.

Lippmann, W. (1927). The causes of political indifference today. *The Atlantic Monthly*, 261–8.

Locke, J. (1712). *Some Thoughts Concerning Education*: London: A. & J. Churchill.

Lynda, M. (1995). *Talking Proper: The Rise of Accent as Social Symbol.* Oxford: Clarendon Press.

Macnamara, J., & Gregory, A. (2018). Expanding evaluation to progress strategic communication: Beyond message tracking to open listening. *International Journal of Strategic Communication, 12*(4), 469–86.

Mansbridge, J. J. (1983). *Beyond Adversary Democracy.* Chicago: University of Chicago Press.

Mansbridge, J., Bohman, J., Chambers, S., Estlund, D., Føllesdal, A., Fung, A., . . . Martí, J. L. (2010). The place of self-interest and the role of power in deliberative democracy. *Journal of Political Philosophy, 18*(1), 64–100.

Marcus, G. E. (2010). *Sentimental Citizen: Emotion in Democratic Politics.* Philadelphia: Penn State Press.

Markell, P. (2009). *Bound by Recognition.* Princeton, NJ: Princeton University Press.

Markman, E. (2004). *The Coffee House: A Cultural History.* London: Orion House.

Massaro, T. M., & Stryker, R. (2012). Freedom of speech, liberal democracy, and emerging evidence on civility and effective democratic engagement. *Arizona Law Review, 54,* 375.

Massumi, B. (2002). *Parables for the Virtual: Movement, Affect, Sensation.* Durham, NC: Duke University Press.

May, R. H. P. T. (2019). *PM Speech on the State of Politics.* www.gov.uk.

McAdams, D. P. (2008). *The Life Story Interview.* Evanston, IL: Northwestern University.

McCloskey, D. N. (1992). *If You're So Smart: The Narrative of Economic Expertise.* Chicago: University of Chicago Press.

McCloskey, D. N. (1998). *The Rhetoric of Economics.* Madison, WI: University of Wisconsin Press.

McClurg, S. D. (2006). Political disagreement in context: The conditional effect of neighborhood context, disagreement and political talk on electoral participation. *Political Behavior, 28*(4), 349–66.

McCombs, M. (2013). *Setting the Agenda: The Mass Media and Public OPinion.* Hoboken, NJ: John Wiley & Sons.

McCormack, C. (2000). From interview transcript to interpretive story: Part 1— Viewing the Transcript through multiple lenses. *Field Methods, 12*(4), 282–97. doi:10 .1177/1525822X0001200402

McCormack, D. P. (2005). Diagramming practice and performance. *Environment and Planning D: Society and Space, 23*(1), 119–47.

Mcdowell, N. (2004). Levelling language: The politics of literacy in the English radical tradition, 1640–1830. *Critical Quarterly, 46*(2), 39–62.

McPherson, M., Smith-Lovin, L., & Cook, J. M. (2001). Birds of a feather: Homophily in social networks. *Annual Review of Sociology, 27*(1), 415–44. doi:10.1146/annurev. soc.27.1.415

Mead, G. H. (1932). *The Philosophy of the Present.* La Salle, IL: Open Court.

Meltzer, B. N., & Musolf, G. R. (2002). Resentment and ressentiment. *Sociological Inquiry, 72*(2), 240–55.

Merleau-Ponty, M. (1964). *Signs* (R. C. McCleary, Ed.). Evanston, IL: Northwestern University Press.

Mertz, E. (2007). *The Language of Law School: Learning to "Think Like a Lawyer"*. Oxford: Oxford University Press.

Mills, C. W. (2000). *The Sociological Imagination*. Oxford: Oxford University Press.

Mills, L. (2009). When the voice itself is image. *Modern Drama, 52*(4), 389–404.

Milroy, J., & Milroy, L. (2012). *Authority in Language: Investigating Standard English* (4th edn). Abingdon and New York: Routledge.

Mishler, E. G. (1991). *Research Interviewing: Context and Narrative*. Cambridge, MA: Harvard University Press.

Montrose, L. A. (1989). Professing the Renaissance: The Poetics and Politics of Culture. In H. Aram Veeser (Ed.), *The New Historicism*. New York: Routledge.

Moore, M., & Ramsay, G. (2017). *UK Media Coverage of the 2016 EU Referendum Campaign*. King's College London.

Morey, A. C., Eveland Jr., W. P., & Hutchens, M. J. (2012). The "who" matters: Types of interpersonal relationships and avoidance of political disagreement. *Political Communication, 29*(1), 86–103.

Morrell, M. (2018). Listening and deliberation. In *Oxford Handbook of Deliberative Democracy* (pp. 237–50). Oxford: Oxford University Press.

Morris, W. (1993). *News from Nowhere and Other Writings*. In Penguin Classics. London: Penguin Books.

Mugglestone, L. (1995). *Talking Proper: The Rise of Accent as Social Symbol*. Oxford: Oxford University Press on Demand.

Mutz, D. C. (2002). The consequences of cross-cutting networks for political participation. *American Journal of Political Science, 46*(4), 838–55.

Mutz, D. C. (2006). *Hearing the Other Side: Deliberative Versus Participatory Democracy*. Cambridge: Cambridge University Press.

Neblo, M. A. (2003). *Impassioned Democracy: The Role of Emotion in Deliberative Theory*. Paper presented at the Democracy Collaborative Affiliates Conference.

Neocleous, M. (2004). The monstrous multitude: Edmund Burke's political teratology. *Contemporary Political Theory, 3*(1), 70–88.

Newman, N., Fletcher, R., Kalogeropoulos, A., Levy, D., & Kleis Niels, R. (2017). *Digital News Report 2017*. Retrieved from Oxford: https://reutersinstitute.politics. ox.ac.uk/

OED. (2018). The Oxford English Dictionary.

O'Keefe, B. J., & McCornack, S. A. (1987). Message design logic and message goal structure: Effects on perceptions of message quality in regulative communication situations. *Human Communication Research, 14*(1), 68–92.

Olson, K. (2011). Legitimate speech and hegemonic idiom: The limits of deliberative democracy in the diversity of its voices. *Political Studies, 59*(3), 527–46.

Orr, L. (1990). *Headless History: Nineteenth-Century French Historiography of the Revolution*. Ithaca, NY: Cornell University Press.

Orwell, G. (1946). *Politics and the English Language*. London: Horizon.

O'Toole, F. (2018). *Heroic Failure: Brexit and the Politics of Pain*. London: Head of Zeus Ltd.

Padel, R. (2008). *The Poem and the Journey: And Sixty Poems to Read Along the Way*. New York: Random House.

Papacharissi, Z. (2012). Without you, I'm nothing: Performances of the self on Twitter. *International Journal of Communication, 6*, 18.

Parkinson, J., & Mansbridge, J. (2012). *Deliberative Systems: Deliberative Democracy at the Large Scale*. Cambridge: Cambridge University Press.

Passy, F., & Giugni, M. (2000). *Life-Spheres, Networks, and Sustained Participation in Social Movements: A Phenomenological Approach to Political Commitment*. Paper presented at the Sociological Forum.

Pateman, C. (1971). Political culture, political structure and political change. *British Journal of Political Science, 1*(3), 291–305.

Pateman, C. (1980). The civic culture: A philosophic critique. *The Civic Culture Revisited*, 57–102.

Pateman, C. (2018). *The Disorder of Women: Democracy, Feminism and Political Theory*. Hoboken, NJ: John Wiley & Sons.

(2013, 23 October). Jeremy Paxman talks to Russell Brand [Television series episode]. In Paxman, J. (Executive producer), *Newsnight*. London.

Penman, R., & Turnbull, S. (2012). From listening … to the dialogic realities of participatory democracy. *Continuum, 26*(1), 61–72.

Perner, J., & Wimmer, H. (1985). 'John thinks that Mary thinks that . . .': Attribution of second-order beliefs by 5-to 10-year-old children. *Journal of Experimental Child psychology, 39*(3), 437–71.

Perrin, A. J. (2009). *Citizen Speak: The Democratic Imagination in American Life*. Chicago: University of Chicago Press.

Piaget, J. (1936). *The Origins of Intelligence in the Child*. London: Routledge & Kegan Paul.

Pinter, H. (2013). *Various Voices: Prose, Poetry, Politics 1948–2008*. London: Faber & Faber.

Pocock, J. G. (1973). Verbalizing a political act: Toward a politics of speech. *Political Theory, 1*(1), 27–45.

Ponder, J., & Haridakis, P. (2015). Selectively social politics: The differing roles of media use on political discussion. *Mass Communication and Society, 18*(3), 281–302.

Poovey, M. (1995). *Making a Social Body: British Cultural Formation, 1830–1864*. Chicago: University of Chicago Press.

Pow, J., & Garry, J. (2019). *What Happens When People Deliberate in a Deeply Divided Place? Evidence from Mini-publics in Northern Ireland*. Paper presented at the International Political Science Association, Sarajevo, Bosnia & Herzegovina.

Prendergast, C. (2000). *The Triangle of Representation*. New York: Columbia University Press.

Preston, D. R. (1999). *Handbook of Perceptual Dialectology* (Vol. 1). Amsterdam: John Benjamins Publishing.

Price, V., Cappella, J. N., & Nir, L. (2002). Does disagreement contribute to more deliberative opinion? *Political Communication*, *19*(1), 95–112.

Probyn, E. (2005). *Blush: Faces of Shame*. Mineapololis, MN: University of Minnesota Press.

Pugh, A. J. (2013). What good are interviews for thinking about culture? Demystifying interpretive analysis. *American Journal of Cultural Sociology*, *1*(1), 42–68.

Rancière, J. (2010). *Dissensus: On Politics and Aesthetics* (S. Corcoran, Trans.). London: Bloomsbury Academic.

Rancière, J., Panagia, D., & Bowlby, R. (2001). Ten theses on politics. *Theory & Event*, *5*(3), 555–68.

Reddy, W. M. (2001). *The Navigation of Feeling: A Framework for the History of Emotions*. Cambridge: Cambridge University Press.

Redlawsk, D. (2006). *Feeling Politics: Emotion in Political Information Processing*. New York: Springer.

Renwick, A., Allan, S., Jennings, W., McKee, R., Russell, M., & Smith, G. (2018). What kind of Brexit do voters want? Lessons from the Citizens' Assembly on Brexit. *The Political Quarterly*, *89*(4), 649–58.

Renwick, A., Palese, M., & Sargeant, J. (2018). Discussing Brexit—Could We Do Better? *The Political Quarterly*, *89*(4), 545–52.

Repacholi, B. M., Meltzoff, A. N., Toub, T. S., & Ruba, A. L. (2016). Infants' generalizations about other people's emotions: Foundations for trait-like attributions. *Developmental Psychology*, *52*(3), 364.

Rich, A. (1986). *Of Woman Born: Motherhood as Experience and Institution*. 1976. New York: Norton.

Richards, S. (2013, 24 July). To emulate Blair, Ed Miliband will have to stop imitating him. *The Guardian*. Retrieved from https://www.theguardian.com/commentisfree /2013/jul/24/blair-ed-miliband-public-personality

Ricoeur, P. (2004). *Memory, History, Forgetting*. Chicago: University of Chicago Press.

Ringrose, J. (2011). Beyond discourse? Using Deleuze and Guattari's schizoanalysis to explore affective assemblages, heterosexually striated space, and lines of flight online and at school. *Educational Philosophy and Theory*, *43*(6), 598–618.

Rorty, R. M. (1989). *Contingency, Irony, and Solidarity*. Cambridge: Cambridge University Press.

Rosa, H., & Wagner, J. (2019). *Resonance: A Sociology of Our Relationship to the World*. Hoboken, NJ: Wiley.

Rowbotham, S., Alexander, S., & Taylor, B. (1979). The Trouble with Patriarchy. *The New Statesman*.

Ruesch, J., & Bateson, G. (1951). *Communication: The Social Matrix of Psychiatry*. New York: Norton.

Sacks, H. (1984). On doing 'being ordinary'. *Structures of Social Action: Studies in Conversation Analysis*, 413–29.

Sayer, A. (2011). *Why Things Matter to People: Social Science, Values and Ethical Life*. Cambridge: Cambridge University Press.

Schudson, M. (1997). Why conversation is not the soul of democracy. *Critical Studies in Media Communication, 14*(4), 297–309.

Schudson, M. (1999). *The Good Citizen: A History of American Civic Life.* Cambridge, MA: Harvard University Press.

Schutz, A. (1964). *Collected Papers: Studies in Social Theory* (Vol. 2).

Schutz, A. (1970). *On Phenomenology and Social Relations* (H. R. Wagner, Ed.). Chicago and London: Chicago University Press.

Scott, J. C. (1990). *Domination and the Arts of Resistance: Hidden Transcripts.* New Haven: Yale University Press.

Scott, J. W. (1991). The evidence of experience. *Critical Inquiry, 17*(4), 773–97.

Searle, J. R. (1969). *Speech Acts: An Essay in the Philosophy of Language* (Vol. 626). Cambridge: Cambridge University Press.

Sewell, Jr. W. H. (1992). A theory of structure: Duality, agency, and transformation. *American Journal of Sociology, 98*(1), 1–29.

Shipman, T. (2017). *Fall Out: A Year of Political Mayhem.* New York: HarperCollins Publishers.

Silverstone, R. (2007). *Morality and Media.* Cambridge: Polity Press.

Sklar, D. (2000). Reprise: On dance ethnography. *Dance Research Journal, 32*(1), 70–7.

Sloterdijk, P. (2012). *Rage and Time: A Psychopolitical Investigation* (M. Wenning, Trans.). Chichester: Columbia University Press.

Smith, O. (1986). *The Politics of Language, 1791–1819*: Oxford: Oxford University Press.

Smith, P. (1992). *The Emotional Labour of Nursing: Its Impact on Interpersonal Relations, Management and Educational Environment.* Macmillan International Higher Education.

Somers, M. R. (1994). The narrative constitution of identity: A relational and network approach. *Theory and Society, 23*, 605–49.

Somers, M. R. (1995). Narrating and naturalizing civil society and citizenship theory: The place of political culture and the public sphere. *Sociological Theory, 13* (3), 229–74.

Somers, M., & Gibson, G. (1994). Reclaiming the epistemological "other". In C. Calhoun (Ed.), *Social Theory and the Politics of Identity.* Oxford: Blackwell.

Soper, K. (1990). *Troubled Pleasures: Writings on Politics, Gender, and Hedonism.* London: Verso.

Sorensen, J. (2004). Vulgar tongues: Canting dictionaries and the language of the people in eighteenth-century Britain. *Eighteenth-Century Studies, 37*(3), 435–54.

Spence, D. P. (1982). *Historical Truth and Narrative Truth.* New York: Norton.

Spinrad, T. L., & Eisenberg, N. (2017). Compassion in children. In D. C. Cameron, E. Seppala, D. James, M. Worline, & S. Brown (Eds), *The Oxford Handbook of Compassion Science* (pp. 53–63). Oxford: Oxford University Press.

Stearns, P. N., & Stearns, C. Z. (1985). Emotionology: Clarifying the history of emotions and emotional standards. *The American Historical Review, 90*(4), 813–36.

Steiner, G. (1975). *After Babel: Aspects of Language and Translation.* Oxford: Oxford University Press.

Steiner, J. (2012). *The Foundations of Deliberative Democracy: Empirical Research and Normative Implications*. Cambridge: Cambridge University Press.

Steiner, P. (2001). The sociology of economic knowledge. *European Journal of Social Theory*, *4*(4), 443–58.

Stephens, B. (2017, 24 September). The dying art of disagreement. *The New York Times*. Retrieved from https://www.nytimes.com/2017/09/24/opinion/dying-art-of-disagreement.html

Stern, D. B. (2009a). Partners in thought: A clinical process theory of narrative. *The Psychoanalytic Quarterly*, *78*, 701–31. doi:10.1002/j.2167-4086.2009.tb00410.x

Stern, D. N. (2009b). Pre-reflexive experience and its passage to reflexive experience: A developmental view. *Journal of Consciousness Studies*, *16*(10–11), 307–31.

Stern, D. B. (2010). *Partners in Thought: Working with Unformulated Experience, Dissociation, and Enactment*. London and NY: Routledge.

Stern, D. N. (2004). *The Present Moment in Psychotherapy and Everyday Life*. New York: W. W. Norton & Company.

Street, J. (1997). Remote control? Politics, technology and 'electronic democracy'. *European Journal of Communication*, *12*(1), 27–42. Retrieved from https://journals.sagepub.com/doi/abs/10.1177/0267323197012001003. doi:10.1177/0267323197012001003

Stromer-Galley, J., Bryant, L., & Bimber, B. (2015). Context and medium matter: Expressing disagreements online and face-to-face in political deliberations. *Journal of Public Deliberation*, *11*(1), 1.

Stryker, R., Conway, B. A., & Danielson, J. T. (2016). What is political incivility? *Communication Monographs*, *83*(4), 535–56.

Suiter, J. (2018). Deliberation in action – Ireland's abortion referendum. *Political Insight*, *9*(3), 30–2.

Swidler, A. (1986). Culture in action: Symbols and strategies. *American Sociological Review*, 51 (2), 273–86.

Swidler, A. (2001). *Talk of Love: How Culture Matters*. Chicago: University of Chicago Press.

Tannen, D. (1984). *Coherence in Spoken and Written Discourse* (Vol. 12). Norwood, NJ: Ablex.

Tannen, D. (2005). *Conversational Style: Analyzing Talk Among Friends*. Oxford: Oxford University Press.

Tannen, D. (2007). *Family Talk: Discourse and Identity in Four American Families*. Oxford: Oxford University Press.

Taylor, C. (1989). *Sources of the Self: The Making of the Modern Identity*. Cambridge, MA: Harvard University Press.

Taylor, C. (1993). Engaged agency and background in Heidegger. In C. Guignon (Ed.), *The Cambridge Companion to Heidegger* (pp. 317–46).Cambridge: Cambridge University Press.

Taylor, C. (1997). The politics of recognition. *New Contexts of Canadian Criticism*, *98*, 25–73.

Taylor, C. (2002). Modern social imaginaries. *Public Culture, 14*(1), 91–124.

Thévenot, L. (2005). Pragmatic regimes governing the engagement with the world. In *The Practice Turn in Contemporary Theory* (pp. 64–82). London: Routledge.

Thompson, E. P. (1978). *The Poverty of Theory and Other Essays.* London: Merlin.

Thompson, M. (2016). *Enough Said: What's Gone Wrong with the Language of Politics?* New York: Random House.

Thrift, N. (2008). *Non-representational Theory: Space, Politics, Affect.* London: Routledge.

Thurlow, C. (2001). Talkin"bout my Communication: Communication Awareness in Mid-Adolescence. *Language Awareness, 10*(2–3), 213–31.

Tolson, A. (2001). Being yourself: The pursuit of authentic celebrity. *Discourse Studies, 3*(4), 443–57.

Tomlinson, M., & Millie, J. (2017). *The Monologic Imagination.* Oxford: Oxford University Press.

Townsend, M. (2016, 9 December). If you're as worried as I am about spending Christmas with your Brexit-voting relatives, here are some helpful tips. *The Independent.* Retrieved from https://www.independent.co.uk/voices/brexit-vote-s upreme-court-remain-remoaners-surviving-christmas-day-debate-family-relatives -top-tips-a7463991.html

Trevarthen, C. (1977). Descriptive analyses of infant communicative behaviour. In H. R. Schaffer (Ed.), *Studies in Mother-Infant Interaction* (pp. 227–70). London: Academic Press.

Van Langenhove, L. (1998). *Positioning Theory: Moral Contexts of International Action.* Oxford: Blackwell Publishers.

Verba, S., & Almond, G. (1963). *The Civic Culture: Political Attitudes and Democracy in Five Nations.* Princeton, NJ: Princeton University Press.

Verderber, R. F. (1994). *Speech: For Effective Communication* (7th edn). New York: Holt Rinehart and Winston.

Waisbord, S. (2018). Truth is what happens to news: On journalism, fake news, and post-truth. *Journalism Studies, 19*(13), 1866–78.

Waks, L. J. (2010). Two types of interpersonal listening. *Teachers College Record, 112*(11), 2743–62.

Walstad, W. B., & Allgood, S. (1999). What do college seniors know about economics? *American Economic Review, 89*(2), 350–4.

Watzlawick, P., & Beavin, J. (1967). Some formal aspects of communication. *American Behavioral Scientist, 10*(8), 4–8.

Wedeen, L. (2002). Conceptualizing culture: Possibilities for political science. *American Political Science Review, 96*(4), 713–28.

Weeden, J., & Kurzban, R. (2016). *The Hidden Agenda of the Political Mind: How Self-Interest Shapes Our Opinions and Why We Won't Admit It.* Princeton, NJ: Princeton University Press.

Weiss, R. S. (1995). *Learning from Strangers: The Art and Method of Qualitative Interview Studies.* New York: Free Press.

Welsh, S. (2002). Deliberative democracy and the rhetorical production of political culture. *Rhetoric & Public Affairs, 5*(4), 679–707.

Wetherell, M. (2012). *Affect and Emotion: A New Social Science Understanding.* New York: Sage Publications.

White, H. (1980). The value of narrativity in the representation of reality. *Critical Inquiry, 7*(1), 5–27.

White, J. (2009). Thematization and collective positioning in everyday political talk. *British Journal of Political Science, 39*(4), 699–709.

Wilkinson, A. (1970). The concept of oracy. *The English Journal, 59*(1), 71–7.

Williams, R. (1974). Communications as cultural science. *Journal of Communication, 24*(3), 17–25.

Williams, R. (1977). *Marxism and Literature* (Vol. 392). Oxford: Oxford Paperbacks.

Willig, R. (2017). An Interview with Arlie Russell Hochschild: Critique as emotion. *Theory, Culture & Society, 34*(7–8), 189–96.

Winnicott, D. W. (1953). Transitional objects and transitional phenomena—A study of the first not-me possession. *International Journal of Psycho-Analysis, 34*, 89–97.

Winnicott, D. W. (1971). *Playing and Reality.* London and New York: Routledge.

Wobker, I., Lehmann-Waffenschmidt, M., Kenning, P., & Gigerenzer, G. (2012). What do people know about the economy? A test of minimal economic knowledge in Germany. *A Test of Minimal Economic Knowledge in Germany* (October 1, 2012).

Worthen, M. (2016, 30 April). Stop Saying 'I Feel Like'. *The New York Times.* Retrieved from https://www.nytimes.com/2016/05/01/opinion/sunday/stop-saying-i-feel-like .html

Yanow, D. (2015). *Constructing Race and Ethnicity in America: Category-Making in Public Policy and Administration.* London: Routledge.

Young, C. (2017, 22 June). Will we ever have civility in American political discourse? *The Hill.* Retrieved from https://thehill.com/blogs/pundits-blog/media/338966-will -we-ever-have-civility-in-american-political-discourse

Young, I. M. (1985). Impartiality and the civic public: Some implications of feminist critiques of moral and political theory. *Praxis International, 5*(4), 381–401.

Young, I. M. (2002). *Inclusion and Democracy.* Oxford: Oxford University Press

Zahn-Waxler, C., & Radke-Yarrow, M. (1990). The origins of empathic concern. *Motivation and Emotion, 14*(2), 107–30.

Zelizer, B. (2018). Resetting journalism in the aftermath of Brexit and Trump. *European Journal of Communication, 33*(2), 140–56.

Zembylas, M. (2006). Witnessing in the classroom: The ethics and politics of affect. *Educational Theory, 56*(3), 305–24.

Zezima, K. (2019, 11 January). Is it possible to resurrect civility amid a tsunami of toxicity? *The Washington Post.* Retrieved from https://www.washingtonpost.com/ national/is-it-possible-to-resurrect-civility-amid-a-tsunami-of-toxicity-this-group-is -trying/2019/01/11/7ccbba7c-15c6-11e9-90a8-136fa44b80ba_story.html

Index

www.ingramcontent.com/pod-product-compliance
Lightning Source LLC
Chambersburg PA
CBHW050432280326
41932CB00013BA/2086